Conversations with Wendell Berry

Literary Conversations Series

Peggy Whitman Prenshaw
General Editor

Photo by Ryan Beiler

Conversations with
Wendell Berry

Edited by
Morris Allen Grubbs

University Press of Mississippi
Jackson

www.upress.state.ms.us

The University Press of Mississippi is a member of the Association of American University Presses.

Copyright © 2007 by University Press of Mississippi
All rights reserved
Manufactured in the United States of America

First printing 2007
∞
Library of Congress Cataloging-in-Publication Data

Berry, Wendell, 1934–
    Conversations with Wendell Berry / edited by Morris Allen Grubbs.
       p. cm.
    Includes index.
    ISBN-13: 978-1-57806-991-0 (alk. paper)
    ISBN-10: 1-57806-991-2 (alk. paper)
    ISBN-13: 978-1-57806-992-7 (pbk. : alk. paper)
    ISBN-10: 1-57806-992-0 (pbk. : alk. paper) 1. Berry, Wendelll, 1934——Interviews.
2. Authors, American—20th century—Interviews. 3. Berry, Wendell, 1934——Homes
and haunts—Kentucky—Henry County. I. Grubbs, Morris Allen, 1963–
    PS3552.E75Z46 2007
    818'.5409—dc22   2007008834

British Library Cataloging-in-Publication Data available

Books by Wendell Berry

Fiction

Nathan Coulter. Boston: Houghton Mifflin, 1960; rev. ed., San Francisco: North Point, 1985.

A Place on Earth. New York: Harcourt Brace, 1967; rev. ed., San Francisco: North Point, 1983.

The Memory of Old Jack. New York: Harcourt Brace Jovanovich, 1974; Washington, DC: Counterpoint, 1999.

The Wild Birds: Six Stories of the Port William Membership. San Francisco: North Point, 1986.

Remembering. San Francisco: North Point, 1988.

The Discovery of Kentucky. Frankfort, KY: Gnomon, 1991.

Fidelity: Five Stories. New York: Pantheon, 1992.

A Consent. Monterey, KY: Larkspur, 1993.

Watch with Me. New York: Pantheon, 1994.

A World Lost. Washington, DC: Counterpoint, 1996.

Two More Stories of the Port William Membership. Frankfort, KY: Gnomon, 1997.

Jayber Crow. Washington, DC: Counterpoint, 2000.

Three Short Novels. Washington, DC: Counterpoint, 2002.

Hannah Coulter. Washington, DC: Shoemaker and Hoard, 2004.

That Distant Land: The Collected Stories. Washington, DC: Counterpoint, 2004.

Andy Catlett: Early Travels. Emeryville, CA: Shoemaker and Hoard, 2006.

Drama

Sonata at Payne Hollow. Monterey, KY: Larkspur, 2001.

Poetry

November twenty six nineteen hundred sixty three. New York: Braziller, 1964.

The Broken Ground. New York: Harcourt Brace, 1964.

Openings. New York: Harcourt Brace, 1968.

Findings. Iowa City, IA: Prairie, 1969.

Farming: A Handbook. New York: Harcourt Brace Jovanovich, 1970.

The Country of Marriage. New York: Harcourt Brace Jovanovich, 1973.

An Eastward Look. Berkeley, CA: Sand Dollar, 1974.

Sayings and Doings. Frankfort, KY: Gnomon, 1975.

Horses. Monterey, KY: Larkspur, 1975.

There Is a Singing Around Me. Austin, TX: Cold Mountain Press, 1976.

The Kentucky River: Two Poems. Monterey, KY: Larkspur, 1976.

Three Memorial Poems. Berkeley, CA: Sand Dollar, 1977.

Clearing. New York: Harcourt Brace Jovanovich, 1977.

A Part. San Francisco: North Point, 1980.

The Wheel. San Francisco: North Point, 1982.

Collected Poems 1957–1982. San Francisco: North Point, 1985.

Sabbaths. San Francisco: North Point, 1987.

Traveling at Home. Lewisburg, PA: Press of Appletree Alley, 1988; San Francisco: North
Point, 1989.

Sayings and Doings and An Eastward Look. Frankfort, KY: Gnomon, 1990.

Entries. New York: Pantheon, 1994.

The Farm. Monterey, KY: Larkspur, 1995.

A Timbered Choir: The Sabbath Poems 1979–1997. Washington, DC: Counterpoint, 1998

The Selected Poems of Wendell Berry. Washington, DC: Counterpoint, 1999.

Sabbaths 2002. Monterey, KY: Larkspur, 2004.

Given. Washington, DC: Counterpoint, 2005.

Nonfiction

The Long-Legged House. New York: Harcourt Brace, 1969; Washington, DC: Shoemaker
and Hoard, 2004.

The Hidden Wound. Boston: Houghton Mifflin, 1970; San Francisco, North Point, 1989.

The Unforeseen Wilderness. Lexington, KY: University Press of Kentucky, 1971;
Washington, DC: Shoemaker and Hoard, 2006.

A Continuous Harmony. New York: Harcourt Brace Jovanovich, 1972; Washington, DC:
Shoemaker and Hoard, 2004.

The Unsettling of America. San Francisco: Sierra Club, 1977, 1986, 1996.

Recollected Essays 1965–1980. San Francisco: North Point, 1981.

The Gift of Good Land. San Francisco: North Point, 1981.

Standing by Words. San Francisco: North Point, 1982; Washington, DC: Shoemaker and
Hoard, 2005.

Home Economics: Fourteen Essays. San Francisco: North Point, 1987.

What Are People For? San Francisco: North Point, 1990.

Harlan Hubbard: Life and Work. Lexington, KY: University Press of Kentucky, 1990.

Sex, Economy, Freedom, and Community. New York: Pantheon, 1993.

Another Turn of the Crank. Washington, DC: Counterpoint, 1995.

Life Is a Miracle. Washington, DC: Counterpoint, 2000.

In the Presence of Fear. Barrington, MA: Orion, 2001.

The Art of the Commonplace: The Agrarian Essays of Wendell Berry. Ed. Norman Wirzba. Washington, DC: Counterpoint, 2002.

Citizenship Papers. Washington, DC: Shoemaker and Hoard, 2003.

Tobacco Harvest: An Elegy (contributed introductory essay; photographs by James Baker Hall). Lexington, KY: University Press of Kentucky, 2004.

Blessed Are the Peacemakers. Washington, DC: Shoemaker and Hoard, 2005.

The Way of Ignorance and Other Essays. Washington, DC: Shoemaker and Hoard, 2005.

Contents

Introduction

Believing that a writer's work speaks well enough for itself, Wendell Berry has traditionally resisted interviews. "It seems curious to me," he told L. Elisabeth Beattie in 1993, "that people who have already had something to say in writing should then be expected to talk, as if in talking they would make a contribution that they haven't already made." Such hesitance to "talk" is perhaps especially true of a poet and fiction writer who is also a prolific essayist. Writers are, first of all, writers. They think best on paper; they work through problems, see connections, arrive at conclusions on paper. As an essayist, Wendell Berry is very much a writer's writer. His prose is spring-water clear, his passion moving, his line of thinking manifest, his evidence convincing. And he stands by his words.

Fidelity to his beliefs, steadfastness to his words—these are Berry's enduring signature traits. It is not surprising, then, that as an interviewee he would prefer careful reflective thinking to extemporizing and that he would request the right to edit his spoken interviews. His careful method is a boon to us, for we see in his interviews the same engaging and consistently thoughtful approach that we see throughout his published work. Not until the 1990s, more than thirty years into his writing career, and during a time when he became increasingly vocal as a cultural critic, did his resistance to the interview genre begin to subside. "Because my essays were controversial," Berry has noted, "I began to feel an obligation to answer questions about them." In reading the interviews, we understand more fully his use of the various genres to express his convictions. His poems testify to the mysteries and miracles of life lived in the effort of harmony with land and neighbors; his fiction explores the difficulties and rewards of—and offers a model for—living a community-minded, peaceable, compassionate life; his essays provide the reasoning and evidence for why we should care about the mysteries and miracles, the community and compassion.

Just as a farmer cultivates the soil or a neighbor cultivates care, Berry has approached interviews with the same desire and heightened sense of responsibility. The interview format often requires of him what he, as an English professor, often required of his students: to answer a question with precision and concision—and with consequences. But his answers offer much more than a compact version or a recycling of his central arguments and themes. His interviews are windows into the myriad forces that have shaped this very rare, very vital writer. Flowing through them are the many streams of influence: ancestors, family, teachers, writers, neighbors living and dead, the natural membership of Lanes Landing Farm, the community of Port Royal. What emerges is that the various currents have achieved an uncommon coherence and expression in Berry. He has, in turn, proceeded in interviews with profound care. The seriousness with which he has treated the genre, like all of his work, is a testament to his respect for and love of the people and places that have informed his life. "All my work comes from my loves and hopes," he told Debra Bendis of *The Christian Century* in 1997. "My essays come from a desire to understand what I love and hope for and to defend those things; . . . My work as a fiction writer and poet . . . is my way of giving thanks, maybe, for having things worthy of defense."

Berry is guided by a vision whose focus is on the health of local community, which he defines as the synthesis of the human and natural members of a place. Perhaps what surfaces most clearly in these conversations is that Berry's central themes—marriage to place, the web-like connections between people and land, reverence for mystery, etc.—are the products of his own local membership. "Coming here did one thing for my writing that I am sure of," he told John Leax in 1999. "It caused me—as you say, as I once said myself— 'to live within my subject.' That means that my subject has never been reducible to mere 'subject matter' or 'raw material,' which is the usage of professionalism and industrialism. Coming here made it possible for me to avoid that." Back in 1969 he had described this betrothal in his first book of essays, *The Long-Legged House*, but with decades of practical evidence to back it up, he can now say it with resounding authority. In his conversations, as in his writing, he invariably returns to several touchstone measures of conduct for what he understands as responsible membership in such a community: What can I learn about a place by living there long enough to see the difference I am making? How can I leave the place better than it was when I came to it? What practices and policies are best for the well-being of my community?

What can I do to help encourage the young to live a life committed to place? These questions and others regarding the links between humanity and nature have prompted Berry to produce one of the largest, most consistently articulated bodies of work in contemporary American literature.

His interviews affirm what his imaginative work implies and his essays evince: his life as a writer and his life as a traditional farmer mirror one another and are inseparable. Here we see that both arts occur in the presence of mystery and miracles; both require large measures of discipline and hope. As he told Gregory McNamee and James Hepworth in 1983, "Neither a farm nor a poem should be made at the world's expense; the world must not be looked upon as a supply of 'raw material' for either. To my way of thinking, any made thing should be made in harmony with its sources, and all things so made will have much in common; they will tend to be analogues of each other." Recent interviews make it even clearer that living *within* his subject continually informs his moral and religious life. "My approach to religion has pretty much been from the bottom up," he told Anne Husted Burleigh in 1999. "I never was very good at the top-down version, and my understanding of religion has grown from my understanding of the things of time, from family and community life." What he has affirmed by living and working in a small rural community is that wisdom and harmony and peace cannot be achieved by retreating into nature or by seeking isolation. These achievements come most assuredly by turning toward loving companionship, self-restraint, pity, forgiveness. He shows us that the best matrix for the cultivation and accumulation of wisdom is small-scale, place-based, neighbor-centered communities.

Not only a local fidelity but also a rigorous practicality pervades Berry's life and work. His and Tanya Berry's decision in 1964 to leave the literary world of New York City and make a home in Kentucky, near the place where he grew up, signaled an abiding commitment to practicality. Even his decision in 1987 to resume his professorship at the University of Kentucky, after resigning ten years earlier, was in service to the practical. Unlike his previous appointment teaching creative writing, he returned to teach courses that would put him in the classroom with future teachers and farmers or anyone preparing to work in practical and comprehensive ways with young minds or with nature. "My approach to education would be like my approach to everything else," he told Jordan Fisher Smith in 1993. "I'd change the standard. I would make the standard that of community health rather than the career of the student. You see, if you make the standard the health of the community, that would change everything. Once you begin to ask what would be the best thing for our community, what's the best thing that we can do here for our community, you can't rule out any kind of knowledge. You need to know everything you possibly can know." All areas of his life are governed by a practical, useful, comprehensive vision. As a grader of student papers, for example, he eschewed theory and abstraction, jargon and indirectness (a lesson I learned as one of his students). As a teacher of literature, he preferred portrayals and explorations of the practical links between humanity and nature. As a small-scale traditional farmer, he has criticized the teaching of agriculture in research universities, which, as he sees it, too often proceeds by way of specialization.

Since Berry looks to nature and to others—writers, friends, neighbors, family—for instruction and encouragement, and since his own writing offers a prescription for healing and a model for wholeness, it follows that interviewers would find him both instructive and encouraging. He is teacherly even in his conversations, often broaching what he sees as critical cultural problems and discussing solutions with doses of wisdom, anecdotes, humor, love. Interviewers approach him with admiration and wonder. "If you've never heard of Wendell Berry," Bruce Williamson prefaces his 1973 interview, "it's probably only because the man hasn't been too worried about becoming famous. It's a certainty, however, that Berry's work as a farmer, neighbor, citizen, activist, teacher, poet, novelist, and essayist is one of those rare collections of experience that touches each of us deep in our lives." He is a writer who has localized his vision and yet has garnered a world of respect and admiration from an international audience. Fidelity to place, to people, Berry told L. Elisabeth Beattie in 1993, "just means making a commitment and hanging on, and never giving up. As long as you've got the life and willpower to continue, you continue. All that's based on a faith that my experience, to some extent, proves out—if you hang on, you'll see your way through whatever it is that's difficult—that there's going to be a reward. I believe that; it's my profoundest operating belief." In an age of escalating divorce, transience, and violence toward each other and the earth, interviewers and readers marvel at a man who is wholly committed to trying to understand and to love one place, a man who is able to steady himself in the rushing drifts of modern life.

Although not meant to be an exhaustive compilation of interviews, this volume aims to provide a solid representation of the inquiry Wendell Berry has faced and the answers he has given. For the seasoned Berry reader, these conversations offer a wealth of information and affirmation. For someone new to Berry, they offer a welcoming introduction to work and author, revealing his complexities and perplexities, his ability to cut to the bottom of an issue, his profoundly grounded thinking, his worries and loves, his endearing humor.

The interviewers are this volume's collective heroes, and I thank each for his and her thoughtful and careful work. I am grateful to my students and colleagues at Lindsey Wilson College in Columbia, Kentucky, for encouraging my abiding interest in Wendell Berry, and to the administration for granting me a sabbatical leave. In particular, I thank Provost and Academic Dean William B. Julian, Associate Dean Lori Sargent, Humanities Division Chair Patrick Shaw, and English Program Coordinator Kerry Robertson for maintaining a nurturing climate in which such work can occur. A senior English major at Lindsey Wilson, Candace Styron, now a graduate student at SUNY–New Paltz, typed many of the interviews, sometimes squinting, I'm sure, to read the tiny print in the photocopies I gave her. Our conversations about Berry's work—and Faulkner's too—have helped clarify and enrich my thinking. At the University Press of Mississippi, Seetha Srinivasan and Walter Biggins moved me expertly through the publishing process; I value their experience and appreciate their guidance. My wife, Anissa Radford, is a loving guide and a keen and trustworthy critic; I can't imagine pursuing such work without her. Finally, I am deeply indebted to Wendell and Tanya Berry, who, along with their children and grandchildren, continue to make my work so instructive and so pleasurable. This book is for them.

MAG

Chronology

1934	Wendell Erdman Berry born on 5 August to John Marshall Berry and Virginia Erdman Berry of Henry County, Kentucky.
1936	Family moves to New Castle, Kentucky, where father practices law and farms; attends New Castle public schools through the eighth grade.
1948–52	Attends and graduates from Millersburg Military Institute in Millersburg, Kentucky.
1952	Enters the University of Kentucky at Lexington.
1953	Publishes first essay, "The Wings of the Future," in *The Green Pen*, the University of Kentucky's annual anthology of freshman writing.
1954	Publishes first poem, "Spring," and first short story, "Summer Crop," in *Stylus*, the University of Kentucky's literary journal.
1955	In fall meets Tanya Amyx, an English major and daughter of University of Kentucky art professor Clifford Amyx and textile artist Dee Amyx.
1956	Graduates from the University of Kentucky with bachelor's degree in English; in summer completes literature seminars at Indiana University School of Letters; in fall enters master's program in English at the University of Kentucky.
1957	In spring completes M.A. in English; marries Tanya Amyx; in summer they live in ancestral cabin, "the Camp," on the Kentucky River near Port Royal; teaches English at Georgetown College in Georgetown, Kentucky.
1958	Daughter, Mary Dee, is born in Lexington; in August moves with family to Mill Valley, California, to attend Stanford Creative Writing Program on a Wallace Stegner Fellowship.
1959–60	Teaches creative writing at Stanford University.
1960	First novel, *Nathan Coulter*, appears in March; earlier in year begins writing second novel, *A Place on Earth*.

1961–62   Travels in Europe with family and lives and writes in
          Florence, Italy, and in southern France on a Guggenheim
          Fellowship.

1962   Son, Pryor Clifford (Den), is born in Lexington; receives Vachel
          Lindsay Prize from *Poetry* magazine; in fall moves with family to
          New York to serve as Director of Freshman Writing at University
          College of New York University in the Bronx.

1964   Moves with family back to Kentucky to teach creative writing
          at the University of Kentucky in Lexington; begins commuting
          weekly to Port Royal to write at the Camp; first two books of
          poetry appear: *November twenty six nineteen hundred sixty
          three* in May and *The Broken Ground* in September; in November
          purchases Lanes Landing Farm, adjacent to the Camp.

1965   Moves with family to Lanes Landing Farm on 4 July; awarded a
          Rockefeller Foundation Scholarship.

1967   *A Place on Earth* (novel). Receives Bess Hoken Prize from *Poetry*
          magazine.

1968   *Openings* (poetry).

1968–69   While on leave from the University of Kentucky, teaches at
          Stanford University as Visiting Professor

1969   *Findings* (poetry) and *The Long-Legged House* (essays). Receives
          National Endowment for the Arts grant; wins Borestone
          Mountain Poetry Award.

1970   *The Hidden Wound* (nonfiction) and *Farming: A Handbook*
          (poetry).

1971   *The Unforeseen Wilderness: An Essay on Kentucky's Red River Gorge*
          (nonfiction, with photographs by Ralph Eugene Meatyard).
          Receives National Institute of Arts and Letters Award for Writing;
          named "Distinguished Professor of the Year" at the University of
          Kentucky.

1972   *A Continuous Harmony: Essays Cultural and Agricultural.*

1973   *The Country of Marriage* (poetry).

1974   *The Memory of Old Jack* (novel). Promoted to Professor of English
          at the University of Kentucky; wins Emily Clark Balch prize from
          The Virginia Poetry Review.

1975   *Sayings and Doings* (poetry). First Prize for *The Memory of Old
          Jack* from Friends of American Writers.

1977   *The Unsettling of America: Culture and Agriculture* (nonfiction) and *Clearing* (poems). Resigns from teaching at the University of Kentucky; serves as writer-in-residence at Centre College in Danville, Kentucky.

1978   Receives honorary doctorate from Centre College.

1980   *A Part* (poetry).

1981   *Recollected Essays: 1965–1980* and *The Gift of Good Land* (essays). Receives honorary doctorate from Transylvania University.

1982   *The Wheel* (poetry).

1983   *Standing by Words* (essays). Publishes substantially revised edition of *A Place on Earth*. Receives honorary doctorate from Berea College.

1985   *Collected Poems: 1957–1982*.

1986   *The Wild Birds: Six Stories of the Port William Membership* (short-story cycle). Receives honorary doctorate from the University of Kentucky.

1987   *Home Economics* (essays) and *Sabbaths* (poetry). Returns to faculty at the University of Kentucky to teach "Composition for Teachers," "Readings in Agriculture," and "The Pastoral"; serves as writer-in-residence at Bucknell University; receives the Jean Stein Award from the American Academy of Arts and Letters, and the Kentucky Governor's Award; receives honorary doctorate from Santa Clara University.

1988   *Remembering* (novel). Receives honorary doctorate from Eureka College.

1989   Receives the Lannan Foundation Award for Nonfiction; delivers Blazer Lectures at the University of Kentucky on artist-musician-naturalist-writer Harlan Hubbard.

1990   *What Are People For?* (essays) and *Harlan Hubbard: Life and Work* (biography/criticism); inducted into the Fellowship of Southern Writers.

1991   *Standing on Earth: Selected Essays* (published in Great Britain).

1992   *Fidelity* (short stories) and *Sabbaths 1987–1990* (poetry). Receives the Victory of Spirit Ethics Award from University of Louisville and Louisville Community Foundation.

1993   *Sex, Economy, Freedom and Community* (essays). Resigns from faculty at the University of Kentucky.

1994   *Entries* (poetry) and *Watch with Me* (short stories). Receives the
        T. S. Eliot Award for Creative Writing from the Ingersoll
        Foundation, the Aiken Taylor Award in Modern American Poetry
        from the *Sewanee Review*, and the John Hay Award from the
        Orion Society.

1995   *Another Turn of the Crank* (essays).

1996   *A World Lost* (novel). Receives Harry M. Caudill Conservationist
        Award, Cumberland Chapter, Sierra Club.

1998   *A Timbered Choir: The Sabbath Poems 1979–1997.*

1999   *The Selected Poems of Wendell Berry.* Receives the Thomas Merton
        Award from the Thomas Merton Center for Peace and Social
        Justice.

2000   *Jayber Crow* (novel) and *Life Is a Miracle* (nonfiction); wins Poets'
        Prize for *Selected Poems*; receives honorary doctorate from
        Western Kentucky University and Samford University.

2002   *The Art of the Commonplace: The Agrarian Essays of Wendell Berry*
        (edited by Norman Wirzba).

2003   *Citizenship Papers* (essays). Receives Lifetime Achievement Award,
        Cathedral Heritage Foundation, Louisville, Kentucky.

2004   *Hannah Coulter* (novel) and *That Distant Land: The Collected
        Stories.* Receives Charity Randall Citation from International
        Poetry Forum; Lifetime Service Award from the Environmental
        Quality Commission; and Eli M. Oboler Memorial Award (with
        David James Duncan) from American Library Association.

2005   *Given* (poetry), *The Way of Ignorance and other Essays*, and *Blessed
        Are the Peacemakers* (selections of Christ's teachings gathered and
        introduced by Berry). Named by *Smithsonian Magazine* as one of
        "35 Who Made a Difference"; receives Lifetime Achievement
        Award from the Conference on Christianity and Literature;
        receives honorary doctorate from Lindsey Wilson College;
        inducted into University of Kentucky Arts and Sciences Hall of
        Fame.

2006   *Andy Catlett* (novel). Named Kentuckian of the Year by *Kentucky
        Monthly* magazine; wins Kentucky Literary Award from Kentucky
        Bookfest; receives The Art of Fact Award for nonfiction at the
        State University of New York at Brockport.

Conversations with Wendell Berry

The Plowboy Interview: Wendell Berry

Bruce Williamson / 1973

From *Mother Earth News* 20 (March 1973), 6–12. Copyright 1973 by Ogden Publishing Corporation (UT). Reproduced with permission of Ogden Publishing Corporation (UT) via Copyright Clearance Center.

If you've never heard of Wendell Berry, it's probably only because the man hasn't been too worried about becoming famous. It's a certainty, however, that Berry's work as a farmer, neighbor, citizen, activist, teacher, poet, novelist, and essayist is one of those rare collections of experience that touches each of us deep in our own lives.

Wendell lives—by deliberate choice—on a Port Royal, Kentucky, farm that he considers his "rightful place in the world," but he does not allow this strong sense of location to draw a curtain of provincialism across his view of life.

Instead, Berry seemingly manages to devote the full measure of his attention both to the well-being of his family and community and to the matters which affect and afflict the whole earth. His concern alternates, as he says, between "the doorstep and the planet."

Wendell Berry's anguish about the greed and hate that too often blight the human spirit, and the warm pleasure that he takes in the earth's natural beauty are captured—to varying degrees—in his five volumes of poetry, four books of essays, and three novels. Berry's devotees particularly recommend *The Unforeseen Wilderness*, about a journey by canoe and foot through the intricate delights of a lovely river gorge threatened by "progress"; *The Hidden Wound*, an accounting of his own heritage of racism; *Farming, A Handbook*, poetry not "incompatible with barns and gardens and fields and woodlands"; *A Place on Earth*, Wendell's richly textured and warmly moving second novel; *The Long-Legged House*, and *A Continuous Harmony*, books of essays ranging from his indictment of strip mining in Kentucky, to "A Statement Against The War In Vietnam," to his attempts to discover the importance of his ancestors in bringing him to the place where he is today. Wendell's "language of permanence" in his most recent book of poetry, *The Country of Marriage*, and his reviews of *Farmers of Forty Centuries* and *An Agricultural Testament* in the *Last Whole Earth Catalog* are also warmly mentioned in any gathering of Berry followers.

Wendell Berry—a man who increasingly seems to articulate the hopes and fears and dreams of people committed to a saner world—rarely grants interviews. He not only agreed to the following exchange with Bruce Williamson, however, but sacrificed much personal time and energy to make sure that the conversation—and the article which resulted from it—was as informative, concise, and precise as possible. Here, then, is Wendell Berry . . . exactly as Bruce Williamson found him in the study of his Port Royal, Kentucky, home.

Plowboy: Mr. Berry, for some time now you've been writing about the meaning of farming in your own life and its importance to the modern world . . . and more and more people seem to be coming around to your point of view. Do you think that small-scale farming is finally being reaccepted as a viable and necessary contribution to the stability of both urban and rural life?

Berry: I'm not sure. When I first started saying that it was important just to grow a garden, it seemed really risky stuff to me. You can defend farming on an aesthetic basis and say it's a great thing to go off into the country and breathe good air and lead a healthy life and grow your own vegetables. That's really nice, really lovely. But to get on from there and say that you can learn things of great practical, moral, and spiritual importance from doing it— that's still going to take a while.

Plowboy: Why?

Berry: It has to do with a breakdown of our language, the way we talk about farming. Our culture today is mainly embarrassed about country things. It no longer realizes or wants to realize that its life still must come from the ground. We can't speak to farmers anymore about their value to us. They no longer have a model or a place that they can look to outside themselves, and say, "Yes, there's a vision of the kind of person I'd like to become." Instead, they turn on the television and see a show like "Green Acres" which represents them as negligible and comical. Back in the works of some of the old writers like Homer and Hesiod and Virgil and Chaucer there's real knowledge of the worth of agriculture and it's combined with high art and theology and love and everything else. Farming's right in there. They didn't have to apologize for it.

Plowboy: That kind of respect was based in part on proximity . . . being physically close to the process of farming. Isolated in a technological society as many of us now are, however, it's not surprising that we often lose the ability to see the beauties of a life close to the land.

Berry: I'd like to get people back in touch with the realities of a farming life. There's a great argument going on today about whether or not the family farm is going to survive or should survive. This argument is extremely important, but it seems to me that all the talk about productivity and markets and feeding the hungry is secondary. The primary concern has to be with the cultural relation between people and land.

We need to be talking about the family farmers who live on and care for small tracts of land out of the motivation that long association and deep knowledge can produce, people who know the difference between duty and love. We need to know what that kind of spirit means for a person as well as a place, and then we'll begin to understand the practical value of the family farm.

Plowboy: In terms of what you've called the "love that enforces care"?

Berry: It's love that keeps you walking over a place, and it's love that makes you imagine what can be done on it. More and more since Tanya and I have lived on this farm, our life has been taken up with imagining what would be possible. And we'll be involved in that until we die, or until our energy plays out. Our life here has developed in response to this place and the potential in it. By now we've realized some of it, but the most exciting thing is that we know we haven't realized very much of it.

Plowboy: But you let the possibilities grow and mature slowly instead of trying to do everything at once.

Berry: That's right, and then you start to make it real. Then you begin to make mistakes too, because that's part of it. I don't know the trees I've set out here and had to dig up because something we didn't foresee happened. But that's part of what you mean by organic. We could have gotten a land-scape architect to come here and put this place together—and then we could have lived here like inmates. But we're living here the way we live inside our skin; it fits us and as we change it changes.

Plowboy: And yet some experts would call this hillside farm "marginal land."

Berry: Land like this—and there's a lot of it on both sides of the river here—seems to me to be important because of what it tells us about the limitations of our agriculture. This land is not suited for agribusiness or even the highly mechanized family farm. Much of it was abandoned because of bad farming methods, and it stays that way because our economy won't permit the kind of farming it requires. But cared for in the right way, it has a tremendous agricultural potential and is extremely responsive land. An Italian or an Oriental peasant would see abundance here and would achieve abundance.

Plowboy: Then why aren't such labor-intensive methods being used?

Berry: It has to do partly with the kind of work most people will do anymore. I think we're developing a society now whose dominant effort is to get out of work. It's probably a measure of our decadence that we can talk about a "work ethic." Work isn't an ethic, work's a necessity.

The agricultural experts have a dream and every now and then you see a magazine article that projects it. Here's a farmer sitting up in a glass-enclosed tower, with a console of buttons and instruments in front of him. He's clean, he doesn't have any dust or sweat on him. There are no bugs crawling down his neck or chaff falling down the collar of his white shirt. Out there in the field are all these menial machines, scurrying about doing his bidding. He's our ideal of a good man, too good to work.

But everybody who's ever worked with machines know they're the most frustrating things going. At certain times not appointed by any expert those robots are going to stop. And it's going to be in the middle of a hot humid July day, and that farmer's going to have to leave his air-conditioned cubicle and go out there and crawl under the machinery in dirt and grease, and sweat and fume and curse and get it running again.

Plowboy: On the other hand, an Oriental farmer—at least those described by F. H. King in *Farmers of Forty Centuries*—takes the time to really care for his land, and can get much more productivity from it.

Berry: That's because he uses every resource available to him and wastes nothing, not even his own excrement. Human wastes are excellent fertilizer when composted properly.

Plowboy: I understand you can speak on that subject from personal experience. You have built your own composting privy, haven't you?

Berry: Yes, although we aren't using the compost on any food crops until we've worked with it for a while and are sure of it. We do put the compost on ornamentals and young trees and it's good stuff.

For us that privy has solved several practical problems. We have a limited water supply from our well and a poor soil for a septic tank system, and we also wanted to stop the effluent from getting into the river. Of course, there are other reasons. In *An Agricultural Testament*, Sir Albert Howard talks about bringing growth and decay into balance. Our society is interested in growth and production but isn't really interested in decay at all. And as long as it doesn't get interested, its excrement and garbage will just remain a nuisance and a danger and never become part of that cycle everybody's talking about.

Plowboy: It's certainly much easier to gabble about our "sewage disposal crisis" . . . while we keep right on flushing the toilet. Do you think most people—people in this country anyway—are really willing to alter their habits that drastically? Can we become realistic enough to swap our flush toilets for composting privies?

Berry: There's a state of mind that has to accompany a change like that. The American mind has been schooled for years to think that you oughtn't to spend time on any regular basis on anything that isn't glamorous. And you especially oughtn't to have to spend it turning manure piles in a composting privy. But once you become willing to involve yourself in the kind of discipline and faithfulness it takes to see to jobs like that when they need to be seen to, then it seems to me you're getting away from the sickness that afflicts the society everywhere and going to work on some kind of cure.

Plowboy: That still sounds pretty idealistic!

Berry: Well, I have an American head like everybody else and there are times when it seems there are better things for me to be doing. Anything you go into regularly is going to lead to a certain amount of disenchantment. The first time you ever clean out your privy, you're going to go down there with great enthusiasm and really throw that stuff out of there. It's going to be a great thing to do. But about the fifteenth time you've got to do it, it's going to be raining or you're going to be in a hurry and you're going to think to yourself—maybe you're a writer—"I could be writing, but here I've got to clean out this old privy."

Plowboy: There are many chores on a working farm that require that kind of discipline.

Berry: It's like having a milk cow. Having a milk cow is a very strict discipline and a very trying circumstance. It means you've got to be home twice a day to milk whether you want to or not, or else the cow will be ruined. Some days you'd rather do anything than go down to that barn and maybe some days you go and you're kind of bored with it. But other days it's a most rewarding thing and you realize that you get the reward and happiness of it because you stuck to it when it wasn't rewarding. There's some kind of wisdom in that fidelity, when you can say, "All right, every day ain't going to be the best day of your life, don't worry about that. If you stick to it you hold the possibility open that you will have better days."

Plowboy: But when people make a commitment to farming, won't their attitude toward the work make it more rewarding?

Berry: If by attitude you mean enthusiasm, then I'm not so sure. I think the popular drug culture and certain aspects of the peace and environment movements have led people to believe there's a great deal you can do with enthusiasm. I have a lot of enthusiasm, but I know how far it will get me. It doesn't last until dark when you've got a full day's work, or three or four days' work, to do in a day. If you get all the way to dark and to the end of the job, then you're going to be operating on something else.

A lot of people have assumed that the main work in changing over from an urban to a rural life is to get out of the city. That's hardly the start. Learning farming is like learning an art; it takes a long time, and a lot of careful work. And we've failed to teach the young people to expect that a worthy thing might be difficult to learn.

Plowboy: Yet many people are willing to make a very serious commitment to the land . . . investing their money and their hopes in the ideal of an independent life.

Berry: Yes, but it seems to me that they shouldn't try to be too pure. That is, to throw over a well-paying job—and training that prepares you for some kind of profession—and go back to the farm and attempt to survive there under conditions that are destroying a lot of experienced farmers. That might be a dangerous thing to do unless you know very well what you are doing and are young. I think it's worthwhile to support your farm by some other work. It's worth it to keep your hands on a piece of land and to keep that part of your life away from the corporations and the speculators and the fools.

If we were willing to isolate ourselves, we could have a lifestyle here that would make us a lot more independent of power companies and machines than we are now. It would also keep us from being useful as strip-mine opponents and airport opponents and that sort of thing.

Plowboy: Airport opponents?
Berry: The Jefferson County Air Board wants to build a jetport on 22,000 acres of good farmland in Henry and Shelby Counties. We've been watching those airport people for a couple of years now, seeing what they were up to and getting ready to move when the site plans were announced. We've already had some meetings.

This airport fight is the largest direct action on the part of the people in these counties for years. And as long as the project lasts I think there'll be people to fight it, because we all have a stake in what's going on. There are a lot of people here who would do a great deal to defend the soil under their feet in Henry and Shelby Counties. It seems to me that this supports my belief that a lot depends on a stable community.

Plowboy: How would you define a stable community?
Berry: You've got to have people who talk to each other a lot and who have experiences in common. In a settled farming community old friends get together to work and one thing they do is tell each other again the stories they already know. This is a complex community function. They celebrate their old acquaintance in that way, they celebrate themselves. They alert each other to the realities of their lives and their history. And the effect that it has on story-telling is that it improves the stories.

But the stories in the media today cater to the wish people have for everything to be new. That's very much the emphasis in our arts today, for example. That's not different at all from the Madison Avenue ideal that thrives on the establishment and immediate wearing out of fashions and fads. Any culture building itself on this kind of novelty is bound to run thin.

Plowboy: In the face of that kind of cultural pressure, it takes a conscious effort to reinstate the ceremony and ritual in our lives. Many intentional communities are trying to generate this kind of awareness and stability . . . .
Berry: But I'm much more interested in the results of accidental communities that have formed by fate and fortune and circumstance. The intentional community seems to me a rather escapist idea, sort of a new version of the white citizen's council. I thought that's what we were trying to get away from. I think the idea that you can have an intentional community is about as misleading as saying you can have an intentional life. If you're going to have a decent and stable community, you've got to produce the cultural and social forms by which to deal with the unexpected and the undesirable. The intentional community idea assumes that when you say love your neighbor as yourself, you have some kind of right to go out and pick your neighbor. I think that the ideal of loving your neighbor has to take on the possibility that he may be somebody you're going to have great difficulty loving or liking or even tolerating.

Plowboy: In your writing you emphasize that the inhabitants of a region thrive on the daily interchange between old and young . . . yet many of these new communities are made up primarily of young people.
Berry: Yes, and that's one of the worst possible kinds of segregation. This is probably the first generation not to have a history. They have their own immediate history but not one that comes from having older people around them. They're coming up to adult life without the awareness that anyone has ever gone through their experiences before, much less learned anything from them. But I know people who as children had their grandparents' memories in their memories, so that in a sense, as young people they had old minds. They had a kind of seasoning.

Plowboy: You certainly talk about your own childhood in that way.
Berry: That's right, although I can't say that I've always agreed with all the older people I've grown up around. I've had the same struggles with them as most people who grow up. Nevertheless I owe a great debt to my elders and I agree with all of them on something or other. I think that my knowledge of them and my association with them has given me a sense of what is possible.

There's a sort of gift to humanity that each generation of young people renews. They feel in their bones what's desirable. "It would be great if we could be free." And the function of older people in the society is not to oppose that, but to qualify it. To say yes, it would be great to be free . . . but there are certain ways to get free that are going to surprise you and make stern demands on you. The man who is most able usually turns out to be the man who's most free, not the one who's the most reckless. The old are the ones who will put their hands on you and say, "Well, be a little steady now," or "No, you can't quit, you're not finished yet."

Plowboy: Have you reached that role yourself?
Berry: Well, my own history as a teacher has had a rather dramatic change along those lines. Back when we were making speeches and holding meetings about the environment and against the Vietnam War, I was sort of looked on as a friend of the good causes. Then last year we had a long struggle in the university about academic requirements. I was holding out for the importance of learning a foreign language, for instance, and overnight I got the reputation of being an "academic fascist." But I would be a lot better off if I knew more languages, and more math and biology, too. That's the message I got from my own experience.

Here it seems to me you have a strange thing. You have young people who want world peace but don't want to learn anybody else's language. A young fellow came up to me after one of those meetings and said, "I've never had a foreign language and I want you to tell me why I should take French. I'm studying agriculture, not literature." "Well," I said, "if you don't know, I can't tell you. That's why you take French for two or three or four years, to learn why you should take it."

The fact is that a great deal that's necessary and satisfying to know is not pleasant to learn. So-called educators have allowed the idea to get around among students that education ought to be constantly diverting and entertaining. That's a terrible disservice to reality. And students then feel affronted by the hardship that's native to education and to the mastery of any discipline.

Plowboy: It's true most educators are jumping on the "relevance" band-wagon. And yet a less didactic approach is certainly appealing to the young person who wants to try new directions in learning.
Berry: What I'm saying is that the young have had lots of praisers and lots of detractors but few critics, which is really a way of saying they've had few

friends. A curious phenomenon of the youth culture thing—and it's full of curious phenomena—is these old sycophants who hang about its skirts and try to touch and kiss the hem of its garment. We see white-haired old men stand up at the university and abdicate their responsibility to the young on the grounds that they (the teachers) have not received the word of God.

Charles Reich is one of the best examples I know of a teacher who's copped out completely by becoming a sycophant of his students. I mean I'm completely against this idiocy of his that says surfboarding is an acceptable way of life. That's utterly absurd. The Greening of America is full of false apologies and excuses for people's failure to be responsible. Surfboarding is not a way of life. People are free to think it is because the care and responsibility for society has been broken up and parceled out to the experts. People who make a life of surfboarding are living off other people. They're leeches of the affluent society. They're parasites of a parasite. As long as we have people making some kind of amusement a way of life, you'll find they're getting their support from something destructive, like strip-mining or needless "development" or war-making.

Plowboy: The most frustrating aspect of this is that the cycle seems so hard to break. We're all parasites in one way or another.
Berry: The only way I can see out of the predicament we're all in is to promote that old ideal of personal independence. I don't mean the kind of independence that makes people act without regard for other people or that makes them assume they can get along without other people. I mean the independence by which a person provides some of his own needs and which permits him to do what he sees to be right without the approval of a crowd. That's why Thomas Jefferson said you need to keep as many people as possible on the land. That's necessary for a democracy. You need to keep people independent in the way that the ownership and care of a piece of land can make them.

If the ideals and aims of young people have lost energy, it's because they haven't the stability of a commitment to one place and one community. I think they're disposed to drift around until they find a suitable community. But no community is suitable. There's plenty wrong with them all. I could construct an airtight argument for not settling in my own community. The fact is that I'm spending my life constructing an argument for being here.

Plowboy: In the sense that you don't plan to ever move away from Port Royal, Kentucky?

Berry: Yes, and we had something happen here not too long ago that kind of served as a test of that decision. We'd been here since 1964 and in that period of time we'd sort of solved a whole set of problems that faced us when we started. We'd become almost self-sufficient as far as food was concerned, and had begun to understand the significance of this place in our lives and in the life of modern America. Suddenly the farm next door to us was sold to a developer. He brought in bulldozers and dumped tons of gravel onto the land to make it some kind of ideal landscape for a trailer court. The machines were roaring and real estate speculators were coming around talking about a hundred lots for house trailers and vacation cabins. We could see the smoke from our neighbor's fire, so to speak; we could see the dust from his bulldozer and we could see his signs.

One of our first thoughts was that we would leave, we wouldn't put up with it, we'd get out of here and go someplace where it was quieter and where we could live the way we wanted to. We'd go west, as they used to say. And then we realized that that impulse went against the current of our lives up to that point.

A farmer, who's a neighbor of mine and probably the oldest friend I've got in the world, had told me, "They'll never do worth a damn as long as they've got two choices." That's the most important thing that's been said to me in the last couple of years. It illuminates the meaning of marriage. When you believe in a thing enough so that you eliminate the second choice, forsake all others, then you're married to it. So we decided that this place would have to be our fate and that we'd stay here no matter what happened as long as life was possible. That decision changed us and became a kind of metaphor of our own marriage. Since then, life on this place has had a much different and fuller meaning for us. (EDITOR'S NOTE: Soon after this interview the Berrys were able to buy the threatened land next door to their farm and are now doing what they can to repair the damage done to it.)

Plowboy: I like that concept of marriage . . . commitment to a place as well as to a person.

Berry: My friend Ken Kesey was here the other day and we were talking about the willingness to make marriage and the importance of that willingness in any kind of credible maturity in a man or a woman. My mother's parents' marriage was a good one and they lived long enough after Tanya and I were married for us to see that it was and to get lots of strength from it, a kind of inspiration. We learned a great deal from them about a certain kind of goodness.

That's one difficulty that today's marriages are laboring under—the failure of any good marriage to communicate its existence to any other. Tanya and I have felt this a whole lot. Marriages are crashing down all around us. We feel like the trees in a logging woods—who's going to be next?

Plowboy: Separation and divorce and estrangement are certainly characteristic of our "modern world."

Berry: It's very much a failing of the whole society. Our culture finds it impossible to deal with the kind of love that keeps a community together and stable. It's embarrassed about domestic happiness and grief. And about any show of genuine feeling and love between men. I don't mean love in the sexual way but in the familiar open freehearted way that would let a man give another man a big hug. My family is always hugging a whole lot, and I'm for hugging. I grew up here around men who weren't afraid to touch each other. When I was a boy, older men were always touching me and patting me. I was pretty skinny and they'd squeeze my leg and say, "Boy, does your leg swell up like that every summer?" There was a great goodness and good-heartedness in that and no meanness at all.

Plowboy: That kind of openness and friendliness does seem more characteristic of the country than the city. Having neighbors like that can make a big difference to a newcomer in an area.

Berry: Sure it can. People who are moving out into the country ought to keep that in mind. They can learn a great deal from their neighbors about conditions of the ground, for instance, and how to work it at certain times. Most people are willing to give that advice. To go into a place and base everything on an assumption of your moral and intellectual superiority to your neighbors seems to me to be the most insulting thing you can do. And it cuts you off from the very things you need to know.

If you're really going to neighbor, you go to them when they need you, and when you need help you call. Two brothers who live up the creek and another friend and I have known each other pretty near always, and we exchange work all the time. We don't keep books. I do all I can for them. They do all

they can for me. And it's a good thing. Who knows what the record is? I
helped one of them put in his crop of tobacco last year. He said, "What do I
owe you?" I said, "Nothing." That's ceremony. He wouldn't want me to think
that I hadn't worked well enough to deserve to be paid, or that he wouldn't
be willing to pay me if I wanted him to. But when hog-killing time came I
had two hogs to kill and he said, "I've fattened you a hog, you need three." He
knew I hadn't had enough bacon the year before. I don't know whether he
overpaid me or I overpaid him or where it stands. And that's the way I prefer
to live. That means our work has escaped from economics and has value in
an altogether different sense, and a much larger sense. Our work for each
other is valuable beyond its practical worth because there's a deep strong
bond of friendship and respect among us. It gives us pleasure to work
together.

Plowboy: Do many of the farmers you know around here use organic methods on their land?
Berry: Not really. In order to change from chemical to organic farming, most
farmers are going to need somebody to prove that it can be done economically. Because of the economic stresses they're under, they're not the ones
who are going to initiate the changes. Most of them have a large investment
in land and equipment and the farm economy is unstable. Labor is scarce
because their sons don't stay on the farm anymore, and because they can't
compete with industrial pay. Chemical methods are attractive because they
take less time. That doesn't mean the farmers always like those shortcuts. But
what choice do they have?

There are farms around the country that are beginning to serve as models
for large-scale organic practices, thereby showing that these methods can
work even with the tight economics and the labor shortages. And these farms
are getting easier to find.

Plowboy: As in the "organic directory" published by Rodale Press?
Berry: Yes. People like the New Alchemists are also contributing something
very important by getting the farmers and gardeners to do the experimental
work themselves. This is exactly where the agriculture colleges and extension
services have failed the farmers. Those institutions develop new varieties and
new methods, and then more or less lose interest in them. I think they ought
to work out programs in which the ag school would invite the farmers to do

the experimenting, and then underwrite the cost of any crop failure caused by the use of the new seed or method. In that approach the experiment would succeed or fail in terms of the practicalities of people's lives. If it succeeded, the knowledge would already be in the community where it belonged.

Plowboy: Besides Rodale Press and the New Alchemists, are there any other groups helping the large farmers experiment with organic methods?
Berry: None that I know of. The big farm magazines are giving their effort to pseudo-experiments and editorial opinions attempting to write off or laugh off the claims that organic methods ought rightfully to have on their attention. They've been bought by the chemical companies and the agribusinessmen.

Plowboy: Your resistance to this sort of domination reminds me of the "mad farmer" in your poetry.
Berry: Well, it seems to me that many of the things we're asked to call the blessings of progress are actually deforming diseases. But as I said earlier, that's not a thing our time has made it easy to just pop up and say. I suppose the mad farmer is one of the ways I made myself able to say it. I think he's the voice of a force in the world and in ourselves that our current civilization has been put together to deny.

The impulses of fecundity and fertility, that other cultures have honored in rites and ceremonies, we've put down and covered up. We don't have harvest festivals anymore. We don't really have anything festive anymore. The mad farmer is full of celebration and he's full of the praise of fertility and rutting and loving and dancing and singing. Some literary critic is always saying that he really is sane. The mad farmer's sane, of course, but he says himself, "To be sane in a mad time / is bad for the brain, worse / for the heart."

Plowboy: Have critics given your work a rough time?
Berry: I remember an attack or two. But the ones I remember best didn't come from critics. A friend gave a copy of *The Long-Legged House* to a professional military person and this person looked in it and took it right down and put it in the furnace. He apparently thought it a piece of Communist subversion. Then another couple gave the same book to some friends who

were kind of radical types, and they wrote back that I was an "anti-communist individualist," which seems to be a term of censure.

But it's awfully hard, when you write arguments, to avoid the tone that implies that you know what other people ought to do. My work is best, I think, when I talk as a person who's not an authority on anything but his own experience. I'm very much aware of this and have quit writing arguments for the time being: After finishing the essays in *A Continuous Harmony*, I went with a great deal of relief back to a novel.

Plowboy: Does your new novel take up the story where you ended in *A Place on Earth*?

Berry: In a way it does. After I finished *A Place on Earth* I could see that I would probably write a novel sometime about Old Jack, and the new book's going to be called *The Memory of Old Jack*. It's about the last day that Old Jack lives and about his life as he recalls it and meditates on it, and about his influence on his friends and his survival in their memories.

I've tried in the figure of Old Jack to write a kind of a criticism and celebration of my grandfather Berry's generation, born about the time of the Civil War. I think that was the last generation in this country until now, and maybe for some time to come, that had a chance to become a truly indigenous agricultural community. They identified with their land and took good care of it, or the best of them did. But then the opportunity that they represented was destroyed by adverse markets and social fashions. They had a terrible struggle, and so when there was a chance opening up in the cities for their children to get away, they couldn't advise them to do anything else. I remember my grandmother saying to me, "Don't ever farm."

But anyway, in this novel I've tried to keep the modern world in mind, and tried to gauge what we've inherited that can stand against it. I finally realized that in Old Jack a rather formidable intelligence comes through, and a kind of tragic experience. He understands that there is such a thing as a modern ignorance that consists of arrogance and the assumption that we can outsmart our nature. His conclusion is that man can't help being ignorant, but he can help being a fool.

Plowboy: In other words, for you, Old Jack is another means of expressing the dignity of a farming heritage and the important rituals that each farmer is a part of.

Berry: That's right. If you come from farming stock you know, for instance, when you plant a row in the garden each spring that thousands upon thousands of your own people have done it every spring, and that you're participating in an act that has had to take place every year since agriculture began.

Plowboy: It's that kind of awareness that's drawing thousands of people back to the land each year.

Berry: Well, I'd be the first to say that there are a lot of people who oughtn't to come to the country, and I devoutly hope they won't come. That solution isn't feasible for everybody. We need people to stay in the cities and make them decent and livable again in order to have a healthy nation. But the city has all the advocates and praisers and critics it needs. The country is pretty well understaffed with advocates at present, and I feel like it's an obligation as well as a privilege to speak from this point of view.

We do need more people who can try and undertake the daily labor of working out a different kind of life. But making a place and holding on to it is not something you can put a guarantee on. Our life here has been lucky and there's no way we can get around that. We've tried to do the work our good fortune has brought us and that, of course, is the crux of the matter.

If you're willing to do the work every day, then as far as you know you're probably worthy of your luck. If you're not doing the work, then you ought to worry that you're betraying your good fortune—and anybody who has a piece of land right now is supremely fortunate.

The Art of Living Right:
An Interview with Wendell Berry

Gregory McNamee and James R. Hepworth / 1983

From *The Bloomsbury Review*, June–August 1983, 23–33. Reprinted in
Living in Words: Interviews from The Bloomsbury Review, *1981–1988*, ed.
Gregory McNamee. Portland, OR: Breitenbrush Books, 1988. Reprinted by
permission of Gregory McNamee and James R. Hepworth.

Wendell Berry is a writer and farmer who speaks to his readers always of
responsibility, of aware participation in the arts of life, be they those of com-
posing a poem, preparing a field for planting, raising a family, working for
the social good, loving. He calls for wise and appropriate technology; for the
continuity of customs that have proven themselves indispensable to living
well and humanely; for honesty and integrity of expression and action.

Above all, Wendell Berry urges us to take stock of ourselves in the world,
to better our social and economic health, to pass on to our children a world
worth living in and a language worth speaking.

Berry's career as a writer began in 1960, with the publication of his first
novel, *Nathan Coulter*. Berry has since written several novels and books of
verse, as well as many essays on the economic and agricultural crises con-
fronting us today. For his distinction in poetry and prose, Berry has gained
both a solid reputation as an artist and an ever-increasing audience. Edward
Abbey has called him "the best essayist writing in America today."

The interview took place in February of 1983.

The Bloomsbury Review: You have written that "learning to write poetry
helped me to see farming as a way of life, not merely as a 'scientific' technique." What do your farming and poetry have in common? Are you the
same person writing poetry as you are, say, when plowing?
Wendell Berry: Farming and poetry are both, to a considerable extent, formal disciplines. In both one must be concerned for the way that things are
joined together, in one's mind and art and in the world. Neither a farm nor a

poem should be made at the world's expense; the world must not be looked upon as a supply of "raw material" for either. To my way of thinking, any made thing should be made in harmony with its sources, and all things so made will have much in common; they will tend to be analogues of each other.

I am not sure that I understand the second part of the question. If I am one person, then I must be the same person, whatever I do, and I have always proceeded on the assumption that I am one person. Sometimes because of work I need to be more than one person, and sometimes because of pleasure, I would like to be.

TBR: You've written novels, essays, poems. Have you come to prefer one form to another? Are there any subjects you would confine to one form, that would only lend themselves to a certain method of expression?

WB: It is a matter of using the proper tool for the job you have at hand. This sort of propriety is going to be defined somewhat by the available readers. I think that most readers now feel, and I do too, that the most direct, most economical way is the best way. And so one would not, for example, write a novel or a poem to discuss a problem of agricultural technology, because that would encumber the discussion with unnecessary details or effects. I don't prefer one literary tool to another any more than a carpenter would prefer a saw to a hammer. A saw is fine for sawing, but you can't drive a nail with it.

TBR: You've said that your poems represent your "least-flawed work." Would you still hold to that statement?

WB: I am becoming less interested in arriving at that kind of statement. It is obviously necessary to try to improve the accuracy of one's judgment of one's work, if only because of the likelihood of error in self-judgment. But the life of the mind and the imagination, I think, bears little resemblance to a contest. My various pieces of writing are not involved in a race for first place, but in something more like a neighborhood; they have been necessary and helpful to each other.

TBR: You seem to be more at home with short lyrics than with narratives.

WB: As has been pointed out often enough, the storytelling ability seems to have migrated from poetry to prose. I would like to see it restored to poetry and have written a few narrative poems, but there are difficult problems.

How, for instance, do you tell a story in verse without either writing prosaic verse or making the verse itself too obtrusive? I wish I knew.

TBR: Which writers do you most admire? Have they influenced your own work?

WB: The companionship of other writers, living and dead, has always been precious to me. But there is no contest here either. To try to rank the writers to whom one is indebted is to risk both forgetfulness and error. The question about influences is another that I think I should not try to answer. It asks me to tell the whole history of my life and a good deal of the histories of the lives of my companions and teachers, and it expects me to be right about all of it.

TBR: With your essay "Poetry and Place" you rely more heavily on references to English literature—Shakespeare, Spenser, Milton, Pope—and on techniques of formal criticism than you generally have in the past. Does this mark a new direction for you? Will you be working more with criticism and literary explication?

WB: I believe that I have always relied on literary ancestors. If that reliance had been absent from my life, I think that writing would have been absent from my life too. In "Poetry and Place," I was trying to understand what certain ones of those ancestors had to say about the proper human connection to the world. My subject was propriety, an old-fashioned concept that I think is renewed by our present ecological concerns; it has to do with the question of how one should act, given one's place both in the world and in the order of creatures. This question was a major enterprise of Western literature from Homer and the Bible until industrialism and romanticism began to mince intelligence into the modern specializations.

Now, for a poet such as Gary Snyder, the question of how to act in your place has become paramount again. Once it is acknowledged that there is a proper way to act, it becomes evident that there are acts that are not proper; it thus becomes possible again to think—to think intelligently—about human conduct. One is brought back to the realizations that so troubled the older poets: there are limits to human trustworthiness with power. We can see now that industrial use of fossil fuels should have brought us back to those realizations. Nuclear power has forced us back to them—if we have sense enough to be scared of our propensity to use reason to justify unreasonable behavior. In "Poetry and Place" I was writing as a man—as a father and grandfather—thoroughly frightened by certain human possibilities. And I was looking back to the old poets for instruction and encouragement.

TBR: How important is a sense of place to you? Can you imagine having done the work you have without it, rootless, as so many of us are? What can city-bound people contribute to the marriage relationship you propose between individual and place?
WB: I have lived mainly in, and mainly know about, one little stretch of country in Henry County, Kentucky, and so I assume that my sense of that place has an inestimable importance to me. To imagine myself without knowledge of that place would be to imagine somebody else.

City people have places—have the earth underfoot—just like country people. In city and country, the most necessary job of work now is to recover the possibility of neighborliness between ourselves and the other people and other creatures who live where we do—both on the earth and in the local neighborhood. That work cannot be done by people who move often, just as it cannot be done by absentee owners, officials, and experts.

As long as there are economic connections between city and country—and there always will be—responsibilities are to be met at both ends. If farmers should produce food responsibly, then city people should eat responsibly. That means buying, so far as possible, fresh food that is locally grown and preparing it at home. And it means, when possible, raising a garden.

TBR: Guy Davenport, a neighbor of yours, has said that "writing is the one social bond and should be objective, useful, instructive." Do you agree? What are the responsibilities of a writer toward his or her audience?
WB: I don't know the context of the quotation, but I respect Guy Davenport and would not be in any hurry to disagree with him. Writing is certainly an indispensable social bond, and for most of us it is the one bond that ties us to our cultural sources. I don't know how a person in Henry County, Kentucky, could learn the stories of Agamemnon or King Lear except by reading. But the importance of writing as a social bond becomes evident in another way when we consider that our laws are all written; we are governed by the editing and amendment and interpretation of texts. And so in a democracy, if we are to have a democracy, the ability to read is paramount. When a society loses its ability to read, as ours appears to be doing, it loses its

ability to re-read—that is, to re-examine and re-think—that is, to read intelligently—that is, to govern itself.

A writer's responsibilities to the audience are to work to tell the truth and to work to keep the language fit to tell the truth. This does not mean that I or any other writer can hope to be entirely truthful, but we must try to be. Anxiety about one's own honesty and the truthfulness of one's language is one of the necessary motives.

TBR: In a talk you gave last year in Colorado, you referred to yourself as a "forest Christian." Could you explain this term and relate it to your work?
WB: I used the phrase "forest Christian" to suggest what has been, for me, a necessary shift in perspective on the New Testament: from that of the church to that of the whole Creation. I don't want to sound too positive or knowing about this, because I hope to understand the problem better than I do, but I feel more and more strongly that when St. Paul said that "we are members of one another," he was using a far more inclusive "we" than Christian institutions have generally thought. For me, this is the meaning of ecology. Whether we know it or not, whether we want to be or not, we are members of one another: humans (ourselves and our enemies), earthworms, whales, snakes, squirrels, trees, topsoil, flowers, weeds, germs, hills, rivers, swifts, and stones—all of "us." The work of the imagination, I feel, is to understand this. I don't think it can be understood by any other faculty. And to live here very long or very well, humans now have to understand it. For us, it is not a question of whether or not we shall be members one of another, but of whether or not we shall know that we are and act accordingly.

TBR: In *The Gift of Good Land* you write that to "defend the small farm is to defend a large part, and the best part, of our cultural inheritance." What are the key points of that inheritance? How should we be transmitting them?
WB: As the rest of the paragraph makes clear, I was saying that values cannot be preserved by division, by specialization. When you have divided one kind of value from another kind, you have already begun the destruction of both. I don't think the small farm can be preserved only as an economic quantity or only as a political idea or only as a family home. The small farm is all of those things and much more, too; to speak of it as if it were only one of them is to make nothing of it. Similarly, the idea of property becomes abstract, tentative, and vulnerable if we try to ground it only in economics or only in law.

In defending the small farm, I am defending the idea that great numbers of ordinary people should own property—not money or stock certificates or insurance policies, but real property, property that can give them direct practical support, the means to help themselves, and so make them to a proper extent independent, both in their domestic economies and in their minds. People who have a measure of economic independence can obviously afford to think and speak and vote more freely than people who do not. To me this modest idea of property is not just legal or political or economic, but is validated also by the long cultural memories and feelings that adhere to the idea of homeland—not a nation to be defended "patriotically," but a place personally loved in the particular terms of its hills and trees and streams, houses and households, where the knowledge and memories of grandparents can pass with clear local references into the minds of grandchildren. The understanding that people need such places and should not be alienated from them for economic or any other reasons, goes back in our culture at least to the institution of the year of jubilee [Ed.: see Leviticus 25:10–13], the fiftieth year, when all properties had to be returned to their original owners—an early and honorable example of an artificial restraint on the workings of an economy. Such ideas are best transmitted by parents to their children, older friends to younger friends. Schools and governments should not be trusted with them. If schools and governments become agents of an economy such as ours, then they become instruments of alienation. That is because alienated people—people without property and without neighbors—consume more industrial services and products than people who are not alienated. People who have no neighbors, for instance, must buy help. People who have neighbors have help. Claims for the benevolence of the industrial economy are disproved by the phenomenon of "unemployment." People become unemployed because of alienation from land and community. People who own even tiny parcels of land on which they can work for their own support, and people who own shops or have trades or skills directly useful to their own communities, are not going to be unemployed.

TBR: Former Secretary of Agriculture Earl Butz and the ideology he represented seem to have been favorite targets of yours for quite some time. Have agricultural affairs improved or worsened since Butz's time? What, if anything, should government be doing with regard to farming?

WB: The increase of farm bankruptcies indicates that the financial plight of farmers has worsened since Mr. Butz's time—and to a considerable extent because of his policy of "full production," which came inevitably to mean overproduction.

The government, I think, needs to recognize that any economy—"free" or not—is an artifact. It is "managed" for the good of somebody or other—for the general good, say, or for the good of a few. If there is a genuine wish to make it possible for a lot of people to own land, then government can do that. It can do it, first of all, by ceasing to favor the large landowners. The Department of Agriculture's new Payment in Kind program, for instance, will pay large farmers more per acre than small farmers. In a democracy, there can be no argument about that. It is simply wrong.

But it is wrong agriculturally too. Soil erosion is one of the most serious threats to this country, and one of its causes is depopulation of the farmland.

I don't know whether or not the government can be expected to see this. It can't see it, I think, until a lot of people begin to see it. In representative government, the government is likely to represent the blindness of the governed.

The government, for instance, thinks that national defense is making weapons, and the people go along and pay for it. But soil conservation is elementary national defense. So is people conservation. So is the conservation of culture and intelligence. So is the conservation of political liberty and of the economic independence of households and communities. If the nation is to be defended, it may need fewer warheads and many more real shareholders, people who own homes, homesteads, small businesses, small farms.

TBR: Is it really possible, as you hope, for America to sustain and maintain a stable, hereditary, healthy farming population, given all the pressures exerted by our economic order and agribusiness? Where do we begin?

WB: We once had a chance to sustain and maintain such a farming population. Now we have a chance only to build one, starting with a farm population that is literally vanishing, for it is now less than three percent of the total population and still going down. That, of course, is a smaller chance. Though I see plenty of room for hope, I see little for optimism.

To begin the necessary change, we must first see what the real situation of agriculture now is: what it requires of land and people, and what it costs, not just in money, but in ecological, social, cultural, and economic results. Second, we must understand the meaning, the terms, the technology, the techniques, and the art of agricultural health. We must understand, for instance, that a good farmer's mind is not simple, but extremely complex and highly accomplished. Third, we must understand that all of us—city people just as much as country people—live from farming and therefore have agricultural responsibilities.

TBR: Your early work was brought out by a variety of small and commercial publishers, but of late you seem to have settled with North Point Press. Have you found a home there?

WB: Yes, I feel I have found a home at North Point. The reason is that I am a small writer, in the sense that none of my books has been a best seller or made a lot of money, and North Point is a small business. What a small writer and a small business have in common is an interest in making money, if necessary, in small amounts. Their interest, in other words, is the same, and so they do not need to have an adversary relationship. A small writer and a big publisher, on the other hand, are adversaries necessarily, because the attention of big publishers is focused on big money.

The Progressive Interview:
Wendell Berry

Carol Polsgrove and Scott Russell Sanders / 1990

From *The Progressive* 54.5 (May 1990), 34–37. Reprinted by permission of
Carol Polsgrove and Scott Russell Sanders.

Wendell Berry was born in Henry County, Kentucky, in 1934, and lives there
still, on a hillside farm above the Kentucky River. In some thirty years as a
writer, he has published twenty-five novels, collections of essays and poetry,
and a nonfiction work on agriculture, *The Unsettling of America*. It would be
easy to mistake him for a farmer who writes, since the subject of his writing
has often been farming and rural life. We see him as a writer who has found
in the country—his particular country—a subject that has engaged him
deeply. He has studied it well, with discipline and feeling, and given us books
that can change our lives: *The Memory of Old Jack, A Place on Earth, The Gift
of Good Land.*

We spoke with him not long before publication of his latest collection of
essays, *What Are People For?* It was a Sunday in early spring, and the wood
stove in his living room gave off a comfortable warmth. His wife, Tanya, and
two granddaughters had left for church. While the stew and apples for lunch
cooked, Berry shared some of his thoughts about culture, country, and
community.

Q: We've had so much media hype on the environment recently—should we
take this seriously as an indication that people are coming to some point of
awareness of environmental concerns?

Wendell Berry: I don't think we can take it seriously until people begin to
talk seriously about lowering the standard of living. When people begin to
see affluence, economic growth, unrestrained economic behavior, as the
enemies of the environment, then we can take it seriously. But people are
saying, "Give us everything we want *and* a clean environment," and that isn't
a possibility.

Q: What are some things they want that they can't have?
Berry: Unlimited amounts of plastic, for one. But almost all manufactured goods are causing pollution. We're in a situation in which we have problems but no environmentally sound solutions.

Q: For instance?
Berry: I went to town yesterday to buy some chalk for a chalk-line, a carpenter's chalk-line. I came home with a bunch of chalk dust in a big plastic bottle. Almost everything you buy now comes in a plastic container. The roadsides are littered with trash—well, you see, you start pulling the thread and you find that everything's connected to everything else. Food from the fast-food places is packaged in plastic trash. People are eating more junk food now—more fast food—because everybody's working. Why, all of a sudden, does it take two people working to support a household when not so long ago, one person working could support a household? Who's getting the money? Why is so much money needed? You can start with an issue of livelihood and wind up with an issue of the environment. And that's the connection that has to be made.

Q: How are we going to manage to make that connection?
Berry: The connection will only be made when people *see* it and act on it. Many millions of people will have to see it and act on it.

Q: What would it take to move millions of people?
Berry: It would take leadership, for one thing. There are two choices. You'd either move people by leadership—somebody in a position like the Presidency of the United States would say, "Look, people, we're destroying our country and we will have to take measures to stop it, and they won't be altogether pleasant measures, but we're going to have to do something." And the leader, thus positioned, would make the arguments and persuade the people to act in response in a rational way.

The other way that the connection is made—acted out, enforced—would be by want. When there isn't any plastic any more, when petroleum becomes too expensive to make plastic, then people will *have* to do something. My worry is that this possibility extends to far more urgent needs than plastic.

Food, for instance. If you destroy the productive capacity of the farmland and the farm people, you will have shortages of food.

Q: Would you want to issue an opinion about the quality of leadership we've received over the last ten years, and specifically from our "environmental President"?

Berry: The quality of leadership we've had for a very long time has been just deplorable. The great effort is to lead people to do what the people already want to do anyhow. And to do everything possible to mollify the people who are already well off. And this is understandable, but to me it's disastrous. I don't think a democracy can be maintained without an intelligent public dialogue about fundamental issues. And we've gone through a number of Presidencies without one.

Q: What about the chances of some kind of grass-roots leadership organized from below?

Berry: That's where the hope is now. I don't see very much chance of the cities producing a grass-roots movement that can directly cause change. The cities may finally exert a grass-roots demand that can cause change, but the cities are helpless. The capacity of people in the cities to do things for themselves directly is extremely limited. They can't produce food; they can't produce building materials; they can't produce the materials needed for clothing; they're so cut off from the natural sources of their livelihood and so cut off from fundamental skills, most of them, that they can't directly do much of anything.

One of the hopes in agriculture, though, is that city people will demand a food supply that's safer and of better quality that the one they have now.

Q: And are there some signs of that?

Berry: There are some signs of that happening. I hope it goes ahead and happens. What I'm looking toward is the possibility that the country people, who do still have some capacity to help themselves directly, will start doing so. I think what this means is simply the rebuilding of communities.

Q: Does that mean people moving to the country?

Berry: Eventually it might mean that. What it means immediately, to me, is that the people who are left in the country are going to have to start helping each other again in practical and economic ways.

Q: Are you talking about co-ops?

Berry: Well, no. I'm not necessarily talking about organizations at all. I'm talking about the unorganized institutions of families and neighborhoods.

It's still an ordinary thing here for farmers to trade work. When there are neighborhood exchanges of labor, that works to the advantage of the neighborhood and not to the advantage of the larger economy.

The situation we have now, it seems to me, is that the larger economy—the national economy—is really being run for the benefit of very few people. It is preying upon and slowly destroying the local communities—everywhere. It's very clear this is happening all over the rural United States. Rural America is a bona-fide part of the Third World. It's a colony. Some parts are recognizably Third World—the Appalachian coal fields and the destroyed farm towns of the Middle West. But all of it is at one stage or another of moving toward Third World status. That is, everything we produce in rural America makes more money for other people than it does for the people who produce it.

They want our products as cheaply as they can be bought. They want to sell us their products as expensively as we can bear. They want our young people. And all this is working. We're destroying rural America and we're destroying the rural American communities.

But these communities still have access to land they can use in their own interest. They have access to materials they can use in their own interest. And they still have, to varying degrees, the fundamental skills necessary to work in their own interest. So the rural communities, it seems to me, are places you could look to for some kind of a new start.

Q: Do you see any signs of that?
Berry: Yes, there are some signs of it. One thing that reassures you, if you travel the country, is that scattered all over are people who are doing good work, who are trying to find the better ways. And they are finding some of them.

So the better possibility exists. The problem is getting the country as a whole to pay attention to it. Or getting *any* leader to pay attention to it. These leaders are a terribly cowardly bunch, by and large. They are terribly embarrassed and ashamed to propose anything different. They think it's unmanly. Don't you think that's it? It's unmanly to come up with something different. The manly thing is to stand on the prow . . . and sail over the edge.

Q: You are a model for us of a person who has looked hard at things and thought and written about them. Could you describe how you go about thinking about things?
Berry: The primary fact about me and my work is that I'm a person who is very badly scared. I've been afraid for a long time. What I've seen is that there

has been a lot of waste and damage to this country, here, that I know as my. . . .

Q: Henry County. . . .
Berry: Well, a smaller territory than that. I can't claim to be an authority on Henry County. I know, intimately, only a few hundred acres, some of these farms that I've worked over enough to have them sort of memorized—to know where the water courses are and what the condition of the soil is and where the old plow marks and dead furrows are and so on. There are places where, if you dig—and I've dug lots of post holes—you are digging in sub-soil, from the top. There are other places where you can go and you can dig—I went to a place right out here that's close to a water course and close to an old road, and I dug a five-foot hole, and I was in topsoil all the way down.

The country we're living in here now is literally not the country that our ancestors inhabited. We're living on a surface that wasn't the surface then. And you begin to think about practices that caused this ruination. If you see that a lot of topsoil is gone, then the thing you've got to do is think a long time about plows and how they are used. What kind of plow was being used at a given time and what was its action on the ground? Where was it used? What was above this field where it was used and what was below it? And what did the water do when it came to it? And so on.

Then you ask yourself: What was in the mind of the man who ran the plow? And you ask what was in the mind of the woman who cooked his meals? And you want to know what they read. Well, you know they read the Bible, so you'd better go there and look. And so on.

What I'm doing is simply elaborating, in essays, my understanding of a few gullies: how they got that way and what can stop them. You can propose that a certain kind of person caused a gully, and you had better think pretty carefully about what went into the making of that gully, the assumptions, the cultural means and derivations that went into it. And then you can propose a person who would come along and stop that gully, and then you're asking what does this person's cultural means have to be? What does he or she have in mind in order to stop it? Because the physical, the practical action of stopping a gully is not all there is to it. It begins far back in the culture. There are two cultural themes here. There's a cultural theme of destruction and there's a cultural theme of preserving and cherishing. And they've existed side by side.

Q: On these acres?
Berry: On these few acres that I know. There have been good farmers here, and there have been deplorable ones, and if you could figure out why, you would know something. It's not any great feat to get as far as I've gotten with it.

Q: Can city people think like this? Or do we have to have gullies?
Berry: City people have *got* gullies. There is suffering and deprivation and waste in the cities, too, and some people know this. And the thing there is the same as the thing here: You can't study these problems from the top, you've got to get down to where they are. It's not the great public figures who are going to get in the gully and figure it out. It has to be done by somebody who's both willing to get in the gully and somebody who is fascinated with the gully. So if you're going to talk about healing the urban equivalent of these gullies, you've got to have somebody like Dorothy Day, who'll get down to where the gullies are.

Q: You obviously think quite differently, dramatically differently, from the bulk of folks in our culture, which is, a lot of time, trouble for people around you. Are there quick ways or fairly simple ways that you can account for your having arrived at a different idea than, say, your neighbors?
Berry: Yeah, there's a quick way—my father. My father served this same agricultural cause that I've tried to serve. He was one of the people who were instrumental in starting the Burley Tobacco Growers Cooperative Association back there in the Depression. He served it, and I think the other people served it, out of a vision of what it meant to have an economy here that could support small farmers and keep them on the land. That was his vision, and my father was a practical visionary.

He saw that vision—it's an agrarian vision—and he served it in very practical and effective ways for fifty years. My brother, now, has succeeded him and is wonderfully effective and practical too. But Daddy taught us both, even against our resistance. We learned a lot from him because he was a very careful talker and he was able, pretty fully, to articulate what he thought and why he did what he did.

Of course, he came out of an agrarian tradition, and he came out of a hard experience. The tobacco farmers in my father's childhood were having a terrible time. My father used to tell this story. The first time he remembered

waking up late in the night was when he was about seven years old.
His daddy sent the crop, put it on the boat here, and sent it to Louisville.
Then the night before it was going to sell, they sat up talking about what
they were going to do when they got the money, and it was kind of a
happy, optimistic evening. Then my father heard his daddy get up, at
probably two o'clock in the morning, to get on his horse to go to the train
and go to Louisville, to see his crop sold. And he got back without a dime.
They took it all. The crop, in other words, about paid the warehouse
commission.

My father saw men leave the warehouse crying and he said, when he was
a little boy, "If ever I can do anything about this, I'm going to." So that's
where I come from—that's where my brother comes from.

Q: What year was that?
Berry: About 1907. Daddy was born in 1900.

Q: I just have to ask you how you deal with the moral question of tobacco
farming.
Berry: I don't think you can defend a crop that doesn't serve any useful end.
And in that way, I would classify tobacco simply with a lot of other products.
However, there are some things that can be said *for* it. One is that it's kept the
small farmers alive in this country. I don't know how long it's going to be able
to do it, but it's still a significant part of the livelihood of many people
who are trying to hang on in farming. So I'm *for* the tobacco program,
100 percent. Another complication for me is that I *love* the crop. And I love
the culture that grew up around it.

Q: You mean you like the way it looks in the field?
Berry: I like the way it looks; I like the way it smells; I like the way it looks
growing; I like the way it looks when its curing in the barn, and so on. It's a
lovely plant. Although, as I say, I can't defend it.

I think it's important that we relieve the small farmers here of their
dependence on it. There ought to be alternative crops. The answer, pre-
dictably, is a more comprehensive one. The thing we need in agriculture, not
just in the tobacco country but everywhere, is some action on the idea of
local food self-sufficiency. If we were feeding Louisville, we wouldn't need
tobacco, probably.

Q: Have you seen any changes for the better in the way agriculture is taught in American universities since you became concerned with it?

Berry: There have been some changes. The universities aren't as solidly in support of industrial agriculture as they used to be. But I don't see much reason to be optimistic, because they are dependent upon industrial agriculture. Chemical agriculture is like the Cold War. Everybody wishes we could be rid of it, but a lot of people are dependent on it. The universities are full of people who just wouldn't recognize themselves apart from chemical agriculture—just as there are people in Washington who don't recognize themselves without a Cold War to lean on.

The grounds for hope are really paradoxical. The grounds for hope are that the situation is getting worse and more people know that it is. And the question is, will enough people understand that it's getting worse in time to do something before it becomes uncorrectable?

Q: I've been fascinated over the years by the metaphor of marriage in your work. How has that metaphor figured for you?

Berry: Why, I suppose it came up because I'm so much involved in trying to make a marriage. But it's sort of a metaphor of final commitment, inevitably, and so when you talk about marriage to a place, you're talking about final commitment. You're not going to leave; you're going to give up that other so-lucrative motive of the industrial world: the idea that you'd be better off somewhere else or with someone else.

And I always have to temper that; you never know what other people are going through. So you can't say that a given marriage oughtn't to end. Or you can't say that anybody ought to stay in any given place. There's no way you can authorize yourself to say such a thing. You can say it for yourself, however.

But anyway, within this issue of commitment, there's a lot of experience that has to be accounted for and dealt with somehow. And it's dire. It's not easy at all. It's a difficult thing to live with somebody who *knows* you and stay in that situation.

Q: You can't keep up a front—right?

Berry: I don't have any front with Tanya at all. There's no way that I can improve the impression I make on her—there's too much experience, too much history.

And this old place here, it's even more difficult to do right by than Tanya, really, because it's abused and it's steep, and I've accumulated a history of wrong guesses here. And so I live in this commitment all the time, knowing very well how attractive mobility is. I'd really like to be loved by somebody who doesn't know me—who would be susceptible to charm. I appreciate how fine that would be, but I know it wouldn't last and that I couldn't disguise myself for more than, oh, maybe forty-eight hours.

And I know how it would be really nice, as I've said sometimes to Tanya, to go and get on the fifth floor of some damn apartment house and quit this getting up at night with the sheep.

But marriage is the inevitable metaphor for the kind of agriculture and community life that I'm talking about, and it's an inescapable preoccupation for a man who wants to be well married. If you're going to sustain anything, you've got to have populations that are totally committed. The idea that you can destroy this place and go to another place is exhausted. We can't do that any more.

This is why I'm turning so much in my mind now to the country people— the people of the fields and the forests. They are the ones who are going to have to recognize this; they are the ones who are going to have to tell these companies, "*No more!* You can't do this anymore; you can't come here and act this way."

A lot of people think that I have escaped out here to this bucolic, pastoral, carefree existence. But there isn't any place, as I hope I've made clear, where you aren't on the front line of the battle. There isn't any place that somebody hasn't picked out for some kind of exploitation. So if you're going to take part in that battle, you're going to find plenty of occasions out in the country.

Interview with Wendell Berry

Vince Pennington / 1991

From *The Kentucky Review* 13.1–2 (Spring 1996), 57–70. Reprinted by permission of Vince Pennington.

In December of 1991 I had the privilege of spending most of a Sunday afternoon on Wendell Berry's farm, along the Kentucky River in Henry County. I found Mr. Berry just as a previous interviewer, Fenton Johnson, had: sitting beside the wood stove in his living room dressed in work clothes and a worn pair of sock-moccasins.

For an hour and a half, we discussed a range of issues but focused on Berry's vision of the "historical community" (a small, agrarian community whose families have lived, worked, suffered, and celebrated together on the same land, generation after generation). An English professor, Mr. Berry took great interest in my academic experiences at Dartmouth College; his fondness for young people was obvious. He also talked about London, Florence, and New York City—where he lived as a young man for two years and which he still finds "exhilarating"—with as much excitement as he did about farming communities like his own Port Royal.

After finishing the interview that follows, Mr. Berry and I spent another hour doing chores on his 125 acre farm. We examined a hillside that is recovering from misuse during the early part of this century, and we fed his draft horses, Nick and Doc. We even devoted a few minutes to training his sheep dog. Mr. Berry, clearly in his element, mentioned that training an animal to work for you is one of the great pleasures of life. Occasionally, he would return to a question I had posed inside his house and would add to his answer or make it more precise.

The following interview is a partial record of our talk.

Vince Pennington: If the past is to serve as our ethical guide, as Aeneas tells his son it must, what, do you believe, are the ethical responsibilities of the grandfather?

Wendell Berry: Well, where else would you look? You can't look to the future for instruction; there's nothing there. The only place we get anything from is the past. We get our language from the past; we get the knowledge of what works and what hasn't worked only from the past. So if you're thinking about practical issues of how you settle in a place, how you establish a human community in a place, and bring about some kind of preserving relationship with that place, the members of the community would have to remember the past. They would have to remember what worked and didn't work in a given place. And then they would have to have an appropriate affection for the dead. By "appropriate" I mean they would have judgments to make and evaluations to make. They would have to be critics. But they would have to care about the people who preceded them.

VP: I wonder whether that looking to the past is somehow a gender-specific endeavor. Richard King's *A Southern Renaissance* claims that the grandfather-father-son relationship is central to Southern Literature. Do you think that in a community's "remembering" the grandfather plays a different role than the grandmother?

WB: I certainly learned from my grandfathers, but many of the things I know I learned from my grandmothers. Now that may just be a family accident; my grandmothers both lived with their mothers-in-law, so they heard a lot of family stories. I was the kind of little child who liked to listen, so a lot of things I know came from mother-in-law to daughter-in-law to grandson. Mothers and fathers, grandmothers and grandfathers are apt to remember different things. It depends on how the occupational lineages are set up. I think that a woman in a community would be tremendously enriched by what she learned from her mother and grandmother about child raising, for instance. If the housewifely business runs down the female lineage, then that's the way that would pass. If it's a farming community, another kind of knowledge would come down the male line, although in this country fieldwork was never exclusively done by men. Women worked too. I *know* that people have to remember. How it will be in the future, I don't know. But you can't imagine a community maturing until there are at least three generations native to it. The connection between grandchildren and grandparents is vital.

VP: How is that relationship different from the relationship between children and parents?

WB: Relationships between children and parents are more anxious. By the time you're a grandparent, you're a little more mellow. You know how wide the margins are around bringing up a child. You know how much room there is to make mistakes. And if you're a grandparent, you're not with the child all the time. Older grandparents have more time, time to sit around and tell things that parents often don't have time to tell. But the important thing to me is that this sort of handed down knowledge is *practically* necessary. If you don't remember the history of fields, for instance, you're going to make the same mistakes over and over again, and they're going to be costly mistakes. If people ever did stay settled long enough—which we haven't done in Kentucky, and we're worse off now than a generation ago—but if we ever did stay settled long enough to learn the best ways of land use, the best ways of forestry, for instance, we could establish a preserving forest economy. That would depend on memory. We would have to have people learning young, and I think that people don't understand how important it is to learn young. We know that it is important to teach musicians from very young. But my experience has been that you've got to teach farmers from very young. People who do hand labor, who work with materials, have to have a kind of physical sympathy with the materials that they're using and the motions of the work and the tools, and so forth. And that comes hard late in life. It has to be learned before the child realizes that he or she is learning.

VP: In *The Memory of Old Jack* the community seems to have only a tenuous grasp of its history. Does that explain the presence of surrogate grandfathers and male figures in the novel such as Ben Feltner, who in some ways operates as a father figure for Jack? Is the substitution of these men a last-ditch attempt to preserve the community's awareness of its history?

WB: It's pretty clear that I'm aware in writing my books that the family is not a large enough vehicle for passing these things down. When it works it works, but it may not work, and you may lose parents or grandparents. In that case you've got to have other people who can step in and do the job. In my own life the influence of parents and grandparents has come to me from people outside the family who were influenced by my parents and grandparents. Being a child in a somewhat established community is like being in a room full of mirrors: things are reflected back toward you from many different directions. You can learn about your parents by seeing what your parents have meant to other people, for instance, and the same for your grandparents. And there are certain things about your parents that you won't learn from them, that other people will tell you. So it would be extremely difficult to mark the real lineages of a person's consciousness. You sit down and try to think, by the time you're my age, who's responsible for the making of your mind, and you face a bewilderment of influences that have been important to you.

VP: And thus the importance of community.
WB: That's right. The community is the vessel of inheritance. Families die out, families come and go, parents and grandparents die, people are orphaned. There are too many bad possibilities. But the community is an adequate vessel.

VP: At one point in *The Memory of Old Jack* a man enters the general store and speaks to Jack. The narrator tells us that Jack cannot remember the man's name although Jack "has known him for five generations, from his grandfathers to his grandsons." Do you think that our society entirely denies this possibility: that a person must be known in relation to his ancestors and descendants? Or do you see any indications that, as a society, we are once again beginning to understand and appreciate these relationships?
WB: As a society we're not. As a society we're disintegrating, we're destroying those relationships. That doesn't mean there aren't individuals and families in the society who understand the relationships and value them and try to preserve them; but the society proceeds on a crude, a very crude, understanding of what goes into the making of a human being. This society proceeds on the assumption that a child is a kind of bottle and that people fill that child up with various ingredients, and that it's all done consciously. It isn't all done consciously. Some of it is, but if we were operating strictly according to the capacities of consciousness, we wouldn't amount to very much. There's much more to it than that. We just don't know how to live, as a people, with good fortune or misfortune or blessedness or chance. We don't know how to deal with mystery; we don't know how to deal with ignorance. All we want to do is draw a little circle around what we are conscious of and try to control that—and, of course, the results are disastrous.

VP: We limit ourselves to just what we can control.

WB: Well, we can control up to a point, but we are blind to the effects of our control. So you can control an atom, within limits, or you can control a coal-fired power plant, within limits, but then the influence of that thing enters the world at large. We're not in control of it anymore. We don't even understand what the effects are anymore. It's like the Gulf War, which was supposed to be an exercise in conscious control, and the results of it have been haywire from the beginning.

VP: That was how the War was advertised, as being a controlled experiment.

WB: That was how it was advertised, and, you see, the advertisement, the public relations part of it, ought to give you a kind of index of what our society is all about: it thinks that pretense is an adequate substitute for reality.

* * *

VP: You're often compared to the Southern Agrarians for obvious reasons, but I wonder how similar you actually are to that group. Your novels, at least, portray the Port William community in the 1930s, '40s, and '50s, and one can't help but get the feeling that—despite the community's problems—it still represents a cultural ideal. The Southern Agrarians, on the other hand, reach back to the "Old South" for their vision of the good life, something you never do. Do you consider this a major difference between the Southern Agrarians and yourself?

WB: I've never really thought of myself as a Southerner in a doctrinaire way. And I think one difference between the Southern Agrarians and me is that I'm much more local than they were. My work comes out of the study of one little place, really just a few square miles. In some senses, it comes out of the study of just a few hundred acres. The Southern Agrarians were approaching the issue of Agrarianism in a more general way; they were arguing Agrarianism as a policy more than as a practice. But I have obvious debts to them. I read *I'll Take My Stand* when I was a student, and I still often go back to it and to Allen Tate's essays about the South and about regionalism. To me, that's an unfinished agenda.

VP: These agrarians espoused a fairly convincing argument for an agrarian way of life, but I don't get the impression that they particularly lived it.

WB: Well, you see, they saw it as a system of values, as a system of political choices. But it all has to rest on practice. If you're going to be an agrarian, you *finally* have to ask how you farm, how you use land, how you maintain a rural community. These are all practical questions, and I really don't think the Southern Agrarians ever got to such questions.

VP: John Crowe Ransom writes that one major problem with our concept of "Progress" is that it "never defines its ultimate objective, thrusts its victims at once into an infinite series." So if you're thinking about having a community that is aware of its history, a cohesive community, what would be its goals or ideals?
WB: The standard is the health of the community, but you have to have a comprehensive enough idea of community. The community is *not* just the human bunch that has established itself in a place. It is *not* just the human neighborhood. It includes everything that's there. And if the community is going to be a healthy community and hope to endure for any length of time, everything that's there has to be healthy. So that's the standard.

VP: Don't you think, then, that many contemporary problems of the human community, such as divorce and the disintegration of the family, are very similar to or related to problems in the larger community, such as pollution?
WB: If all the other relationships disintegrate, then the human relationships finally disintegrate. So, you see, you can think of divorce as a kind of principle that we're operating on here in this society: things that ought to be together are separated, or permitted to be separated. We tend to think—the people in Washington, for instance, the people in state houses, in capitals—that there can be a distinction between people and the air they breathe, for instance, or people and the food they eat, or people and the water they drink. And obviously this is an absurd distinction: there is no line that you can draw between people and the elements they depend on. That's why this term "environment" is so bothersome to me. "Environment" is based on that dualism, the idea that you can separate the human interests from the interests of everything else. You *cannot* do it. We eat the environment. It passes through our bodies every day, it passes in and out our bodies. There is no distinction between ourselves and the so-called environment. What we live in and from and with doesn't *surround* us—it's part of us. We're *of* it, and it's *of* us, and the relationship is unspeakably intimate.

VP: In your work one central aspect of a couple's marriage is their mutual relationship with the land they live on. Does this mean that a couple must only share and enact a similar attitude toward the land—or does it suggest that the man and woman ought to have grown up in the same region?

WB: Well, I married a woman who was born in Berkeley, California. I think you have to be practical about these issues. The first thing that I want to do is go to see what the practical issues are. It seems to me that if you are going to be practical, a marriage is in many ways an economic relationship, or it ought to be. In other words, if a family is not held together by a family or household economy, then there really isn't any reason for the family to stay together. The same way with a marriage. People who love each other need to have something they can do for each other, and it will need to be something necessary, not something frivolous. You can't carry out a relationship on the basis of Christmas and anniversary and birthday presents. It won't work. You have to be doing something that you need help with, and your wife needs to be doing something that she needs help with. You do needful, useful things for each other, and that seems to me to be the way that the union is made. You're not in control of a union that's made partly as an economy, as a domestic economy. You're being shaped by it, you're not shaping it. You're being made into a partner by your partner's needs and the things that you're required to do to help. Our society assumes that a profound human connection can be made on the basis of psychology, which somebody is going to dope out, and I don't believe it. Love is *not* just a feeling; it's a practice, something you practice whether you feel like it or not. If you have a relationship with anybody—a friend, a family member, a spouse—you have to understand by the terms of that relationship to do things for those people, and you do them whether you feel like it or not. If you don't, it's useless. You're not always going to feel like it. This is what you learn as soon as you become a farmer, for instance. Once you get into a relationship with even so much as a vegetable garden, you realize that you have to do the work whether you want to or not. You may have got into it because of love, but there are going to be days when you are sick and you're going to have to do your work anyhow. With animals, the work is even more inescapable. There's no way out if you have a milk cow, no reprieve. A cow doesn't know that you're sick. She doesn't say, "Well, since you're sick I just won't make any milk." She makes the milk, and you've got to go get it.

VP: In *The Unsettling of America* you claim that the disintegration of marriage completes the disintegration of community. Might this be equally true the other way around? Might the disintegration spread from the family outward?

WB: You could argue it the other way, and I can kind of see how you could do it. But marriage happens because of the community. In our rather superficial approach to the issue, we think marriage happens because people fall in love. It *doesn't* happen because people fall in love. It happens because the community steps forward and asks us, if we love each other, to be responsible, to take responsibility—not just to each other, but to the community. In marrying, a young couple marries the community, saying, "We will keep our vows to each other, not just because we love each other, but out of respect for the community." So, to me the community is the vessel in which marriage is made. The expectation of the community surrounds a marriage with a kind of pressure, like the atmospheric pressure that balances the internal pressure of our bodies. One thing that marriages do by nature is generate pressure, and if you remove the community the marriage naturally blows up.

VP: Several times you have depicted a hierarchal view of society using concentric circles. I've wondered whether that model is at all similar to the Great Chain of Being. One difference between the two models, I think, is that a given circle in a series of concentric circles affects both the circles inside and outside it, whereas with the Chain of Being only everything *below* a given point is affected by a given incident.

WB: I'm no authority on the Great Chain of Being even though I wrote at some length about it once in an essay called "Poetry and Place." Humans, at least, have responsibilities that go above and below. We're supposed to be humble and reverent toward the things that are above us and magnanimous to those things that are below us. Any representation of the real order is going to oversimplify it. The Chain of Being is an oversimplification; so are those concentric circles that I drew. All you're doing is representing graphically some aspects of the relationship. You're drawing out what you understand. It's invariably more complex than that.

VP: You frequently use the metaphor of marriage to describe the relationship between the various circles. How could you define those connections in religious terms?

WB: Of course the Chain of Being is a religious idea: it goes up to the throne of God. There are other ways to look at it, and they probably aren't diagrammable. The 104th Psalm says, "Thou sendest forth thy spirit, they are created." And there's a verse in Job that says that if God "gather unto himself his spirit and breath; all flesh shall perish together, and man shall return again unto dust." And Genesis says that we are living souls made of dust and God's breath. So if everything participates, as those passages say, in the being of God, there really isn't any diagram that's adequate. According to that, each thing lives to the extent that it participates in God's life. That's an idea that makes all the diagrams crude.

VP: What do you think are the shared characteristics of all these types of marriages: between husband and wife, farmer and field, an individual and his community?
WB: Well, marriage is something that in the first place is lived out, acted out. It's a practical connection between man and woman. A practical agreement, making its vows and promises. It's a contract. And, as I said, it's a contract with the human neighborhood. From then on, when you talk of marriage of other things, you're speaking metaphorically. But the idea does have metaphoric power and so the relationship between a man and a woman is a very proper and instructive metaphor for anything else that a person keeps faith with or attempts to live in any kind of loyalty to.

VP: Why do you think that, as a society, we have such a hard time making these lifelong, or even short-term, commitments and then living them out?
WB: One large reason is that the educational system is geared to individual careers. In general, the education system doesn't educate people to be members of communities. The educational system is not saying we must teach these people what they must be loyal to, or how to be loyal to the things they want to be loyal to. There is no loyalty. How could you be *loyal* to a corporation, for instance, that you *know* will fire you as soon as you become dispensable?

VP: Is that loyalty not taught because, from an industrial or career-oriented point of view, it is limiting? To teach a person loyalty to his community to some extent restricts the "career track."

WB: Yeah, the idea of community loyalty removes the whole glamour of ambition from education, and it makes education a desperate undertaking. If you're trying to teach people to maintain the indispensable things of human culture, you know immediately that it's a desperate business. You've got to teach like fury. Most teachers now don't want to teach very hard. So they learn to teach literature, for instance, as if it were simply a matter of curiosity—what people thought in other, less enlightened historical periods.

* * *

VP: In *The Wild Birds* Wheeler Catlett is referred to as the "preserver and defender of the dead." You write of him concerning the inheritance of the Coulter farm: "How, thinking of his own children and grandchildren, could he not insist on an orderly passage of these frail human parcels through time?" Now, it's easy enough here to see how Wheeler tries to maneuver to protect the farm, but in general how does Wheeler or anybody go about promoting an "orderly passage of these frail human parcels through time?"
WB: There are two commitments involved in that story. That story is almost a controversy between the spirit and the letter, love and the law. Burley knows that the inheritance is wayward, as he says, that it comes down wanderingly. Wheeler, as a lawyer, is a man of order. He's trying to see that it does come down in an orderly way. Burley says that it doesn't, and it can't, and therefore you have to do the best you can, for one thing. For another thing, finally, Burley says we have to forgive each other. That's all. The two points of view are necessary. I think that Wheeler's argument is valid; you have to try for order. Burley's argument is valid: as far as human order is concerned, it's a failure. It doesn't work, what we consciously want; other things happen. Burley is really, in a profound way, Wheeler's teacher in that story. He says, "The way we are, we are members of each other. . . . The difference ain't in who is a member and who is not, but in who knows it and who don't." And then he says that they've got to forgive each other.

VP: I could be wrong, but I think I remember your saying somewhere that Wheeler had to leave his way of life to protect it. But it doesn't seem to me that Wheeler has left his way of life, although he often wishes that he were on his farm rather than in his law office. Wheeler strikes me as being a terribly important character because, reading your work, one sometimes wonders whether one can be a good person without being a farmer. Wheeler is a good man.

WB: Yeah, and Wheeler is conscious of the losses, and he has a political consciousness. And I think he's very important. I don't remember where it says that, Vince, but I'm not a very good expert on my own work.

VP: Is there much autobiographical material in *The Wild Birds*? I know, for instance, that, as lawyers, both your father and brother have represented agrarian interests.

WB: I return over and over and over again to the question of what is the proper relationship between imagination and reality. In one sense it's true to say that there are autobiographical things, that things get into my stories that really happened. On the other hand, you imagine stories because you know that reality never gives you a complete story. You never know enough and so you imagine, and once you give yourself over to imagination, it's a different story. In a sense, some things in my stories have happened before; in another sense, they never happened at all until I wrote them down: what's written is something else. The story of "The Wild Birds" never really happened, so far as I know.

VP: But it would be impossible, wouldn't it, to separate entirely the events of your life from some of the episodes in your stories? These events made you the person you are, and you made the stories what they are.

WB: If I hadn't known my father I would have never written about Wheeler. There's no real life counterpart to Burley Coulter, though.

VP: A person often hears that it is good to go away from home to learn about home, and I've thought about that a lot since going away to college. But you've written that you learned far more about Kentucky when you returned than while you were away. What is the difference between what you learned about Kentucky while you were away and what you learned upon your return?

WB: Well, when you're away you're going to generalize, almost inevitably, and there's nothing to measure your memories against. As a child growing up you do the same thing, you generalize. You don't pay conscious attention to any-thing. You know it so well, you don't pay any attention to it. As a child your sense of things is subordinate to your parents' sense of things, to your elders'

sense of things. What happened to me when I came back in 1964 was that
I just suddenly saw the country as if for the first time. I saw it in detail.
I saw that there was just more here than I had ever dreamed there was, and I
really liked it. It has been really important to me to do my work right in the
presence of what I've been writing about. That has spared me the illusion, for
instance, that a work of imagination could be an adequate substitute for the
world. It isn't. What's here is immeasurably more complicated and immeasurably dearer, finally, than what I've managed to write down. And also it's
important for somebody who writes about agriculture to be involved with it.
I probably wouldn't have written about agriculture if I hadn't come home.
Being here has been a necessary discipline and corrective throughout all that
because farming is easy to sentimentalize. We've got a tradition for the senti-
mentalization of farmers and we've got another tradition—these always go
together when you're dealing with oppressed people—for the denigration of
farmers. They exist side by side, and they're very dangerous to somebody
who has farming as a subject. So it has been a godsend that I've had farmers
right in front of me all my life, and that I have, in a small way, been a farmer.
I don't think that I've sentimentalized. There is a sense in which my work
idealizes certain relationships. I've tried to ask myself sometimes, not what
the actual community I know is like, but what it would be like if people were
to keep fully conscious of, say, the worth and obligation of their friendships
to each other. That's what I was doing in that long story, "The Wild Birds."
Suppose I have an argument between two people who know very well that
they love each other, and that they're not going to do anything but love each
other if they can help it. That kind of problem in an imagined story is going
to press you a little toward idealization. The last thing I was worried about
there was what two *actual* people would *actually* say to each other.

VP: The "Mad Farmer" encourages us to "Be joyful / though you have
considered all the facts." Do you often find that hard to do?
WB: *Sure.* But it's an obligation. What a horrible thing if you gave up on joy
just because of facts. Joy is possible, you see, and it is possible in astonishing
circumstances sometimes, astonishingly bad circumstances. So to give up on
joy is really to give up on life. You never know when joy is going to hit. People
have been joyful in the bitterest of circumstances. See, we think we can plan
joy, get all the terms and circumstances together—and we're terribly disappointed. It doesn't happen that way. That's why people are in such trouble

now, I think. People are terribly disappointed. It seems to me that most people realize in their career as teenagers that when they try to plan the most wonderful party that they've ever had, it turns out to be a bust; and sometimes parties happen because people just happen to be together, and they have a marvelous time. It's a mystery.

VP: Many people are disappointed and frustrated when joy doesn't come according to the terms they anticipated, but never acknowledge the joy of pleasant surprises.

WB: That's right, and they're just unwilling to live loose enough to take it when it comes. My friend Wes Jackson has a friend who argues, really very well, that we must not pursue happiness. I guess his language comes from the *Declaration*, and I don't think he was quarreling with the political principle. But he says if you pursue happiness, you just never find it. It just doesn't happen. I've tried to write about this a time or two. Some of the best parties I've ever been to have taken place when we were at work in tobacco barns or tobacco patches in miserable conditions, and all of a sudden everybody gets a big joke going, and everybody is laughing and happy right in the midst of what the modern world would consider the most miserable conditions: sweaty, hot, no air conditioning, no rest, everybody tired and smelling bad. So it happens.

* * *

WB: I've got old enough that a lot of people have died who have meant a lot to me. You think, "Well, pay attention to these old people and get them to tell you everything they know," and one of these days they're dead, and you think, "Why didn't I ask?"

VP: You always want their opinion.

WB: That's right. But one of the mysteries of community life, I think, is that you don't get the essential learning by anybody's intention. If you stay around, things turn up in conversation. I've learned things about my family, things that I never would have had sense enough to ask about, simply because I was on hand when people were talking. For instance, I learned that my mother's grandfather used to carry a pocketful of locust seeds, and every time he passed a damaged spot or a washed spot on his land he would throw down a few seeds. You can work your way to an ethic, a whole pattern of insights that he'd had, from that, and it's very important for me to know. The organizations of learning assume that you can give somebody a tape recorder and they can dash out in the country and talk to all the old people and get the vital stuff. *They don't know the questions to ask.* Mary Austin said, "You must summer and winter with the land and wait its occasions." You don't make the occasions, you see—that's her point. The occasions come.

The Art of Place: Interview with Wendell Berry

Marilyn Berlin Snell / 1992

From *New Perspectives Quarterly* 9.2 (Spring 1992), 29–34. Reprinted with permission from Blackwell Publishing Ltd.

A poet, essayist, and author of 25 books, including the novel *A Place on Earth* and the collection of essays titled *What Are People For?*, Wendell Berry has lived on and farmed a hillside in his native Henry County, Kentucky, for 27 years.

In the following conversation with *NPQ* Senior Editor Marilyn Berlin Snell at his home overlooking the Kentucky River, Berry proceeds from one of his fundamental precepts: that one cannot talk about culture without talking about agriculture (and vice versa).

NPQ: One of the defining elements of contemporary culture is its rejection of heroic modernism, the belief that some master plan—whether Le Corbusier's high-rise public housing, Marx's historical materialism or Malraux's design for art—can heal our collective ills.

Few today defend modernism's "abstract globalism" or "grand narrative," but what we are left with in its wake is a kind of anarchistic pluralism. Do you believe there to be a transcendent ethics and story, or are there only local, plural stories?

Wendell Berry: First, we must define what we mean by "pluralism." The pluralism that extends hospitability to just anything is not valid. There are standards. Real pluralism extends respect—not tolerance—toward all rooted, locally adapted cultures that know what works and what doesn't work in a given place. That kind of pluralism doesn't exist now. In fact, as soon as a culture becomes rooted, our so-called pluralism *withdraws* its respect, labeling it provincialism or anachronism.

Today, local economies are being destroyed by the "pluralistic," displaced, global economy, which has no respect for what works in a locality. The global economy is built on the principle that one place can be exploited, even destroyed, for the sake of another place. That is a bad kind of pluralism.

There are standards relating to culture that go beyond the self-interest of any group. We must, first and foremost, ask what objective measures we can use in our efforts to live in the world without destroying it. We must ask how, in this place, we may live with each other and with nature. There is no reason why one culture can't learn from another, why what happens in one locality can't be instructive to people elsewhere. But to attempt, as we have been doing, to impose on localities a centrally devised idea, culture, technology or economy means that the localities will be destroyed.

NPQ: There must be standards, a transcendent narrative if you will, but not a universal narrative, which can never accommodate the needs of individual localities?

WB: Yes. We must support what supports local life, which means community, family, household life—the moral capital our larger institutions have come to rest upon. If the larger institutions undermine the local life, they destroy that moral capital just exactly as the industrial economy has destroyed the natural capital of localities—soil fertility and so on. Essential wisdom accumulates in the community much as fertility builds in the soil.

NPQ: How does one square "ecology" in the strict sense you use the word as a rural Kentucky farmer, living in a region where cause and effect are palpable, with the ecology implied by the vanishing ozone layer? Don't some problems demand global solutions? Or is Gaia a quaint Greek myth that has no modern resonance?

WB: What you call "Gaia" I call "the creation," and I understand it to be a harmonious and beautiful whole. I am happy to honor it. However, that the whole exists is not something anybody is ever going to know for certain. We sense that the whole exists because we have experienced the intricacy, wonder, and mystery of its parts. So a valid "globalism" must be based on an absolute willingness to destroy any part of the globe. If we want to use the world without destroying it we must apply our minds to the nature and needs of *places*.

NPQ: One could argue that Georgia, Croatia, and other ethnic enclaves around the world represent the extremes of just this logic.

WB: I'm afraid that their centrifugal momentum may be wrongly impelled. People rightly want the freedom to determine their own lives, to be free of illegitimate rule. But are they willing to do what it takes to be truly free? Are they willing to shorten their supply lines, to establish authentic local economies?

It is one thing to establish nations and quite another to establish local, reasonably self-sufficient and ecologically sane economies. If these freedom fighters extricate themselves from the old guard only to rest their hopes on the industrial superstition that if they don't have what they need where they are they can import it from somewhere else, then they will never come to the fundamental accommodation that is necessary between a people and their land.

NPQ: How are the responsibilities of freedom to be conveyed—not only to the newly independent states around the world, but to stable democracies such as our own?

WB: The first task is to dispense with several deadly superstitions: that there can be adequate central planning; that people can be adequately governed by a government; that private motives and public methods are adequate; that we can be taught in a school everything we need to know; that everything necessary *can* be known; that we are smart enough to work on a large scale.

Further, one must acknowledge that there is a religious as well as an educational dimension to freedom. How will those who want some kind of independence in their own country, in their own place, learn to think of themselves as irremediably dependent people living within—and, to a considerable extent, by—a beneficence that is mysterious?

Such questions lead directly to others of the most insistently local and practical kind: What should we plant here? Where should we locate this workshop? Where should we build our fences? What should we plant on each of these specific parcels of land? What breeds of livestock are desirable?

In other words, how do we hear what our place has to say, and then respond in the most considerate and conserving manner?

NPQ: As advanced industrial society becomes more removed from the foundations of culture, does the need for intermediaries, translators, increase? As a poet and novelist you convey certain responsibilities of freedom through your work. Do writers and artists become more important as we become more alienated?

WB: It depends on what you mean by important. In a disintegrating, shallowly pluralistic society such as ours, the artist's role gravitates toward a kind of nonessential entertainment, which merely distracts us from things that matter. In a truly grounded, locally adapted culture, the artists would be the rememberers. They would memorialize great occasions, preserve necessary insights and so on.

Emerson wrote: "I grasp the hands of those next to me, and take my place in the ring to suffer and to work, taught by an instinct, that so shall the dumb abyss be vocal with speech." He was referring to common experience and common effort on a common ground—that is, to an intact community. One can see the artist's role in this community as that of rememberer.

NPQ: From the contemporary "abyss," most of what is heard is neither reverence nor even remembrance, but a deep and abiding ahistorical cynicism. It is far more *de rigueur* to discuss the death of both the story and the storyteller.

WB: Ever since I have been conscious, intellectuals, critics, and artists have been talking about the death of *something*. I have yet to attend the funeral of anything worthy that has been declared dead by these fellows, though I am aware that much is in jeopardy: marriage, family, community, the entire farming class, for examples.

In my own life, the arts are very much alive. I have returned endlessly to books, paintings and pieces of music for instruction and reassurance, and for the kinds of sustenance that one can't so easily call by name. We can speak of the arts only within limits but we can certainly see that they are essential to our lives.

But when I speak of "arts" I would prefer to mean simply "the ways of making things." We have been using the term in the sense of fine art, but when a culture is doing well, all its artifacts are made well and afford the kind of solace that only beautiful work can give.

If our museums are utilized to protect exemplary works so that the ways of making a sculpture, a bowl, or a painting have a better chance of survival than in the places where the work is currently done, then the museum has a legitimate function. But if our ability to make things has degenerated to the point that we must go to our museums to see art, then we no longer *have* art. Our museum is our mausoleum.

NPQ: . . . It is not the totem—the Picasso, O'Keefe, or Giacometti—that matters, but the tribe. . . .

WB: Both matter. But if the person who looks at a work of art in a museum comes from some place that he or she cares about and wants to see survive and flourish, then the museum simply cannot confine that work of art; it becomes an influence. On the other hand, if viewers see the world and their place in it as arbitrary or irrelevant to themselves, they will see the work as a dead relic of a useless past and an irrelevant humanity. And so they will be unable to feel its influence or be inspired by it. But then I would argue that the spectator is in peril.

The last time I was in New York I went to a hideous show at the Museum of Modern Art. I asked a guard how anybody could like this work, and he said, "Because they don't have to stay here very long," which I thought was a fine piece of art criticism. If you were an artist of any kind, whether you were a furniture maker, a potter, a poet, or an oil painter, you would want people to be able to live with your work—or so it seems to me.

When I think of art, I think of my home and what I want to live with. Made things can be either degrading or instructive, boring or uplifting. Behind my judgment of art is really a judgment about what kind of community I want to live in.

Ananda Coomaraswamy says that the mission of art is to delight, instruct, and move. I would add that the best art involves a complex giving of honor. It gives honor to the materials that are being used in the work, therefore giving honor to God; it gives honor to the people for whom the art is made; and it gives honor to the maker, the responsible worker. In that desire to give honor, the artist takes on the obligation to be responsibly connected both to the human community and to nature.

NPQ: French philosopher Regis Debray argues that a worldwide aesthetic does not exist: "The eclecticism of modern art collections, where the fetish from the Island of Tonga gazes upon the most recent Buren, with a Stella and a Soulages between them, calls forth naught but indifference. Coldness and courtesy."

Do you believe that the well-crafted pottery from the Indian village speaks to the Parisian, say, as eloquently as a Rodin sculpture, or is it somehow compromised in the translation? Can art transcend its place?

WB: Of course it can. When we think of a piece of work as exemplary we have snatched it from the specialized category people are referring to when they speak of lifeless art. In the process, we have also separated ourselves from those who equate sophistication with cynicism and misanthropy.

At this point I must use the word "love." I know that when one works out of love—for family, community, craft—one is strong. I don't mean love as a feeling, but as a practice. Sometimes in the practice of love, one doesn't have the feeling.

To me, love is the source from which all else springs, and that is why the modern "sophisticated" exploitation of sexual love is so regrettable, depressing and, I think, dangerous.

NPQ: AIDS would attest to that.

WB: The sexual revolution, based on the superstition of safe sex, is as big a failure as the "peaceful atom."

In the last 400 years, our attention has moved from the countenance to the specifically sexual anatomy. When we read Shakespeare or Chaucer, we find that the great source of power is in the eyes.

In *The Merchant of Venice*, for example, Portia says to Bassanio, "Beshrew your eyes, / They have o'erlook'd me and divided me . . ." She is not speaking of him as a seducer because the same thing has just happened to him. "One half of me is yours," she says, "the other half is yours." This is happening because they have looked at each other. Their eyes have met with a certain complex understanding. Our obsession with the quantification of the figure—the measurements, the body parts—is another thing.

This change in the focus of sexual love from the countenance to the genitals means that certain responsibilities are being refused. The countenance involves the spirit, the soul. If you deal with people in terms that require you to meet their eyes, you are dealing with them as living souls, not just as bodies. Further, if you deal with them as living souls you recognize instantly that certain things are demanded; for one, you must acknowledge them as people with lives, needs, problems.

Of course, if we can keep the countenance out of it, we don't have to take responsibility for the complexity of the encounter. We can remain in our "animal nature." However, once we exclude responsibility from the encounter, we have also obliterated its power.

If we actually saw actors play that scene from *The Merchant of Venice* between Portia and Bassanio, actors who understood what was happening, it would be hair-raising. It would be far more powerful and erotic than explicit love scenes in modern movies or pornography.

NPQ: In your essay "Writer and Region" you write that "We have hardly begun to imagine the coming to responsibility that is the meaning and the liberation of growing up. We have hardly begun to imagine community life and the tragedy that is at the heart of community life." What is the importance of the tragic sensibility in both personal and community life?
WB: The tragic sensibility simply accepts mortality as an inescapable condition. In a sense, it is the necessary counterbalance to the tradition of seeing the other as a living soul; it applies a sense of time and finitude to our relationships.

The tragic sensibility sees and accepts that as we live we are going to live into the deaths of people we love and it accepts that the condition of our love for those people is that we will lose them—or that they will lose us. The practical aspect of the tragic sensibility is that it infuses both a necessary seriousness and a joyful appreciation.

NPQ: Carlos Fuentes has written in *NPQ* that the task of literature has heretofore been to remember and represent the constant truths of our civilization. In modern times ruled by the linear thinking of progress, literature has had to remember the tragic perspective. His argument is that now literature is faced for the first time with the fact of earth's frailty and the task of imagining a time beyond tragedy.
WB: I agree with him up to the point at which I quit understanding him. The time beyond tragedy is a time when nobody is there. What then is there to write about . . . ?

NPQ: . . . He ends the passage by saying, "At long last, the hubris of the Homeric hero can be satiated—we are now capable of destroying nature; nature like the hero can now know death."
WB: There isn't any question about it, but this is not new. Since the Revelation of St. John we have thought about the end of things. I grew up around elderly women, black and white, who dwelled on the end of things in

a fairly bloodcurdling way. I have been used to these premonitions for a long time.

What happens after the end of things is, I am sure, extremely important, but to my way of thinking it isn't my responsibility. I would like to prevent an end of things that would be a human artifact. I revolt against that possibility, and, in order to keep it from happening, I think we have to accept our lives in real terms, which are mortality, fallibility, ignorance, tragedy, grief, and joy.

NPQ: It seems your notion of tragedy is more akin to James Joyce, who wrote in *Portrait of the Artist as a Young Man* that "the tragic emotion is the face looking two ways: toward terror and toward pity." In Joyce we see the tragic emotion as a bonding agent: in terror we are bonded to the unknown, in pity we are bonded to one another.

Both the religious and the empathic bond seem to have been broken in contemporary society.

WB: I agree.

There is a wonderful story by Frank O'Connor called "Guests of the Nation" in which some rather innocent Irish Republic Army soldiers have to kill two British captives they have come to like. After the first has been shot, the other looks at the body lying at his feet and says, "Poor bastard, we don't know what is happening to him now." That is the terror. The immensity of death will touch even the most insignificant life—even an insect. Sooner or later, it will overtake us, and it will be momentous in a way that ordinary daily reality doesn't prepare us for.

Then there is pity. Cynics have made much of the selfishness of grief. First, such an attitude doesn't acknowledge the naturalness and appropriateness of a certain selfishness. Second, these cynics don't seem to understand how we imagine our way into the lives of those we care about. There isn't any clear line to be drawn between ourselves and the people we love. We *are* them in a certain sense; if we weren't we wouldn't mind what happened to them.

NPQ: Joyce also said that the tragic emotion was static, whereas other emotions and the arts that excite them are "kinetic"—that is, they inspire desire, which urges us to possess, to go to something, or they inspire loathing, which urges us to abandon, to go from something. He contrasts this kinetic sensibility with the static, eternal moment of "aesthetic arrest."

WB: I too believe in the eternal moment, but I am not sure I understand it as a stasis, though I do see that the artistic moment is different from the lived moment.

Let's take the moment when Portia and Bassanio look at each other, or the moment when Emma tells Mr. Knightly in Jane Austen's novel that, after all, they are not too much brother and sister for her to be able to dance with him. And Mr. Knightly says, "Brother and sister! No, indeed."

Those moments are eternal in the sense that they represent powerful realization. We take them into our minds as artifacts and return to them again and again to find them unchanged but always replete with renewing power.

The moments of great power and feeling that we live through, such as moments of great grief, seem to me to be relentlessly kinetic, to use Joyce's term, or dynamic. They carry us into another world; they change our lives. That power is going to remain an emotional power within us.

The eternal moment in art is not personal. It can affect us personally but it has a kind of loftiness and serenity to it that grief doesn't have. Grief rubs you into the ground. It isn't lofty and serene, though it certainly tells us something about eternity.

NPQ: The eternal moment of art and the lived moment of, say, great grief are powerful enough to collapse the time of past, present, and future—though one is transcendent and one is very personal.

What do you think happens to contemporary culture as it loses its connection to the past and its faith in the future, residing more and more in the avaricious present? Instead of aesthetic arrest we have dizzying market-driven change and the acceleration of time . . .

WB: . . . which seems to me to be a hell of a bad mistake, made on the basis of several illusions that evaporate when one tries to impose them on one's work or on nature.

You see, when you have a farm, it doesn't make any difference how wound up you are. If you are going to grow corn, you have got to slow down to the speed of corn. If you are an artist you have a certain capacity to work well, your own speed and endurance.

I have never bought the argument made to me repeatedly that if I had a computer I could write faster. I know beyond any doubt that I can write as well as I can write at a sustained rate of two or three pages a day. If I wrote more than that my work would be worse, not better. The refusal to speed up, to hitch yourself to these mechanisms that impose speed on you, is simply a way of staying within real time—the time in which things grow, in which good work is done. Taking the adjective "good" off the process might speed things up, but if you aren't interested in working well, why work?

I have been reading a fascinating book about wine, *Adventures on the Wine Route* by a Californian named Kermit Lynch. He writes that specialists are now telling vintners how they can speed up the wine-making process with heat and chemicals. The point that Mr. Lynch makes is that one can speed up the wine-making process, but what one has as a result is not, properly speaking, wine. It is a kind of expensive mouthwash.

Lynch talks about wine as an artifact and about how "impressionable" it is. Real wine—good wine—is something that comes about in its own time. If the vintner wants real wine he or she will have to accept its rate of becoming.

NPQ: In a sense, the task of the vintner, no less than the poet, is to pay respectful attention to the rhythms of their creative activity?
WB: That's right. Coomaraswamy says that we want art but are not willing to pay attention to the things that make for art, just as we want peace but are not willing to pay attention to the things that make for peace. In art, the process is much longer than a lot of people think, and the beginning is much further back than the addicts of technological acceleration are willing to acknowledge. It begins in the ground with anything that grows, including artists, which means it began eons ago.

NPQ: . . . and not thirty minutes ago at the beginning of the television program. . . .
WB: That's right. The older I get as a writer, the better I understand how long the process is. I understand that I am writing things that come out of years of preparation not only in my life but in my teachers' lives—my father's, my mother's, my grandparents', my friends', the lives of people I ran into in school.

As an individual I can plot out my lineage. As an artist my lineage is much more complicated, but I must always work to acknowledge formative influences and affirm their importance. Otherwise, there is only the ego.

NPQ: In one of my favorite lines from your work you didn't say "a good poet"—you said "a good poem exists at the center of a complex reminding."

WB: That is right. I have read poetry that has meant a good deal to me, so that as I work on my own poetry I am aware that much speaking is going on. My work is being moved in many ways—by inspiration, by technical fascination, and by the other people who have spoken to me in writing or conversation. I am working deep in my own awareness of history.

NPQ: In a sense, as the rememberer, the artist *is* the community . . .
WB: There is a very arrogant way to answer that question. But there is also an humble response, which sees the artist not as an isolated, preeminent genius who materializes ideas from thin air, but as a person who has been in a community a long time, has been attentive to its voices . . .

NPQ: . . . and who is prepared to pass on what has been heard.
WB: Yes. There are two things the artist must do: pass on all that is involved—the art, the memory, the knowledge. And take responsibility for his or her own work—that is the reason the work is signed, and that should be the only reason.

Wendell Berry

L. Elisabeth Beattie / 1993

From *Conversations with Kentucky Writers*, ed. L. Elisabeth Beattie. Lexington, KY: UP of Kentucky, 1996, 2–21. Copyright © 1996 by The University Press of Kentucky. Original copy of interview in the Kentucky Writers Oral History Project, Louie B. Nunn Center for Oral History, University of Kentucky Libraries. Reprinted by permission of the University Press of Kentucky and University of Kentucky Libraries.

Berry: My name is Wendell Erdman Berry, and I was born August fifth, 1934. My mother's maiden name was Virginia Erdman Berry, and my father's name is John Marshall Berry. My father was a lawyer and also a farmer, and my mother is a housewife still. My father is dead.

Beattie: What was your childhood like?
Berry: I had, I think, a wonderful childhood. I grew up in the little town of New Castle, Kentucky, where my parents moved in 1936. I went to school at New Castle School until 1948. But I also grew up on farms. My father continued to be a farmer, and both sets of grandparents were on the farm. I had what I think was a very free childhood, a lot of swimming and riding on horses and wandering about.

Beattie: Did you help your father much with the farm?
Berry: Well, my father was often involved in things that he couldn't be helped with, but I helped other people on the farm. I helped my father sometimes. There would be days when he would take time off from his office, and we would work through a bunch of cattle or something like that. He was a good teacher. But my father was very busy in his law practice, and for fifty years he was involved with the Burley Tobacco Growers Cooperative Association as counsel, as vice-president, and then as president. So the opportunities for working with my father weren't all that available, but there were other people I worked for and with from the time I was very young.

Beattie: Did you think, when you were a child, that you might be a lawyer or a farmer?
Berry: I thought off and on that I might be a lawyer. I always wanted to be a farmer from the time I was a little boy.

Beattie: What was your early schooling like?
Berry: I had some good teachers. I wasn't a very tractable student, and after about the second grade, I began to cause a lot of trouble.

Beattie: In what way?
Berry: Oh, being uproarious, doing the things kids do who are not very happy to be in school.

Beattie: Do you remember liking any subject better than any other?
Berry: Not early. I liked to read from a very early age, but reading I did on my own. I had also found out very early what it was like to be at large in the countryside, and what it felt like to be at work in the countryside, and that made it difficult, I think, for me to be at home in school. I always thought that there would be a better place to be, and I'm not entirely convinced that I wasn't right. So I'm not sure that I had a favorite subject for a long time.

I loved to read from early in my life. I loved being read to, and my mother loved to read and loved to read to me. She really was the one who gave me a love of books, and who gave me books to read. It was a wonderful thing to be sick and home from school with her, because we would read. We read about King Arthur's knights and Robin Hood and other wonderful things.

Beattie: Do you remember other books that either she read to you or that you read yourself?
Berry: *The Swiss Family Robinson* was a very big book with me. My mother read it to me, and then I read it over and over and over again for myself. And *The Yearling*. My mother gave that book to me, and it was another book that I virtually memorized. I didn't try to read a lot of books. If I found a book I liked, I just read it and read it and read it. A little later I read Mary O'Hara, *My Friend Flicka*, and *Thunderhead*, and later *Green Grass of Wyoming*. I nearly wore out *My Friend Flicka* and *Thunderhead*. I still know all about those books. So I took spells at reading, but I never much liked to read assignments.

Beattie: Because they were assignments or because they just weren't very interesting reading?

Berry: Well, I don't very much like to read my own assignments. The sense of having to do it is damaging to reading, in a way. You ought to read freely, and I still do that some.

Beattie: That goes along with the psychology of reading with a flashlight under the bed covers, doesn't it?

Berry: I did a lot of that. The flashlight was a great boon to me. I read a lot of comic books that way, but also real books. My mother was convinced that we ruined ourselves with comic books, which, of course, made them irresistible.

Beattie: Did your sisters and brother read as much as you did?

Berry: Not as much as I did. My mother read to us all, of course. I was the one who became a bookworm.

Beattie: What about athletics or other things? Did you do that sort of thing in school?

Berry: There wasn't much in the way of organized sports for young kids at school. There was some organized play, and I did some of that, but mostly we played on our own. We played hours and hours of basketball in people's yards, throwing a basketball through old buckets and makeshift hoops, but we played all the time. That was real play. I mean, it's real play when kids get together and play a game. It's not real play when they get together under supervision of adults and are made to do it the right way and all that.

Beattie: You just went through eighth grade in New Castle. Where did you go after that?

Berry: I went to Millersburg Military Institute. It was very confining and military, of course. I never liked the military part of it. I did have some good teachers there, and I began there to read more seriously than I had before. In high school I began to have a favorite subject: literature.

Beattie: When did you start your own writing?

Berry: I wrote a few poems and other things when I was in high school, but I didn't begin to write knowledgeably until I was well along in college. I had a very good teacher—who just died—at the University of Kentucky in my second semester, Thomas Stroup. He taught Milton and other seventeenth-century writers. But he also taught a course at that time called "Introduction to Literature." It involved reading and writing about poetry. He used that old textbook, *Understanding Poetry*, by Robert Penn Warren and Cleanth Brooks. It's still referred to, I think, as "Brooks and Warren." I would carry Stroup my awful poems, which he very patiently read and criticized and made fun of a little bit. But that was when I first began to write with the idea that there might be a way to do it that I needed to learn.

Beattie: Had you ever written poetry or done any kind of writing on your own in elementary school or high school?
Berry: A poem or two, as I said, and articles for the school paper. I began to feel then that it would be a good thing to be a writer. I had been a bookish little boy. I would imagine how it would be to write about what I was doing. I would say it over to myself the way I thought a writer might write it. But there were times when I didn't read at all; my mind would be on farming or hunting. I wound up at military school because I was so much more interested in hunting and trapping and that sort of thing than I was in school. My parents thought something had to be done.

Beattie: Did you go directly from the military school to the University of Kentucky?
Berry: Yes, the next fall.

Beattie: Why did you choose the University of Kentucky?
Berry: I didn't give the subject very much thought; the University of Kentucky was just there, and I went to it. I had begun to think that I wanted to be a writer, and I had the rather naive assumption that the business of the University of Kentucky was to make me into a writer. Of course, that wasn't its business, but I found people there who helped me. Tom Stroup was the first, and then Hollis Summers, and after Hollis there was Robert Hazel— people who treated me very kindly and taught me a lot.

Beattie: Were you involved in any extracurricular pursuits there, such as the newspaper or literary magazines?
Berry: I was involved with the literary magazines. They used to have a fresh-man magazine called the *Green Pen*, and I helped to edit that. Then I was

involved in [the literary magazine] *Stylus*, as a contributor, and then as editor.

Beattie: Several other people I've interviewed for this project have talked long and fondly about their time with you at UK and at Stanford, Ed McClanahan and Gurney Norman and Jim Baker Hall.
Berry: Jim Hall, oh yes.

Beattie: Even Bobbie Ann Mason.
Berry: We were all together there. But Bobbie Ann Mason was Gurney's contemporary, and Gurney was just coming in as I was going out. I didn't meet Bobbie Ann until 1963 or '64, in New York. I stayed [at the University of Kentucky] five years and got an M.A. Jim Hall and I were friends from at least the time I was a sophomore. We got to know each other in one of Hollis Summer's creative writing classes, and we were very close friends. We were together all the time, talking about writing, poetry, T.S. Eliot, and Ezra Pound and the poets of that generation who were such monuments to kids in school at that time. Ed came as a graduate student in 1956, it must have been. He'd been to Stanford. Ed had been around quite a bit, much more than I had, heaven knows. We became friends at that time and stayed friends. I went, the next year after I was a graduate student, and taught at Georgetown [College]; and if I'm not mistaken, Ed was still working on his M.A.

Beattie: This is Georgetown, Kentucky?
Berry: Yes. And Ed and Kitty, his first wife, were living out at Bryan Station Spring, in an old ice house. We visited a lot at that time. The next year Ed went to Corvallis [Oregon] to teach, and I went to Stanford as a Stegner Fellow.

Beattie: Your decision to go to Stanford, did it have anything to do with their having been at Stanford?
Berry: Jim Hall went to Stanford as a graduate student the year that I taught at Georgetown, and he told me about those fellowships. Of course, I wanted to go where he was, and also my wife, Tanya, grew up in California. She loved it out there, and it was attractive to me to go out where she had been and was at home. It was a very fortunate thing, really, that I did get to know that part of the world that meant so much to her.

Beattie: When did you meet and marry your wife?
Berry: I met Tanya at the University of Kentucky in the fall of 1955.

Beattie: What brought her from California to the University of Kentucky?
Berry: Her father [Clifford Amyx] taught in the art department. Tanya and I got married on the twenty-ninth of May, 1957.

Beattie: What was your master's thesis on?
Berry: I didn't do a thesis. That got me into trouble with some people, but Jim Hall and I had gone the year before, the summer of 1956, up to the School of Letters at Indiana University. We took a course in Joyce and Yeats from Richard Ellman, and a course in modern poetry from Karl Shapiro. I picked up six credit hours that way, you see. Then along in my year as a graduate student I found out that you could do six extra hours of credit in lieu of a thesis. I just took that option.

At Georgetown College, I taught three courses of freshman composition and a course of sophomore literature. I enjoyed the teaching a lot, but we were required to attend chapel and so on. I was the way a young man is supposed to be; I was rebellious, and didn't like to be required to do things.

Beattie: When you went to Stanford, I know you had Wallace Stegner as a major professor. You've written about what a wonderful teacher he is. Will you talk about your relationship with him? Also, you've described Stegner as a regional writer who has escaped the evils of regionalism. Will you describe those evils?
Berry: Well, the evils of regionalism all have to do with thinking that special virtues come with your region, and that's something you have to get over. You're not going to be a better writer or a better person because you are a Kentuckian. The other evil is offering your region and people as curiosities. We've had a good bit of that in Kentucky, people offering Kentuckians as stereotypes, as what other people think they are, so that those other people can say, "Oh, look at the quaint, backward, ignorant Kentuckians."

Beattie: Would you say, too, that whatever a piece of writing is in terms of being regional, that it has to be universal to have any kind of real value?
Berry: No, I don't agree with that entirely. It has value in itself. I mean, this is my assumption, that all creatures are uniquely valuable, individually. They

don't get their value by virtue of belonging to a category. There has to be this appreciation, which is one of the most precious things in our tradition, this appreciation of the value that inheres in us by virtue of our being what we are individually.

Beattie: I agree with that. I just meant in order for other people to appreciate individuality, there has to be something . . .
Berry: Oh yes, there must be recognition. If you're absolutely unique, you're absolutely lonely. So there is shared . . .

Beattie: Humanity?
Berry: Yes.

Beattie: What about Wallace Stegner? What was he like in your relationship with him, the student-teacher relationship?
Berry: Wallace Stegner was a man of great personal dignity and a lot of reserve. He wasn't the kind of professor who let you get to be his pal. You weren't going to drop in on him for an informal chat, or at least I wasn't. But implicit in that reserve was an expectation. I don't mean to say that he was not generous; he was absolutely generous, and he would help you to no end. He's helped me, goodness knows, without reservation and without limit, so far as I know. Every time anything good has happened to me, he has turned out to be behind it somewhere, a letter of recommendation or something. But, he kept his distance. I always felt in his reserve an expectation that people ought to live up to what they'd been given, not just to a fellowship, but to the whole tradition of literature and culture in the West, in the world, even. He made me feel that there was no excuse for doing less than I could, and no excuse not to give honor to the things I'd been given.

Beattie: Do your classmates share your feelings about Stegner?
Berry: I don't know. I never did ask them. We didn't gossip about him very much. If he had involved himself with us on a more familiar basis, we might have gossiped about him, but I don't remember very much gossip at all about Wallace Stegner, which is rather remarkable. I also had another wonderful teacher at Stanford, Richard Scowcroft. I have a large debt to him, also, and remain his friend.

Beattie: What sort of writing were you doing when you were in the work-shop [at Stanford]?

Berry: I was working on *Nathan Coulter*, my first novel. I had about half of it written when I went out there, and I just continued to work on it.

Beattie: I wondered when reading that novel, if you, in your childhood, experienced the death of someone similar to the powerful scene in the book where the mother is in the parlor?

Berry: No, I didn't experience anything like that. You mean the death of the mother.

Beattie: Yes.

Berry: No. I experienced the deaths of loved ones early, but not of my mother. People immediately said that *Nathan Coulter* was an autobiographical novel, but it's not an autobiographical novel at all. Nathan, as I figured, was born in 1924. So his early experience was actually of a more unadulter-ated rural life than I ever knew.

Beattie: Ed McClanahan and Gurney Norman have talked about the good times they had living out in California. Were you ever part of that, with Ken Kesey and the psychedelic bus and all of that?

Berry: Well, Ken Kesey was part of that seminar that I was in at Stanford, in that year of '58 and '59. Kesey was living on Perry Lane during those years. I lived in Mill Valley, though, and commuted, because Tanya's uncle and aunt had a little place there that they would rent to us. It was attractive to be there, so that's where we stayed. I guess it must have been '63 or '64 when Gurney and Ed made me aware of Kesey's exploits. But no, I missed that.

Gurney, Jim, and Ed came there as fellows after I left, so Kesey had flow-ered more fully during their time than he had during mine. I have always been friends with Ken, but I never was a prankster. Kesey and I are the only two people that Tanya and I knew in college who are still married to the same women. Very different styles of matrimony, I suppose, but it's a fact.

Beattie: What about your children? Were they born while you were in California?

Berry: No. Mary, our oldest, was born in Lexington in May of 1958. She went to California with us as a little baby, in August of that year. Then Den was born, also in Lexington, in August of 1962.

Beattie: Where were you living?
Berry: When Den was born, we weren't really living anywhere. We had come back from Europe. We were staying in a borrowed house that belonged to some friends of Tanya's parents.

Beattie: When you were in Europe, was that just vacation or were you studying there?
Berry: I got a Guggenheim in 1961. We went to Europe that August and came back the next July.

Beattie: Where were you there?
Berry: Mostly in Italy, in Florence, but we also spent two months in southern France and some time in Paris and London. I was writing a book, or so I thought, and I did work on it some, but not very effectively. I had begun *A Place on Earth* in California in January of 1960, and I carried it on in Europe as best I could. I wanted to write not so limited a book as *Nathan Coulter* had been, and I didn't know how to write a less limited book. There was a lot of awkwardness in the writing of *A Place on Earth*.

Beattie: But you were able to use parts of what you'd written?
Berry: I believe I was. I don't think I wrote anything that was very good when I was in Europe, but I think I salvaged some of it.

Beattie: Then you went to New York to teach?
Berry: Yes, at the University College, so called, of NYU, which was up in the Bronx, in University Heights. I taught freshman English. I was the director of freshman English.

Beattie: How long were you there?
Berry: Two years, until the spring of '64.

Beattie: What was the experience like?
Berry: Well, I enjoyed all of it, pretty much, being up there. I learned a lot that has been indispensable to me.

Beattie: In terms of what sorts of things?
Berry: Living in a great city and working in a great city and being used to being a part of a great city. Just knowing your way around and being equal to

the things you had to put up with. We lived in an old loft on Greenwich
Street, 277 Greenwich Street, down by City Hall and the Washington Market,
an exciting part of town to live in. Then I got acquainted with museums and
art galleries. The city offered a lot, and I took advantage of a good bit of it.

Beattie: But you decided you didn't want to stay?
Berry: Yes, I got an offer to come back to teach at the University at
Lexington—thanks, I later found out, to Wallace Stegner.

Beattie: Had you not gotten that offer, do you think you would have stayed
in New York?
Berry: I have no idea. I had assumed for a long time, because of the way I'd
been taught by schools, that I would never amount to anything if I stayed at
home. So when I got to New York I sort of assumed, well, this is what one
does. Then when I got the offer to come back to Kentucky, we knew, first of
all, that we wanted to come back. Also, it had become fairly plain to me that I
was a Kentucky writer; I wasn't going to be a New York writer. I'd just lived in
Kentucky too long. My mind and my life were formed here in Henry County,
my allegiances were here. All my kinships were here, and several of my dear-
est friendships. So I wanted to come back, and teaching at the University of
Kentucky would make it possible. So I did return to Kentucky. I certainly
didn't feel that I wanted to spend a lot of my life living in New York. I liked it,
it was exhilarating, it was wonderful, but I think a lot of my excitement
depended on my understanding that I didn't have to stay, that I'd find some
way to leave if I wanted to.

Beattie: You talk about realizing that you were a Kentucky writer and that
you wouldn't be a New York writer. When you were in New York, did you
write or attempt to write things that were centered in Kentucky?
Berry: I worked on *A Place on Earth*, and, of course, always on poems. I've
always written poems, off and on. They would come to me. But I was busy
writing *A Place on Earth* all the time I was in New York. I finally sort of
learned to write it when I was up there. I finally began to feel that I knew
what I was doing. But, of course, *A Place on Earth* is about my part of
Kentucky, and it was pretty plain by that time that what I really wanted to
write about was this place here, these few square miles that I'd known all my

life. What I loved most was this, and that was what I most wanted to serve. Of course, we had no idea what our life was going to turn out to be.

Beattie: Had you attempted to write stories or poems with other settings, such as New York?
Berry: Oh, I wrote a few New York poems. I'd written a few West Coast poems, and I still occasionally write a poem about someplace else. But I don't have the permanence of commitment and interest elsewhere that I've always had here. My father had a commitment to this place and to small farmers, to the way of life that was practiced here, and I have followed him in that.

Beattie: Sounds like your father gave you the impetus to be what you are, and your mother showed you the way to be who you are.
Berry: It would be hard to unravel my debts to them. My father, of course, thought that I was going to starve to death as a writer, and he didn't very much favor my choice. It was something that I now understand. If I had a child who came in and said he wanted to be a writer, I would be scared to death. It would not be something that I would want to encourage very much, because it's so chancy.

Beattie: Have either of your children wanted to write?
Berry: No, my children are farmers. My daughter and son-in-law live at New Castle on a farm, and my son and his wife live near Lacie on a farm. Right here, ten miles away, and about four or five miles away.

Beattie: It's rare to be able to say that today.
Berry: It is. It means we have our grandchildren.

Beattie: When you returned to the University of Kentucky, what were you teaching?
Berry: I taught the writing courses, mainly.

Beattie: You have written about and talked about creative or imaginative writing being another form of good writing. How did you teach those classes, and don't you still teach at the University of Kentucky?
Berry: I don't teach those classes any more, and I haven't since 1977. I quit in 1977, and stayed quit for ten years. When I went back, I started teaching other things. I don't like teaching so-called creative writing anymore.

I've been teaching, since the fall of '87, a course called Composition for Teachers, for people who are going to teach English in the public schools. Then I've taught, usually, a literature course of some kind. I taught a course called Readings in Agriculture, which is probably too complicated to explain this afternoon, and a course in pastoral literature.

Beattie: You didn't particularly enjoy teaching creative writing?
Berry: I enjoyed it. I actually had a very good time doing it, but the course worried me all the time I was teaching it, because it was a little hard, given the assumption that people came into the course with, to make them concentrate as much as they needed to on the technical issues of writing. I was always a little uneasy about the justification for such a course.

Beattie: Did you ever have any students that were very promising writers?
Berry: I had some very good students. Lynn Hightower's the one I think of immediately, and I'm sort of out of touch with the people I taught all those years ago. It's been fifteen years now since I've taught one of those courses. I'm not sure what's happened to all of the students I had. Some of them were very good writers. But, you see, preparing people to be novelists and poets and that sort of thing, is hardly the same thing as preparing somebody to be a doctor or an engineer or a lawyer, or a teacher even, because there are just not any significant number of places that are dependably available. So really, in terms of the life of the student, you're working in the dark. You don't know what you're doing, and that's why I always insisted that I would rather make a good writer and a good reader than to make a published writer, because you'd be lucky, unless you were someplace like Stanford, to make very many of them.

Beattie: I'm always surprised at the number of would-be or creative writers who are not readers and who don't see why they need to be readers.
Berry: Yes. Well, I can explain that, but I suppose there's not much use.

Beattie: I was wondering if you ran into that when you were teaching creative writing.
Berry: I've run into people who were afraid that if they read any poetry, they would destroy their originality. You'd always find that such people were writing under the influence of cigarette commercials and that sort of thing. It's

hard on people of romantic sensibility to face it, but the fact is that writing comes out of writing, just as talk comes out of talk. If you didn't hear other people talk, and study their ways of talking, you'd never get to be a good talker. The same goes for writing.

Beattie: In one of your essays you were quoting, I believe it was Adrienne Rich, talking about not needing to know Yeats's voice.
Berry: Well, that wasn't an ignorant statement; it was a political statement, and I understand that. But there are people who think they don't need to read Yeats or Shakespeare or Milton. Some people who think those people don't need to be read are teaching literature in English departments.

Beattie: A lot of people think they shouldn't be read because they're "dead white men."
Berry: They are dead white men.

Beattie: So that somehow negates them.
Berry: Yes, and people who talk that way don't acknowledge their very considerable debts to dead white men who, after all, kept alive this idea of individual worth, and individual dignity, and individual freedom.

Beattie: It's replacing one prejudice for another.
Berry: Yes, all that's very regrettable. The question of who is alive can't be settled by category. Some allegedly dead white men are more alive than some people who are allegedly living.

Beattie: When you were a student yourself, did you ever feel a need to choose a genre that you were going to write in?
Berry: I sometimes wondered whether I would be a poet or a novelist. It didn't occur to me that I might be an essayist. Because you're in a school, you know, you're under the influence of specialization, and, without anybody ever telling you, you're made to feel, by the system itself, that someday you'll have to choose. I remember sitting around wondering, "Well now, what'll I choose?" But in practice the problem gets resolved fairly naturally. I've used the various genres that I've used simply because I've had a use for them. Occasionally, I'll get a review that makes me think, "Well, this person is really saying, 'What's this essayist doing writing a novel?' or 'What's this novelist

doing writing a poem?' or, 'What's this poet doing writing about agriculture?' "

Beattie: I'm sure there are people who know you mostly by your writing and people who know you as a neighbor and farmer. Are your neighbors very familiar with your writing?
Berry: I know that there are people in this community who read my books. But it's not a thing that I'd be very comfortable in trying to find out much about. You can't walk up to somebody and say, "Have you read my book?"

Beattie: They don't come up to you and talk about your writing?
Berry: Occasionally they do, and occasionally I hear back things that people have said that they didn't say to me. But really, in a way, I don't want to be dealt with by my neighbors as somebody who publishes books. I don't want to be dealt with by my children as somebody who publishes books, or by my wife. And a fat chance there'd be of that. I want to be dealt with as a person who's living through the same life that these other people are living through, and dealing with the same difficulties and hardships and griefs and joys that they're dealing with. Being a writer has to be incidental to that.

I ought to say, though, that when I know that my neighbors read my books, or when they occasionally say they think I've done well, it's just an unspeakable pleasure to me.

Beattie: More than a *New York Times Book Review*?
Berry: Yes, a lot more, because love is involved in it here. You see, it's a different emotion.

Beattie: All of your books—novels, essays, poetry—deal with your concern for community. Will you discuss that concern, and do you think it's more probable or even possible that an increasingly urban and centralized and specialized society can return to or can achieve true community?
Berry: Well, of course, willy-nilly, I've been part of a community. It hasn't been a thriving community since the end of World War II. Rural communities have been in rapid decline since about then.

Beattie: Port Royal [Berry's home]?
Berry: Port Royal, New Castle, the little towns that I've known. The economic integrity of these communities has been destroyed. When I first knew

them, you could hardly drive in these little towns on Saturday night. It would have been a problem to drive through Port Royal, as small as it was. The places were jammed with people who were talking together, visiting, doing their buying. You couldn't draw a line between the economic life of the community and its cultural life. It was all happening at the same time. Increasingly, that life has been destroyed. These little towns are dead as a wedge now on Saturday night.

I've been, in a way, a peculiar defender of community, because I'm pretty much a solitary person; I have never been a person who enjoyed institutional affairs or group activities much. But it affected me very much, especially after I came back here to live, to see what was happening to the communities.

Or, you can come to it in another way. You think, well, you would defend the small farm, the small family farm as a thing that's needful for various reasons. But then you finally see that the family is not an adequate vessel. Families deteriorate, or they perish altogether. So a larger container has to be proposed, and the only other one, of course, is the local community. The community survives the deaths of families, or it can.

So, in those various ways, I've slowly come to think of community. My novels and stories have all proposed a community that's more or less conscious of itself, its people conscientiously helping each other. I've learned a lot from the participation of my own family in community life. Tanya's involvement in the church up at Port Royal as member and musician matters to me and has taught me a lot.

I don't know, of course, what's going to happen, but it seems to me imaginable that a time could come when we will either have to achieve community or die, learn to love one another or die. We're rapidly coming to the time, I think, when the great centralized powers are not going to be able to do for us what we need to have done. Community will start again when people begin to do necessary things for each other.

Beattie: In your essay, "Poetry and Place," you argue that too often contemporary poetry lacks narrative, and instead focuses on autobiographical or psychological confessions, which you imply are self-indulgent and not universal. But I'm wondering if you think that sense of alienation—of geographical and spiritual hunger—expressed in so much contemporary poetry is universal? Is it a way of achieving an ironic sort of community between and among alienated poets and alienated audiences?

Berry: There may be something to that. But the alienated are going to be a network at best. You can't start a community with that. Finally, it comes down to whether you want to be alienated or not, and whether you're willing to join yourself to the things that you have to join yourself to in order not to be alienated. This probably means that you're going to have to love people who don't have college degrees and who may appear to be not as smart as you, only to prove later, perhaps, that they are smarter than you, but in a different way. The community, you see, is a practical idea. The network is not necessarily practical at all. The community has to begin in practical matters. One of the things that a community has to do is make some kind of practical working peace with its place. If it's going to be a real community, a great diversity of people are going to have to know and cherish what they have in common, which of course would be their place, first of all.

This is what American multiculturalism is finally going to have to face. The question that is finally going to have to be asked and answered is not, what is your economic relationship to your place of origin, or what is your relationship to your ancestors, or what is your relationship to your old-world culture. The most important question, and ultimately the undodgeable question, is what is your economic relationship to this place where you are now? That would give us authentic cultural diversity, you see, because of the great diversity of places. Cultures and communities that were authentically adapted to their places would be authentically different.

Beattie: According to your definition of communities, a community has to be composed of different types of people, not, for instance, of people just in the same church congregation or people in the same school. It has to extend to include a variety of types of people and ways of life?

Berry: Well, it would have to include a variety. Now, you have to go beyond that and say that it won't, maybe, work in the right way, or it may fail to work with absolute impartiality toward all its members. It may fail to love everybody that it includes. It may make it hard on some people and force them to leave. All kinds of bad possibilities inhere in the idea of community. But all kinds of bad possibilities inhere in human nature, and you have to do the best you can to correct them. My argument with these people who are by principle alienated from any kind of community life is that they're using inevitable human failings as a kind of escape. They're not facing up to these bad possibilities that inhere in human nature.

Beattie: In *What Are People For?* you write, "To be creative is only to have health," and in another place you say, "Order is the only possibility of rest." Both of those quotations interested me in conjunction with the question, "What is the nature of creativity?"

Berry: I know less about creativity than I know about anything. It really is a mystery. I mean, where does it come from, how does it happen? I don't know. It's not rational, it's not subject to rational scrutiny. If you had only to think of what you wanted to think of, what you described to yourself ahead of time as a desirable thing to think of, there would be no such thing as so-called creativity. I wouldn't deny the involvement of my own history in what I have written, or my conscious reasons. Nor would I deny the absolute importance of workmanship, of technique, in the study of the art of writing. But I don't think that's all the story. It certainly isn't for me. Ruskin says that artists are moved by love for things that they want to preserve, or to preserve them at least in memory. That appeals to me. But I believe also in inspiration.

You have to have a routine. You've got to work. You've got to be able to work deliberately. If you write anything that's very long, you've got to work every day. But it depends, too, on serendipity, on felicity, on inspiration. When the poets invoke the Muse, or the Heavenly Muse, or the Holy Spirit, I take them very seriously, because I know that things come. Things come that you can't account for. When I write well, I'm writing, I think, far beyond anything you would expect from knowing me.

Beattie: Would you call it intense concentration when the writing just seems to come and you don't even know exactly what it's going to be until it's done?

Berry: Occasionally the language itself will come. For me, it never comes in great quantities, but occasionally, something—a line or a sentence or even a passage—will come, and the sentences that come are the sentences that you really have to pay attention to.

Beattie: Do you find that sometimes you're in the middle of writing before you know what it is you're going to write?

Berry: Not so much anymore. Occasionally, I'll find that I've wasted a little work at the beginning. But I no longer try to write. I mean, I don't try to make myself think of something to write. If I don't already have something to say, I've got other things that I'd rather be doing. I don't ever ask myself, "Why don't you get an idea?" I just deal with what comes, and when it comes, then I try to do the best I can with it. But the essays I'm writing now are pre-pared for by years of other essays and thought and reading and worry, and the other things that go into essay writing. When I write stories, I'm apt now to be writing stories that I've had in mind for years, and wondered if I would ever be able to write. Sometimes the stories often come from thinking about real stories that I've known maybe for fifty years. In poems, I occasionally will wind up someplace that I didn't know I was going. You never have in your mind ahead of time, or in actual experience, a whole story. What has to come in order to make it a whole story is often a surprise. But I don't hanker enough to be a writer to write to see if I have something to write. I like the assurance of having a job of seeing the work pretty closely ahead of me.

Beattie: The meaning comes first and the form follows.
Berry: For me it's words. I mean, the writing has to offer itself as something that can be said, that I'm now feeling close to having the power to say. As a young man, I had enough of the feeling that I had a wonderful thing to say and no ability whatsoever to say it. That's just a terrible fix to be in.

Beattie: *Fidelity*, the title of your most recent book of short stories, seems to me to describe an essential aspect of your character in relation to your com-munity, your farm, your family, and your friends. Will you talk about what fidelity means to you?
Berry: It just means making a commitment and hanging on, and never giv-ing up. As long as you've got the life and willpower to continue, you con-tinue. All that's based on a faith that my experience, to some extent, proves out—if you hang on, you'll see your way through whatever it is that's diffi-cult—that there's going to be a reward. I believe that; it's my profoundest operating belief. Something will come. Out of the impasse, something will come that you'll be glad to know. I don't have enough faith in myself to believe the next choice I would make would be better than the ones I've already made.

Beattie: Or maybe you have more faith in other people?
Berry: I have faith in God. I have no faith at all that I could find a better woman than Tanya, or a better place than this to live, or different work that I could do as well as the work I've already chosen. It just makes no sense to me to assume that I could. I'm not talking out of a life that I think is perfect, or

that has been always easy and rewarding. I think that I've been blessed in all the choices I've made, but I don't think that I would have found out that I was blessed if I hadn't kept to those choices.

Beattie: It seems to me that so many people don't put time or energy into things that require work or effort.
Berry: I would never, by the same token, have faith enough in myself to say to anybody that he or she absolutely ought to stick to any choice that he or she has made. Because you never know what the other person is suffering, and you understand that a fidelity that's imposed by somebody else's advice is not what fidelity is, anyway. It has to come from inside the person. So although you can lament the statistics of divorce and mobility and all the rest of it, you can't really say that in any particular instance people oughtn't to get a divorce or move to a new place. Or I can't. I know that things are happening to men and women, between men and women, now that are just awful, and the statistics are terrifying. The divorce statistics are terrifying. The impact on children is absolutely terrifying. Yet, you can't just go up to people and say, "What you're doing is, in your case, wrong."

Beattie: I think I've read recently that something like twelve percent of all families in this country are the traditional, two-parent households now, which *is* pretty scary.
Berry: As a teacher, over and over again, I've seen young people who I thought must have needed their fathers at critical times in their lives when their fathers weren't there, and now I'm afraid we're going into a time when we'll see students who needed their mothers at such times. I don't think it's a great improvement for men to be working away from their families; having made that judgment, I can't say that I think it's a good idea for women to work away from theirs. It's just too clear that raising a child is not a job for one person. It isn't even a job for two people. It takes a lot of committed people. This is another argument for community. A well-raised child would be raised by the community, a community in which a lot of people feel privileged to correct that child. I think that was the great good fortune that I had in my growing up, that I had fathers and mothers wherever I looked. Some of them remained parents to me until they died. They would say, "Wendell, I think you're not right about that. I think you'd better think again about that."

Beattie: In your introduction to your 1975 book *Sayings and Doings,* you write, "Memorable speech is measured speech," and you indicate in several of your essays irritation with people who speak constantly. You also refer to a silent time returning home in a wagon with your granddaughter as a special time. Do you sometimes find more communion in silence than in speech?

Berry: Oh, yes. And the inadequacy of language is the first thing a writer ought to know, or a speaker. The condition that language has to exist in and make the most of, be disciplined by, is it's own inadequacy. It just isn't adequate, and silence is the way we acknowledge that. Finally, you can't say all that needs to be said. To pretend to be able to say all that is necessary is what modern reductiveness is all about. To think that when you name a person or a creature or a condition or a feeling, you have somehow done justice to it is foolhardy. I really resist and resent this claim that so many people make so readily now: "Oh, I understand." Mostly, we don't understand. We may know, but we don't understand, and can't prove that we do by talking.

Beattie: Maybe they really mean, consciously or subconsciously, "I want to understand it," or "I want to communicate . . ."

Berry: Sure, or they mean, "I understand a little bit of it," or they mean, "I sympathize," or "I feel compassion," which is another matter altogether. That wonderful story "A River Runs Through It" is about that very thing, the necessity to love without understanding.

Beattie: Will you comment on your writing habits and your views on the interconnectedness of all work?

Berry: Well, if I *had* writing habits, it would be easier to comment on them. I have desires. The best way for me is to write half a day and work outdoors half a day. But that's not always easy to do. Sometimes, other things have to be put first. But an ideal day for me in the winter would be to write through the mornings and get outdoors in the afternoon. In summer it would be good to do it the other way around, work outdoors in the morning and write in the afternoon. But, as I said, it's not always possible. I write with a pencil. I erase a lot and cross out a lot. Then, sooner or later, Tanya types a draft.

Beattie: You referred to Tanya as your best critic.

Berry: She's my best critic, because she's my most faithful reader. I usually read my longhand drafts to her, and then she types them, so she knows what

I've done. I don't agree with all her criticisms, but she's the first line of defense against my partialities and bad habits.

Beattie: Was she an English major as well at UK?
Berry: Yes. She was also a music major for a while.

Beattie: Do you ever discuss what you write before you begin to write with her, or does she first see your work after you've completed it?
Berry: Occasionally I have. We talked, for instance, about that story "Fidelity" before I wrote it. But I don't really like to talk about what I'm writing until I've finished my longhand draft. It's a bad thing to talk about what you're going to do.

Beattie: I've heard writers say that if they talk about writing beforehand that they can't write about it when they finally get down to doing it.
Berry: I don't know if that would be true with me or not, but I never have liked the idea of talking about what I'm going to do. The thing is to do it, and then talk if you want to. But if you do it, you don't need to talk. But I did talk about "Fidelity" a good bit with Tanya. Also, with my brother and sister-in-law, because it's a complicated plot and legal and medical issues were involved. My brother is a lawyer and my sister-in-law is a nurse, so I got some very necessary help.

Beattie: You have, in many places, written about the integrity of all types of work. Will you comment on that?
Berry: If any kind of work is done well, it will have integrity. Work that's done poorly or done in fragments by various people who don't have responsibility for the result has no integrity.

Beattie: You've also talked about, or written about, craftsmanship having integrity if it's done for a useful purpose or if it's done for a purpose other than just for art's sake.
Berry: Yes. I think that art comes about in answer to a need. At least, mine does. The community needs to talk about itself, needs to remember itself. It needs to recall the significant things that have happened, and to mull them over and figure out what the significance is. You see this working in the old ballads, in the Homeric epics, in the Greek tragedies. In my work, that need

certainly figures. Not that the community has to ask me to perform this function, but that I, as a member of the community, have these needs in mind. There's never a very direct correspondence, I think, between anything I've written and anything that really happened, or any actual place. But I write about an imagined community that's something like my actual community.

Beattie: What about the need for beauty itself, the human need for the aesthetic, even if it's not usable? I guess it's arguable whether a painting is *useful*.
Berry: Well, you don't need to define use as utilitarian. All made things don't have to be commodities or tools. I mean a story, for instance, has no immediate utilitarian value, but it can inform the minds that use things. It's a part of the circumstance that finally determines how things will be used. A community is deeply dependent upon the stories available to it, and not just its own stories. The same thing would apply to painting, I would think, and painting had a carefully understood use for a long time. Paintings were a way to teach scripture. The churches of the Middle Ages were books in which the illiterate could read the stories of the Bible. Later, as in the Palazzo Veccio in Florence, the painters were painting their city's history to remind the people who held the public trust of the origins of that trust.

Beattie: Is there one piece of writing or one task that you would like to tackle more than any other?
Berry: I have some projects lined up. I don't suppose it would be much fun talking about them. I'd like, before I die, to finish my series of Port William stories.

Beattie: Do you enjoy the type of writing, or the genre, in which you are engaged at the moment most, or do you have a preference?
Berry: I never write without some pleasure. The pleasure of essay writing is diminished when you're trying to meet a deadline, or trying to fulfill an obligation that you're sorry you ever took on in the first place. But yes, I enjoy it. I like to meet the problems and work them out, and make the transitions, make the connections, figure out how I'm going to get two apparently disparate things in the same work.

Beattie: You've written repeatedly about your admiration for numerous writers from Homer, to Blake, to Yeats, to Gary Snyder. Are there Kentucky writers whom you particularly admire?

Berry: My friends, I particularly admire my friends. I've learned a lot from them and things that they've done.

Beattie: Are you talking about Ed McClanahan and Gurney Norman and . . .

Berry: And James Baker Hall. It would take a lot of talking even to acknowledge my debts to those three. James Still is a Kentucky writer whom I profoundly admire. I think he's one of the best short story writers that ever was. He's capable of such delicacy and at the same time such power, and he's a man who really has mastered the art, the craftsmanship. I admire Harriette Arnow, although not exactly for the same reason. I don't think she's as good a writer as James Still, but *The Dollmaker* is one of the great stories. It's one of the archetypal stories about our age, and one that everybody ought to know. Allen Tate is another Kentucky writer I admire, and one to whose work I often return.

Beattie: You refer to poetwatchers as the sort of people who hang onto poets' words as though poets are somehow more prophetic than other people.

Berry: Did I say that?

Beattie: well, something like that.

Berry: People who see poets as privileged oddities.

Beattie: Even though poets may not be any more special or prophetic as human beings than are other people, don't you think that people are drawn to poets' particular articulations of the human condition, and often want to hear their own experiences voiced? And do you think that the act of publishing, of offering one's thoughts for public consumption, almost invites such recognition?

Berry: Oh, it does. It invites it. The problem is that . . . Well, there are a number of problems. One is the problem of recognition that's not critical enough, that's too deferential. The other problem is that a poet is a maker of work, and the attention ought properly to be on the work. If more attention is paid to the person than to the work, then you've got an obvious absurdity. I think, myself, that writers are asked to talk too much. The thing that they are known for, if they're known, is writing. It seems curious to me that people who have already had something to say in writing should then be expected to talk, as if in talking they would make a contribution that they haven't already made.

Beattie: You've written strong essays on the lack of standards in education today and on the harm caused by teachers of literature attempting to remain objective. Do you see any hope that this will turn around in Kentucky or in the nation?

Berry: Not very soon. The problem with the way literature is taught now is that people don't teach it as something that's of great importance. It's taught as a "subject" and as a specialty. I think a great change would come about if literature were taught by people who believed that it's of great importance to everybody, that it's necessary to everybody, that it says things that are indispensable to us.

Beattie: Morally as well as aesthetically?

Berry: Yes. That it can be read for *both* instruction and delight. I've always read for instruction as well as for pleasure. It seems to me I've learned a lot from Shakespeare, Jane Austen, and other people, and not just about how to be a writer, but about how to be a person, how to conduct my life, how to be a husband and a father and brother and son and friend and the other things that I've been.

The idea that education ought to be painless and fun all the time is something new. Nobody with sense and experience has ever believed that. Some things are hard to learn, and if they're going to be learned, the student has to submit to difficulty. And that, again, is an issue of faith. One teaches that way with the faith that a time will come when that student will be glad to have made the sacrifice. You can't learn a language easily. You can't learn to read Milton and Shakespeare and Chaucer easily. It takes some trouble, and there are rewards for that trouble. If there weren't, nobody would teach it. But you have to have authority as a teacher that does not come from an individual, but comes from a community that says, "These are beloved things, they must be passed on; these are the indispensably beloved, and everything will suffer if they are not learned."

I'm finding this dichotomy of objective and subjective less useful all the time. Literature does have a value that exceeds the value assigned to it by anybody out of whims or tastes. For want of a better standard, we have to use the standard of endurance. The so-called classics have meant a lot to a lot of people for a long time, and that is why we teach them. If they hadn't meant a lot to a lot of people for a long time, we wouldn't teach them, obviously. My good teacher, Tom Stroup, told a class one time, "I love these things I'm teaching. If I didn't, why would I have devoted my life to them?" The justification of schools is the body of work that needs to be passed on to another generation. We claim now that we have schools in order to help all these people to have careers. But not much will get passed on in that way.

Beattie: In 1992 you received, from the University of Louisville, the Victory of Spirit Ethics Award. What did receiving that award and other such honors mean to you?

Berry: Well, I'm grateful for honors. I don't know that they have much of an influence on me. I would have gone right ahead and done what I've done, whether I'd been honored or not, or I hope so. Honors warm your heart and make you grateful, and people are nice to you, and all that counts, but what interests you is not what you've already done. Or that's the way it is with me.

Beattie: Do you feel the same way about the process of writing a piece versus its publication? That it's much more exciting to write it than to see it completed?

Berry: The excitements lasts a while. You have people you show your work to, and they're usually the people whose opinions matter the most to you. But by the time you've written a book and revised it and proofread the manuscript and gone over the copy-edited manuscript and read the galleys, you're pretty well worn out with it. You're very much ready to go on to something else. That is, if you're alive. I don't want to sound ungrateful for publication or honors, but if I'm ever going to amount to anything ever again, those things can't count very much. You don't say, "Oh, this confirms everything. Now I will live happily and then die happily." It doesn't work that way. If you're a living person, you're still underneath the same problems you were under when you started out, and you have the same obligation to work and get on.

Field Observations: An Interview with Wendell Berry

Jordan Fisher Smith / 1993

From *Orion* 12 (Autumn 1993), 50–59. Reprinted by permission of Jordan Fisher Smith.

I. *On a winter afternoon*, Wendell Berry and I go for a walk on his farm in the Kentucky River Valley. The low sun flashes through the breaks in the bare hardwoods as we hike up out of Berry's upper pasture into the forested uplands. Berry is trying to teach me to recognize nineteen kinds of bare trees by the color and texture of their bark, size and growth habit, where they occur, and the dead leaves on the ground beneath them. I make many mistakes, and he patiently points out the trees again and again as he strolls his long legs ahead of me up the hollow. Berry says the names with appreciation: tulip poplar, wild cherry, black walnut, red, white, chinquapin and shumard oaks, pignut and shagbark hickories, ironwood, hornbeam, beech, sugar maple, sassafras, honey locust, black locust and cedar, water maple and sycamore. He knows them not as a botanist, but the way a country boy who grew up to be a farmer knows trees. "These are the first to grow back in an abandoned tobacco patch, you see," and "These make fine lumber that will last outdoors for generations without rotting," and "These grow in the poor ground of old overgrazed pastures."

We climb to the top of the slope and catch the panorama of the river valley spread out below us, like a Hudson River School painting in grays and light browns, I think. I can see the Berrys' rich bottomland, and that of the neighboring farms, in the river's floodplain. The rows of last summer's croplands look like corduroy at this distance.

"What I'm going to do here," says Berry, stopping to show me the view down into a fine stand of medium-age trees, "is grow an old-growth forest. It will take about two hundred years, and I won't live to see it, but there will be some nice trees here, if somebody doesn't cut them down."

Berry leads the way out along the edge of the uplands, beneath a line of huge old trees spared, says Berry, by the farmers who worked the adjoining slopes as late as World War II. In between the trees are mossy piles of rocks, some quite large and heavy, carried from the fields as the plow turned them up.

The country in front of us now falls off steeply toward Cane Run and the horse barn. Berry says he hunted squirrels here as a boy. As we begin to descend, I am thinking about boyhood and Berry's poetry, and I ask Berry if he agrees that school children should be reintroduced to the lost institution of memorizing and reciting poems.

"Yes," he replies, "you've got to *furnish* their minds."

The idea of poetry as furniture expands within my imagination, and for weeks I think about a poem committed to memory as an old chest of drawers in the corner of a child's room. At first the thing is simply a place to put clothes. With time, the grown man, or grown woman learns to see more of it: toolmarks left by the hand of a long-dead craftsman, a cornice molding around its top in a shape found on ancient Greek temples. And by gazing at its sturdiness for so many years, he or she knows something about how to make things that last.

II. *Late evening*, and Berry has carried wood from the box next to the wringer washing machine in the back porch, and stoked the two wood burners to capacity. He sits reading with his feet up in a large comfortable chair in the living room, in front of a full wall of bookshelves. I sit on the opposite side of the stove reading a copy of Virgil's *Georgics* I have brought with me in a cardboard box of books from home. (Like bringing coals to Newcastle, I think, after taking one look at the Berrys' place.)

Berry's wife, Tanya, a graceful, purposeful woman from a family of artists, with a pretty face and calm green eyes, leans into the room from the kitchen with a newspaper in her hand. She says something to Berry about the funding for NASA being cut. Berry looks satisfied and replies that he thinks this is a good move.

I decide to probe Berry about his attitudes on the widely accepted virtues of the view of fragile Earth from space. Berry has a certain puckish grin when he is out to puncture some popular icon, which spreads across his face as he drawls, "That view didn't do much for me; it looked like a poor old Christmas ornament." I ask him if he doesn't find, as I do, the experience of flying over a piece of country particularly beautiful and enlightening about, say, the geology, hydrology, vegetation patterns and so on. Berry chuckles.

"Tanya will tell you about me and flying. As soon as that thing takes off, I'd just as soon lie down in the aisle between the seats like an old dog (pronounced "dawg") and go to sleep until it's over."

Then he looks at me and, a little more seriously now, polishes his argument.

"Let's say you were from somewhere else, seeing this Earth from space for the first time. I don't know about you, but I wouldn't be satisfied with that view; I'd want to get closer, walk around on it, even get down on my hands and knees. That's how I prefer to see the Earth."

III. *On a cold and windy day*, Berry loads up some tools into his pickup truck. I squeeze into the cab next to two of his granddaughters, and Berry drives us to a graveyard. There, we join a group from town who are clearing brush in the back part of the burial ground, where the graves of Berry's people lie next to others, who lived before the Civil War.

We work for a while gathering up the brush into piles and set fire to the piles. We begin to stand around them to warm ourselves as the wind picks up. Berry is paying close attention to an older farmer in a pair of mechanic's coveralls and a ballcap, who has begun to tell stories about the people buried around us. The man is close to seventy, but he's muscular, and has a very smooth, unlined face. He's chewing a wad of tobacco, and he spits occasionally. The tales seem to have a formula, featuring the remembered person as a comic character at the center of some hilarious misadventure. A couple of the other men have gathered to listen and poke at the fire with sticks and hand tools. Everyone bends toward the old man in the wind as he delivers the punch line, and then they explode outward in laughter.

Berry takes me back to the graveyard a day or two later. I remark that the stories of the dead people seem to have been preserved as comedy.

"For some reason," Berry says, "that's the way the men remember things, but the women tell stories about the sad things that happened, and there are plenty of sad stories in this graveyard, people who died young, women who died in childbirth. . . ."

His voice trails off and we fall silent for a long time. Berry turns the pickup around and drives us home to supper in the gray evening light.

IV. *On a frosty, sunny Sunday*, Berry and I sit at the kitchen table, after milking, chores, breakfast and a couple of hours of writing. Brilliant red cardinals are pecking around outside in the sun between the kitchen window and the cistern on the uphill side of the farmhouse. Berry's two sheepdogs are hanging around the back door waiting for something to happen.

Berry wears faded blue farmer's overalls, with several pens and a pair of glasses in the bib pockets, a khaki workshirt and a red cardigan with a bookstore's logo embroidered on it. He regards each question, even the poor ones, seriously and slowly. He waits patiently as I paw through my papers, looking for a note about something I wanted to ask him. Berry's rich voice—it would be called a baritone if he were a singer—and his Kentucky accent make the English language prettier, it seems to me. At one point he stops in mid-sentence and looks out the window, to watch his ewes crossing above the house on their way from the barnyard into the upper pasture.

Jordan Fisher Smith: In your poem "In Rain," you wrote: "I walk this ground/of which dead men and women I have loved/are part, as they/are part of me. . . ."

From what I see of your life here, it would be hard to walk a few steps in any direction without finding something to remind you of someone who lived here and has gone now. What happens to us if we forget the dead?
Wendell Berry: Well, if you didn't know any of the past, you literally wouldn't know anything. You'd have no language, no history, and so the first result would be a kind of personal incompleteness.

But practicalities are involved also. If you had a settled, a really settled, thriving, locally adapted community, which we don't have anywhere, you wouldn't just be remembering the dead. You'd remember what they did and whether it worked or not. And so you'd have a kind of lexicon of possibilities that would tell you what you could do, what you could get away with, and what penalty to expect from what you couldn't get away with.

So the memory that a community has of its dead, and of the pasts of the living would be a precious sort of manual—a kind of handbook, a kind of operator's manual for the use of the immediate place. That's the only kind of operator's manual for the world that we're going to have.

JFS: And it's largely oral, isn't it?
WB: It would necessarily be largely oral, because there simply wouldn't be people to write all of it down and there would be little point in writing it down, because it would be too particular to be of much use to the people who lived in other places. It would be extremely local and extremely particular at its best, because it would consist of information about the history of

various fields and patches of forest and that sort of thing. It would be too local to need to be preserved for but local posterity.

JFS: There's a passage in your story "Fidelity," where the narrator says of his grandfather: "When I sat down beside him, his hand would clap lightly onto my leg above the knee," and goes on to say, "The shape of his hand is printed on the flesh of my thigh as vividly as a birthmark. This man who was my grandfather is present in me, as I have always felt his father to be present in him." Along with the beauty of that passage, there seems to be a sense of obligation on the part of the older man, if he's to be remembered that carefully. You're a grandfather now. Can you tell me something about what you feel the obligations of the older man are towards the younger?

WB: The obligation is very great and moves two ways. The old have an obligation to be exemplary, if they can—and since nobody can be completely exemplary, they also have an obligation to be intelligent about their failings. They're going to be remembered in one way or another, so they have an obligation to see that they're remembered not as a liability or a great burden, but as a help. And of course the young, the inheritors, have an obligation to remember these people and live up to them—be worthy of them. So it's an obligation that goes both ways, and it's inescapable. Once you become involved in this sequence of lives, there is no way to escape the responsibility. You inherit, and in turn you bequeath an inheritance of some kind.

JFS: Isn't there a wholesale attempt to escape these obligations underway now? I'm reminded of the bumper stickers I see on retired people's motor homes on the highways, which say, "We're spending our children's inheritance."

WB: We've noticed that bumper sticker too. The problem with that is that it's a lot truer than the people who fly that particular banner understand. They're not just spending the money that a particular set of young people would inherit, but they're participating, as we all are, in the squandering of our natural and cultural inheritance. So, that's passed off as a joke. But, of course, most people have no choice; they simply can't escape this escape from history and responsibility. They're not just moving around, they're *being moved* around. This phenomenon of mobility is now maybe our major social institution.

JFS: Who is benefitting from all this mobility?

WB: I don't see how anybody benefits from it, really. It can't do anything much for the people who are moving around, and it's bound to depress the quality of work. For work to get good, it has to be carried on for generations, not just for a few years until you get tired of it.

JFS: Many people who would agree with you in principle don't have the benefit of what you were born into, this ancestral relationship with a place. They find themselves living far from where their ancestors are buried, in unfamiliar land that they didn't grow up with, and don't know much about. How would you advise them to begin deepening their relationship with place?
WB: Well, I think that I would give the same advice as Gary Snyder. Stop somewhere! Because you can't recover what's lost. There's no going back to get it. You just have to start again, and I think what people have to experience—have to let themselves experience—is the knowledge and understanding and even happiness that come with long association with people and places and kinds of work.

Of course, along with those enrichments there are griefs and worries too. As you learn what's involved in a place, or in a personal relationship, or a kind of work, you come to understand the dangers, the shortcomings, the damages that already have been inflicted, and so on. And if you stay in a place and make connections, make relationships, you experience losses that are difficult to bear.

What we're really talking about is faith, the faith being that if you make a commitment, and hang on until death, there are rewards. The rewards come. Nobody has ever said that this was easy to do, but I think that everybody who has done it has done it out of this faith that there are rewards. My experience suggests very powerfully to me that there are rewards.

JFS: The phrase you just used, "make a commitment and hang on until death," reminds me of marriage. Something like half of all American marriages will fail, and forty percent of all adults are single now. That's a larger proportion than any time in this century. Is there a relationship between the present failure rate in marriage and families, and the failure to form a sustainable human relationship with the land?
WB: As I see it, there is. People pursue perfection, and I suppose that's a thing that humans have a duty to do, in a way. But there's a tendency now to misunderstand this obligation to pursue perfection as a right to be perfect, to have perfection given to you. And so people enter into their relationships with one another and with their places with the idea that they have a right to expect those places and those people and those connections to be perfect, and then

when imperfection appears, as it inevitably does, they feel that they have a right to be offended, and they don't see the arrogance and the condescension in that.

It's not up to the other people and the places and the relationships to be perfect. It's up to every participant to make the relationship and the place and the other person as perfect as possible. We don't have a right to give up on our choices and our places and, indeed, our cultural inheritance because it's not perfect. We don't deserve that they should be perfect. We have an obligation to make them perfect, if we can.

JFS: Is this expectation of perfection in one's marital partner, and in one's land, a form of narcissism?
WB: Well, you expect the thing you have to be a perfect replica of the thing you desire. I suppose there's some narcissism in that. It also is condescending and arrogant.

JFS: . . . and childlike, in a way?
WB: Very childlike, and it results in childish disappointment and frustration. The other thing is much more difficult because to submit to the job of making perfect a relationship or place or another person means that you must submit to correction yourself. You must submit to the agony of being made perfect yourself, and that's terrifying and extremely difficult. It means you have to face failure over and over again—to realize that you never will really succeed, but this is the necessary work of the world.

JFS: Which is?
WB: To take what we've got and make it better.

JFS: You have written that it's useless to try to develop far-reaching plans about how to survive for the next 100 years. Many people would say that it's precisely this lack of planning that has caused the environmental mayhem that we find ourselves participating in. Why shouldn't we be planning intelligently for the future?
WB: In the first place, to try to imagine people who aren't born yet is inevitably sentimental. It's sentimentalizing about something you don't know, which you have no right to do.

I love my little granddaughters, but to try to sit here and imagine the people they'll grow up to be, even though they're already here and certain things can be known about them, would be sentimentalizing. It would also be a form of oppression.

The first characteristic of a plan is that it won't work. The bigger the plan and the more far-reaching and "futuristic" it is, the less likely it is to work.

There isn't a person who is alive and who has any appetite for living, who doesn't make plans. I make a plan for every day I live. I've got certain things I want to do that day, and if I didn't, I suppose I wouldn't do anything. But I can't help but notice, and I've been noticing for a good many years now, that my plans almost *never* work out. The day almost *never* exactly fits the plan. Some days depart wildly from the plan. So I conclude that even though you're going to make plans, if you're a live human being, one of the things you must learn to do is to take them lightly.

A plan is really useful for signifying to yourself and other people that you like living, that you're looking forward to living some more, that you have a certain appetite to continue the enterprise. But one's real duty to the future is to do as you should do *now*. Make the best choices, do the best work, fulfill your obligations in the best way you can, and work on a scale that's appropriately small. Make plans that are appropriately small. If you do those things, then the future will take care of itself. But if you don't do those things, then you build up a debt against the future, which is what we're doing now.

If we were willing to live by the rule, for instance, that it's a sin and a crime to waste things, we would be enacting a far greater kindness toward the future than we would by making a lot of big plans for it. C. S. Lewis pointed out in *The Abolition of Man* that if your choices are on a grand enough scale, it's possible to make choices for people unborn that they perhaps wouldn't make for themselves. We've done that over and over again. For example, we've filled the world with poisons and have thereby chosen that our children, for generations, will live in a poisoned world. They can't choose not to live in a poisoned world.

JFS: What, in your opinion, are the most dangerous superstitions, as you refer to them, of modern industrial culture?
WB: That industry will inevitably come up with solutions for the problems that it has created; that knowledge is neutral or value-free; that education is good; that education makes people better; that you can make people better by means of technological progress. Those are some of them.

JFS: The superstition that knowledge is neutral reminds me of a discussion you and I had last month, about the Luddites in early nineteenth-century

England, who broke up machines and burned factories when faced with new weaving machines which, they felt, would disrupt their way of life. I notice that the term "Luddite" has a kind of sting in popular usage. . . .

WB: Luddism has been far too simply defined. It doesn't mean just the hatred of machinery. Luddism has to do with a choice between the human community and technological innovation, and a Luddite is somebody who would not permit his or her community to be damaged or destroyed by the use of new machinery. The Amish, for instance, have succeeded simply by asking one question of any proposed innovation, namely: "What will this do to our community?"

That, to me, is an extremely wise question, and most of us have never learned to ask it. If we wanted to be truly progressive, if we were truly committed to improving ourselves as creatures and as members of communities, we would *always* ask it. I think some of us are beginning to ask it. The question isn't often spoken outright, but it lies behind a lot of these grassroots movements to save forests and rivers and neighborhoods and communities, and so on.

JFS: Much of this environmental action seems to focus on legal remedies: lawmaking if there's time, or lawsuits if there's not. In the long run, the aggregate of our attempts to control the effects of economic activity on culture and on nature seems to result in a body of regulations and an expensive bureaucracy to manage them. Is there an alternative way of controlling what is done for profit?

WB: The alternative is the revival of the idea of community.

I don't think you ought ever to give up on the law, and on the public effort to improve law and to improve the effectiveness of it—to try to see that the government acts truly and effectively in the interest of the people. But that kind of effort obviously isn't enough.

The real way for these bad innovations to be prevented is for the communities to refuse them, and that's happening to some extent. Communities do refuse bad innovations. There's a lot of scorn now toward people who say, "Not in my backyard," but the "not-in-my-backyard" sentiment is one of the most valuable that we have. If enough people said, "Not in my backyard," these bad innovations wouldn't be in anybody's backyard. It's your own backyard you're required to protect. Of course, it's better if you defend your own backyard with the understanding that in doing so, you're defending everybody's backyard. Or with the understanding that you may need help in defending your backyard, or that you may need to help others defend theirs. But the "not-in-my-backyard" sentiment is an altogether healthy and salutary and useful one, and I'm for it.

However, a community has to understand that if it refuses the public proposal, then it has to come up with something better. And if the government or a corporation comes in and says, "We want you to have this obnoxious installation because it will employ your people; it will bring jobs," then the community has to have an answer to the question: "Where are we going to find jobs?" Sometimes it won't be an easy question. Sometimes it will be a devastating question, but the community nevertheless has to begin to look to itself. It has to look to itself for the answers, not to the government—and not to these corporations that come in posing as saviors of the local community, because they don't come in to save the local community.

So the communities have to begin to ask what they need that can be produced locally, by local people and from the local landscape, and how it can be produced in a way that doesn't damage the local landscape or the local community. And by local community, obviously, you can't mean just the people. You mean the people and the natural communities that are supposed to exist there—the trees, the grasses, the animals, the birds, and so on. Everything has to be included and considered.

JFS: But I notice that there is not much of a constituency for coyotes in this part of Kentucky, especially around your sheep. The restoration of populations of wolves is not a popular idea in the cattle country of the northern Rockies, and I've seen sea lions and otters dead from gun-shot wounds along the Pacific Coast fishing grounds, all the way from California to Alaska. How do you address this apparent failing, in practice, of the stewardship ethic you are proposing? Such an ethic seems to favor those things for which you have, what you call, "affection."

WB: Well, we obviously have to enlarge affection so that it includes more than those things that are most congenial or profitable. Stewardship means simply the care of something that doesn't belong to you. Originally, it meant the care of property belonging to God. The most suggestive and comprehensive understanding of the world is that it's God's property, but of course we could understand it also as belonging to our children and their children and their children. Beyond that, we have to understand that human interest can't be the definitive interest. If we're not going to be religious about the world, we have to see that it is a property belonging to itself—a stranger and riskier proposition, it seems to me, than the theological one.

If the coyotes are getting your sheep, as experience has shown, a very impractical approach is to say, "Well, we'll just kill all the coyotes," because you're not going to kill them all. They seem to be a species that thrives on human malevolence.

A better question is how can you raise sheep in spite of the coyotes, and there are ways of doing that. Here we use donkeys and a guard dog, some electric fence, and we're saving our sheep. All kinds of questions are involved in any of these issues, but the important thing to me is to define the issue with a due regard for its real complexities.

The inherited approach to this kind of problem in America is that if you're in the sheep business and coyotes eat sheep, then you must kill coyotes. But that isn't corrected by adopting the opposite one. The opposite approach espoused by some environmentalists is that if you like coyotes and there's a conflict between coyotes and sheep, you ought to kill the sheep. The necessary, and the most interesting, question is how these two things can exist together. It may be that in some places this effort ought to be given up. I thought when the coyotes came in here that this might be one of those places.

JFS: Thus the question of "What is possible here?"
WB: Right. What's the nature of the place? The proper approach to any kind of land use begins with that question. What is the nature of this place? And then: What will nature permit me to do here? There was a lively interest in such questions in the poetic tradition from Virgil to Pope, and it undoubtedly goes back well beyond Virgil. That way of thinking continues in the work of some modern agriculturalists—Albert Howard and Wes Jackson, among others—whose approach is to ask what the nature of the place is, what nature would be doing here if left alone. What will nature permit me to do here without damage to herself or to me? What will nature help me to do here? And those latter questions imply another one: How can I make my work harmonize with the nature of the place? Wes Jackson and Albert Howard would argue that farming in a place ought to be an analogue of the forest, or the prairie, or whatever naturally occupied the place before farming began.

JFS: I want to question you a little more about this idea of identifying with and defending the specific region where one lives, as opposed to a "global" sort of environmentalism. It seems there are at least two more problems with this.

First, what about areas that are not really any particular group's domain? And second, what are we to do if we see someone else failing in their responsibility? It seems to me that if we are to take regionalism or bioregionalism seriously, we must respect other people's sovereignty. Yet if the Koreans, for example, are mining sea life with huge drift nets against international accords, or people in southeast Alaska are removing the rain forest there at an unsustainable rate, shouldn't people in Kentucky do something about it? Do others have a greater right to destroy what is in their charge than we have to defend it?

WB: Nobody has a right to destroy anything, and everybody has an obligation to defend as much as he or she possibly can. But sooner or later you'll have to choose. You can't defend everything, even though everybody has an obligation to be as aware as possible, and as effective as possible, in preserving the things that need to be preserved *everywhere*. But I've argued over and over again that the fullest responsibility has to be exercised at home, where you have some chance to come to a competent and just understanding of what's involved, and where you have some chance of being really effective.

Let's understand that a little more carefully. Another superstition of the modern era is that if you don't have it here, you can safely get it from somewhere else. A corollary superstition is that it's permissible to ruin one place for the benefit of another. So you can wreck eastern Kentucky in order to supply coal to the industrial cities of the Northeast, or you can contaminate a nuclear waste site in order to supply power to some other place.

Those two superstitions lie behind this willingness of any community to destroy the basis of its economic life. Any fishing community that fishes destructively is undermining its own existence, obviously. But it's doing that because of these superstitions I'm talking about: "Well, if we use this up, we'll do something else. If we ruin this place, we'll go to another place."

JFS: But that superstition you are talking about goes so far back that all of our enterprises seem to be built upon it. Take, for example, the rich tradition of pastoral writing that your work follows. The construction of the library at

Alexandria in third century B.C. Egypt, and the pastoral poetry of
Theocritus, were made possible by ruinous taxation of the production of the
agricultural people that pastoral writing celebrates. How do you expect to
root out something so ancient and fundamental to Western culture as this
superstition you are talking about?

WB: Yes, Rome destroyed itself by undervaluing the country people, too. I
guess we should leave open the possibility that we'll be too stupid to change.
Other civilizations have been. But at least it's more obvious now that this
superstition is a superstition, because now there's no place else to go. The
"other places" are gone. If we use up the possibility of life here, there's no
other place to go, and so the old notion is bankrupt, though it still underlies
most destructive practice.

"Space," I guess, is the new "other place"—places for a few privileged people to get government subsidies, take souvenir photographs, and have expensive mystical experiences. But it's important to see that all these "other
places" have been bad for us. They have been the poor excuses that have
allowed us to ignore the limits of nature and our own intelligence, and so
avoid our responsibilities. One of the oldest American assumptions is that
if you don't like where you are you can move: if you don't like Virginia, go
to Kentucky; if you don't like Kentucky, go to Missouri; if you don't like
Missouri, go to Texas or Oregon or California. And that assumption has done
damage everywhere it has gone.

But what if people gave up that idea or began to move away from it, and
began to ask, "What can we do here?" and "What that we need can we produce here?" and "What that we need can we do for each other here?" In the
first place, there would be less incentive for those people to over-fish their
fisheries because we'd be promoting local consumption of local food right
here. I mean it's not just enough to find out which tuna fisheries are killing
the dolphins. If you really want to get radical, the question is what have we
got here that we can eat instead of tuna fish?

JFS: To, as you say, shorten the lines of supply?

WB: That's right. Shorten the supply lines. Bring your economic geography
back into your own view. That's not to say that we don't need tuna fish here,
but even if we were catching ocean fish in the least destructive way, it would
still be wrong for us to be too dependent on tuna in Kentucky. We ought to
eat more catfish.

We ought to see to it that our rivers are unpolluted here, and eat the local fish from them. And we ought to fish in a way that preserves the supply and, therefore, preserves the livelihood of fishing. What I'm trying to talk against is the idea that a so-called environmental problem can *ever* be satisfactorily reduced to a simple moral choice. It's always complex in its causes, and so its solutions will also have to be complex.

JFS: It seems to me that you've turned these words "complex" and "simple" upside down, in terms of their usual positive or negative values. You've said you wish to complicate, not to simplify, every aspect of daily life.
WB: Absolutely! Simplicity means that you have brought things to a kind of unity in yourself; you have made certain connections. That is, you have to make a just response to the real complexity of life in this world. People have tried to simplify themselves by severing the connections. That doesn't work. Severing connections makes complication. These bogus attempts at simplification ignore or despise the real complexity of the world. And ignoring complexity makes complication—in other words, a mess.

JFS: But that complication is considered to be outside the accounting?
WB: It's left out of the accounting. That's right. People think either that they'll die before the bill comes due or that somebody else will pay for it. But the world is complex, and if we are to make fit responses to the world, then our thinking—not our equipment, but our thoughts—will have to become complex also. Our thoughts can never become as complex as the world is— but, you can see, an uncanny thing is possible. It's possible to use the world well without understanding it in all of its complexity. People have done it. They've done it not by complicated technology, but by competent local adaptation, complex thought, sympathy, affection, local loyalties and fidelities, and so on.

JFS: I don't expect to see those words you use, "sympathy, affection, loyalty, and fidelity," appearing this week in a business or scientific journal. Our Western cultural inherence seems to have been bifurcated between the time of the scientific revolution in the sixteenth and seventeenth centuries and the time of romanticism in the early nineteenth century, into one side which is the manipulative and the *effective*, science and industry; and another side which is the feeling and *affective*, art, spirituality, and the emotions. How does this play out in the current trouble that we're in with nature?

WB: It plays out in the construction of tools that *can't* be used sensitively. People try to conduct their lives, say, as whole human beings, and yet do their work in ways that are unfeeling and violent. And that won't work.

How can technology be sensitively and intelligently applied? How can it be used with the utmost intelligence and sensitivity? You can make your equipment so powerful and so big that it, itself, institutionalizes the impossibility of using it sensitively and intelligently.

JFS: So you're saying the separation of art and science isn't necessary?
WB: The separation of art and science is impossible.

JFS: But, in fact, that's the way the world is organized right now, isn't it?
WB: Yes. It's organized on the superstition that these two things are separate. Another superstition is that they are separable. Science means "knowledge" and art means "doing" or "making." Obviously you can't know without doing or do without knowing.

JFS: What about how young people come to know things? You've taught for many years, and you've been critical of the education system. What would be your approach to improving education?
WB: My approach to education would be like my approach to everything else. I'd change the standard. I would make the standard that of community health rather than the career of the student. You see, if you make the standard the health of the community, that would change everything. Once you begin to ask what would be the best thing for our community, what's the best thing that we can do here for our community, you can't rule out any kind of knowledge. You need to know everything you possibly can know. So, once you raise that standard of the health of the community, all the departmental walls fall down, because you can no longer feel that it's safe not to know something. And then you begin to see that these supposedly discreet and separate disciplines, these "specializations," aren't separate at all, but are connected. And of course our mistakes, over and over again, show us what the connections are, or show us that connections exist.

JFS: So this calls into question, doesn't it, the whole structure of postgraduate work where people find a tiny specialty to become the world's foremost expert on it?

WB: It calls into question the whole organization of intelligence in the modern world. We're teaching as if the purpose of knowledge is to help people have careers, or to make themselves better employees, and that's a great and tragic mistake.

JFS: I have trouble visualizing how the body of knowledge would continue to grow if everyone was a generalist. Isn't this incremental contribution to the body of knowledge in the form of obscure studies a necessary activity?

WB: Adding to knowledge is not the first necessity. The first necessity is to teach the young. If we teach the young what we already know, we would do outlandishly better than we're doing. Knowing is overrated, you know. There have been cultures that did far better than we do, knowing far less than we know. We need to see that knowledge is overrated, but also that knowledge is not at all the same thing as "information." There's a world of difference—Wes Jackson helped me to see this—between that information to which we now presumably have access by way of computers, libraries, and the rest of it, great stockpiles of data, and that knowledge that people have in their bones by which they do good work and live good lives. The knowledge that a good farmer has, for instance, is a far different thing from the knowledge that most university experts have. For one thing, a farmer's knowledge is usable knowledge; a lot of it comes from experience, and a lot is inherited. The knowledge of most university experts is self-centered—committed to their own advancement in their careers and therefore, indifferent to the effects of the work they're doing or going to do. And they're usually not committed to any community.

There's a difference between thinking about problems and having problems. Where experts are thinking about problems, the people who have the problems are usually absent, are not even well represented. The only way out of this is for the teacher, the person of learning, the researcher, the intellectual, the artist, the scientist, to make common cause with a community. They must commit themselves to a community in such a way that they share the fate of that community—participate in its losses and trials and griefs and hardships and pleasures and joys and satisfactions—so that they don't have this ridiculous immunity that they now have in their specializations and careers. Then they'd begin to learn something. New knowledge would come from that, and it would be better than "information."

JFS: It seems to me that one of the problems with this strong identification to the local community, in practice, is that it seems to have resulted throughout history in a strong self-other distinction, and caused internecine warfare. For example, take the struggles of ethnic groups in Eastern Europe after the decline of communism. What about this apparent nasty side of strong local identification?

WB: It's an old problem, and it has an old solution.

For a long time, we've had this understanding that our humanity is damaged and stunted by being, in this bad sense, provincial or chauvinistic. Of course, you can make a chauvinistic, xenophobic stranger-hating little old small town. You can also make a large city or a whole nation that hates strangers and is xenophobic and chauvinistic and arrogant and condescending—genocidal in fact. So, when you say that one of the dangers of community life is xenophobia, I say of course that's one of the dangers. That's the very job of work we're talking about, not just to become a community, but to become a good community, and a *good* community has to imagine the strangers that come to it; it has to imagine its misfits and its enemies; it has to imagine its natural membership.

JFS: So your vision is not, as a shallow reading of your work might make somebody think, regressive, a kind of nostalgic longing for a rural nineteenth-century ideal with horse-drawn equipment? But in fact, the kind of community you envision hasn't existed yet. Is that right?

WB: That's right—at least it hasn't existed in America yet—but there's no way to defend yourself against a shallow reader. If your work includes a criticism of history, which mine certainly does, you can't be accused of wanting to go back to something, because you're saying that what we were wasn't good enough. There is no time in history, since white occupation began in America, that any sane and thoughtful person would want to go back to, because that history so far has been unsatisfactory. It has been unsatisfactory for the simple reason that we haven't produced stable communities well adapted to their places.

What I'm talking about in my work is the hope that it might be possible to produce stable, locally adapted communities in America, even though we haven't done it. The idea of a healthy community is an indispensable measure, just as the idea of a healthy child, if you're a parent, is an indispensable measure. You can't operate without it.

The *Bluegrass* Interview: Wendell Berry

Katherine Tandy Brown / 1993

From *Bluegrass* magazine, 6.3 (Winter 1994), 22–28. Reprinted by permission of Suzanne Concannon Cassidy (editor of *Bluegrass*) and Katherine Tandy Brown.

Long before it was fashionable to talk about the environment, Wendell Berry was writing elegant essays about the subtle ways we are bound to the land. Long before family farms became the story of the hour, Wendell Berry was writing with quiet passion about the need for a local economy. On his 125 acres of Henry County hillside overlooking the Kentucky River, Berry lives in the community where his family has lived since 1803, and he writes honestly about what he sees around him. Occasionally, he leaves to teach at the University of Kentucky, to lecture or to read from his work. Berry's commitment to bedrock values and his ability to speak the truth as he sees it, make him an eloquent spokesman for conservation and community values. His ability to think to the bottom of an issue makes him a philosopher. And his ability to move people to change makes him an activist. He has helped us understand the many minute ways we are linked together.

From his office at Patterson Office Tower overlooking Lexington's burgeoning skyline, Wendell Berry spoke to *Bluegrass* about a few of Kentucky's—and the nation's—critical problems.

Bluegrass: In your writing you stress the importance of environment, community and autonomy. What's your perception of what's wrong with our society?

Wendell Berry: That's a great big question. You could make a list, but the fundamental thing that's disturbing, I think, is that we've lost the sense of connection between ourselves and the natural world. Even though we have a good many people who "love nature," we still lack, and lack increasingly, any precise sense of our connection to nature. And this connection is economic, necessarily. That is, we live from the natural world one way or another. And because of the relative ease of (and cheapness of) transportation, and because of our mobile and unsettled population, we have extremely extensive personal economies; we don't know where the things we consume come from. And so it's not just that we don't care what the ecological costs of those products might be; it's also impossible for us to know these costs because we're so far removed from the economic sources of our lives. That's not all that's wrong, of course, but a lot of the other things that are wrong relate to that problem.

Bluegrass: So it's more a not knowing than not caring?
WB: If you care and don't know, it doesn't make any difference whether you care or not. So you see, this issue of caring depends on the other issue of knowing. And of course, one of the responsibilities of a culture is to see that people know enough to care. And our educational system doesn't deal with that problem. Really, as a system, it hasn't heard of that problem.

Bluegrass: That leads directly to my next questions. What is the lifestyle in which we can be in harmony with our environment? How can we as individuals stop abdicating our responsibilities for the environment and thus stop suffering the consequences of abuse of our natural resources? Obviously, looking to the schools is one answer.
WB: If I were to give you a complete answer to that question, you should get up and run, because I would be crazy. I mean, it's possible to sit here and define a large problem, but then if you sit here and begin to give large solutions, in the first place, you're immediately out of your depth. And in the second place, people with large solutions are dangerous.

Bluegrass: Perhaps like trying to become God?
WB: Yes. Well, it's like trying to become at least a dictator. So you can say, for instance, that one thing we need to do is shorten our supply lines. I talk a lot about this in my new book, *Sex, Economy, Freedom and Community*, and I'm going to continue to talk about it. I'm arguing in many of the essays in that book that people need to live from their local landscape and their local countryside as much as they possibly can, as much as they reasonably can. For instance a lot of the Kentucky cities—Louisville and Lexington

certainly—are surrounded by good farmland, and they should be eating from that land to the extent that it's possible for them to do so. The idea that a city surrounded by fertile farmland that's well-watered should be importing food 2,500 miles is preposterous.

Bluegrass: Thus driving the cost out of the ballpark.
WB: It drives the cost up and it removes from the consumers all the powers of choice, of knowledge and of judgment. The consumers who import foods from long distances eat what they're given to eat, what they're sold. Many things would improve if they ate closer to home, including the local farm economy. So I'd like to see Kentucky agriculture become diversified enough to go a long way toward feeding Kentucky. And I would like to see Kentucky consumers as devoted to Kentucky food products as they are to Kentucky athletic teams.

Bluegrass: What a gift that would be.
WB: It would be wonderful because the quality of our food would go up. As the distance that it's transported decreased, the quality would go up, and it would also go up as it came more and more under the influence of the con-sumers. Consumers don't eat hard, tasteless, characterless tomatoes because they choose to. They eat those tomatoes because those are the only tomatoes they're offered.

Bluegrass: That's what they get.
WB: That's what they get. And so one thing we're talking about when we talk about a local food economy is a kind of freedom that we're very rapidly losing.

Bluegrass: So local support would be a great help as far as focusing the econ-omy back in the area?
WB: You're talking about a different kind of economy, really. If you're talking about a local food economy or any other kind of local economy, you're talk-ing about an economy that's going to have to run a considerable extent on cooperation, not on competition between consumers and producers. You're talking about an atmosphere of good feeling in which people try to find out what they can do well for one another. The local consumer is going to have to be concerned that the local producer have a livable income. The local

consumers want the best products possible and the local producers are going to have to be interested in supplying the most desirable products possible to the local consumers. So if you're going to succeed, it can't be a situation in which everybody is in an economic war against everybody. That's a description of the global economy.

The advantage of the local economy is that it gets you out of the global economy. You can secede from the global economy if you have a local economy. The global economy is going to be an economy that permits the exploitation of everybody and everything for the benefit of relatively few.

Bluegrass: Is that what you mean when you talk about community? Your definition of community seems to be in the best sense of the word. It's not the little town we live in, necessarily.

WB: No. What I've tried to do is work out a definition of community that's not sentimental and is not metaphorical. There's a lot of sentimentality about community now. It's a cliché: "I love my community." Well, a community is not something you love all that simply. A community is going to present you with problems, and some of them are going to be big. Some of them are going to be terribly discouraging. Some of them may be insoluble.

People use the term metaphorically when they talk about "the community of business leaders" or the "community" of some professional group. In other words, community is used as a synonym for what's better called a network. But community in the real sense is a commonwealth. It's a holding in common of many different things of value.

So a community is, for one thing, an economy. And if you have a community but no economy—if you have a local community but no local economy—then your community is seriously impaired. It becomes a thing of feeling only. And you can't exclude any members from a community. If a community becomes false, it becomes artificial, and is in danger the way all false things are. A community can't exclude the nonhuman creatures, for instance, if it hopes to last. It can't exclude the streams and rivers and other bodies of water. It can't exclude its climate. It can't exclude the air. All these, in a real community, are members. So if you are careful enough in defining a community, you see that it's a pattern of practical relationships. It's also, of course, a pattern of loyalties and it's an emotional pattern. It's a cultural pattern. It's a known thing. It depends on being commonly known by its members.

Bluegrass: The title story in *Fidelity* seems to be a primary example of sense of community, of the caring for one of its own. Previously you mentioned a sentimental side of community; that's not what takes place in that particular story, is it? Isn't it more what you were just talking about—a commonality?

WB: It's a little bit wrong to read that story as an illustration of an idea of community. It's a story, and a story is always larger and more interesting than its theme. If it were merely an illustration, you wouldn't read it. But that story is certainly a story that's informed by an idea of community—by the thinking that I've done over a good many years now about what it is to be a member of a community. It seems to me that we belong to each other and to God. If that's accepted, there are many practical things that you are committed to do. You see that nobody gets hungry, for instance. You see that nobody sleeps in the street. You see that children are taught—not just enough to get them a job or get them a diploma—but taught enough to function as responsible, affectionate members of that community. They'd be taught the community's history. They'd be taught the ecological limits of the local countryside. It would be a matter of great importance that children should know what their grandparents and great-grandparents did. They would be taught what has gone wrong. They would be taught what's worked. All that in addition to the larger cultural inheritance that they're going to need. It's a complex commitment.

And I think the educational system, whatever it would be, should take into consideration the complexity of that local commitment. Of course, our educational system has failed completely to do that. We're educating kids to live anywhere, not somewhere in particular.

Bluegrass: So this education is generic, sending them off to practice it wherever they may choose, rather than their having this commitment?

WB: This generic education is like distilled water, as opposed to water off your own roof or out of your own well, tasting of your local bedrock. . . .

Bluegrass: The distilled water is depleted, whereas your own is much better for you and can help you grow.

WB: Yes, and is pleasant to drink, too.

Bluegrass: A good analogy, which leads to the next question. In this disposable society, why should those who lead seemingly comfortable lives begin to prefer and choose this quality over quantity? To say no to their technologies? To get the focus off the dollar? How will it behoove them in the long run?

WB: We've been taught over and over, by our cultural tradition, our religious tradition, and so on, that great quantities are not safe. You gather up, for instance, a great stockpile of food, and that stockpile of food is subject to all kinds of mishaps. Insects can get in and eat it. Water can get in and spoil it. You can have a power failure, and it can spoil in your freezer.

Bluegrass: Or it can lose its vitality by freezing.

WB: It can lose its nutritional value. Somebody can steal it. Somebody can burn it up. Lightning can set the building on fire. That stockpile of food is subject to every imaginable calamity. It can be destroyed in many ways. And so if you're going to think about economics or culture or education, you've got to contrast that stockpile of food with the ability to grow food; that ability is a present power in people, in the community, and in the land.

So you have to make a choice: are you going to trust the stockpile, or are you going to trust this continuing potentiality that people and the landscape possess? And I'm taking the side of the potentiality. You can't make the future safe, because you don't know what the future's going to be. We really don't owe the future anything except to do the right thing now, which is to take good care of what we have and to protect this power to grow and make the things we need, which doesn't exist in humans alone, or in the world alone, but in both together in specific localities.

Bluegrass: And only both together?

WB: Only both together. If you're a splendid farmer, and you have no land, you have no potential as a food producer. And if you have excellent land and you're not a farmer, you come up with the same zero, the same failure. The world approaches starvation every year in spite of the stockpiles. We are dependent on a present, continuously growing supply of food, as we are continuously dependent on our beating hearts.

Bluegrass: It seems an imbalance in that we have stockpiles that are spoiling, yet people are starving every day in parts of the world.

WB: Yes, that's right. You can't despise charity, which is a good thing. But charity as a permanent condition is a bad thing. The question of whether or not people are hungry is a short term question. The long term question is whether or not a given people or a given community and their land have the capacity to produce food. And this is a capacity that we're very rapidly destroying in the land and in people too. And so however much money they have or however large their stockpile is, people are unsafe if they don't know anything about where their food comes from, or if too many of them at a given time don't know how to produce it. Anybody can eat a potato, but we have a larger percentage of people now than ever before who don't know how to grow a potato.

Bluegrass: Doesn't it get back to the sense of community and the importance of values in that?
WB: Yes. The community is the vessel that preserves these things. The family can't do it because families die out, and a family, even an extended family, isn't large enough to do all the necessary jobs of work. Finally, these possibilities have to be preserved in the community. The community has to be the organism, so to speak, that does the remembering, that does the teaching.

Bluegrass: So it's the community that's really the heartbeat behind continuity?
WB: That's right.

Bluegrass: A learning and a teaching of what's right and what's important and then the continuity of the same?
WB: That's right. And if the things that need to be remembered are forgotten, then the learning becomes more costly than it ought to be.

Bluegrass: Seems like that's on lots of levels.
WB: The costs are paid all the way from the individual person to the ecosystem, and they're insupportable costs. I mean, neither the world nor the community can afford a trial-and-error education in these practical things every generation.

Bluegrass: So finding the heartbeat, finding what's important and using what's tried and passing that on is the only thing that can work?
WB: You have to remember what you tried and you have to remember whether it worked or not. If it failed, then the community has to build into itself the authority to say to the young people, "No, that won't work."

The grownups have to have the guts to say, "You mustn't do it because I say you mustn't, because I remember. I remember, and you don't."

Bluegrass: That's a concept that seems often to get lost in today's automated, technological society.

WB: Well, we're assuming in this society that we can "access" the necessary information. But "accessing" the information takes time. And then determining which information is pertinent is an impossible task if you're overloaded with information that you don't know how to apply.

Bluegrass: Which we are.

WB: Which we are. So there's a difference between so-called information and the knowledge that is shapely in the mind of a good worker. That knowledge is immediately available because it lives not just in the mind and the memory, but in the body and hands of the person doing the work.

Bluegrass: Therefore, it could be that education today is solely for getting by, whereas knowledge is forever? That knowledge is for processing all of this, for helping to stop the depletion of natural resources and for helping to provide the sense of community?

WB: It's for taking care—taking care of things that are worth taking care of. Education now, you see, works toward the idea of making people able to take tests, or to meet the needs of an employer. And this means that education's going to run to minimums. It runs to the minimal fulfillment of whatever requirement is hypothesized. An educational system that concentrates on the minimum is going to reduce the minimum.

So there has to be a better standard, and the better standard, I think, is the health of the community. If the standard of education is job qualification and an intelligence test or a college entrance examination, then education's going to get worse. If you have an educational system that's not prepared to ask every student to get better no matter how good he or she already is, then you've got a failing system.

Bluegrass: Do you think that strengthening the sense of community within each individual can possibly help strengthen the quality of education? Or is it entirely up to the community?

WB: You can't make it work the way you think it ought to work. I mean, the first rule of education is that it's not going to work the way you think it's going to work. You can set up an ideal system; you think, "Well, I know how to do it this time," and the first thing you know you have to quit fooling yourself. It's not going to work ideally. A lot of things you do are not even going to work pretty well. I'm not ever, in anything I've written, trying to say exactly how anything ought to be done. I mean, I don't have a program. My argument is that if you change the standards of your work, you'll finally change your work. If you're a teacher and you're trying to teach to the career needs of every individual student or you're trying to teach to the presumed career needs of a conglomeration of young people, then you're not going to do well. If you're a teacher and you make the health of the community the standard of your work, then you're going to teach better. If you teach with the good health of your community in mind, you're going to try to make every one of your students the best possible member of the community. You're going to fail a lot, but you're going to change the way you teach and maybe you'll succeed some, too. If you suppose to yourself, "Well, when these kids graduate, that's probably the last I'm going to see of them," you're going to teach differently than you would teach if you assume that you're going to spend the rest of your life with these people. These kids are going to grow up. They're going to take their place in the community you live in. They're going to be your fellow citizens, your fellow members.

Bluegrass: And then you can see that it's to your benefit to do the best job you can.
WB: That's right. It's going to get urgent.

Bluegrass: That sort of answers the next question: Can individual change really make a difference on the grand scale?
WB: It doesn't have to make a difference on a grand scale. It has to make a difference on the individual or local scale. You don't have any obligation to save the world. Edward Abbey said that saving the world is a good hobby, by which he meant you shouldn't take it too seriously. But I think that changing yourself—by doing the best work you can—is of major importance.

Bluegrass: You have partially answered this already, but what led to your present concerns about the environment? Why did a Stegner Fellow at

Stanford choose to come back to a rural environment, instead of "going on to fame and fortune" in New York City as a writer? That definitely could have been an option for you. And how would you respond to people who feel that you avoided an actual hands-on dealing with issues by escaping to your Henry County farm, a peaceful place?

WB: Well, there isn't any peaceful place, you see. People often assume that there's some place where you can get away from the problems. But there isn't any such place. Air pollution is universal. Acid rain is everywhere. Water pollution is everywhere. Soil erosion is everywhere. Bad education is everywhere. Crime and violence are everywhere. People who move to the country to get out of the war really are moving to the front lines. That's where much of the damage is being done.

Bluegrass: So that is where, on an individual basis, you can get into the trenches and start fighting the war.

WB: Well, if you have any conscience at all, it's impossible to live anywhere and not fight. I don't mean violent fighting, but the confrontations have to take place if the world isn't going to be completely destroyed. People have to face their enemies and do what they can. Well, I've been involved marginally or more than marginally in several fights that have been successful. We beat the jetport that was going to be built out east of Louisville. We beat the Marble Hill Power Plant. We beat the Red River Dam. We beat the Eagle Creek Dam twice. So it's possible to be successful in these things, but anybody who thinks there's a place you can go to escape problems had just better go and find out. There isn't any "best place." There are many good places, and they're all under threat. Every one of them. And they need people in them willing to fight.

Bluegrass: It seems that often people who live in cities feel a lot more helpless, feel that perhaps there isn't as much that they can do on an environmental level as those in the country.

WB: That's not right. You are not helpless unless you think you are. Most people live in cities now. Most consumption now takes place in cities, and that consumption is damaging just about to the extent that it's ignorant. People buy ignorantly. They eat ignorantly. They don't know what they're doing when they consume. That's why the damage gets done.

Bluegrass: It's the age of plastic. It's so easy to use, so easy to toss, and so hard to bring back again.

WB: Plastic is a horrible substance. I don't know what we can do to be forgiven for plastic. It's everywhere. It wasn't but a short time ago when the Kentucky River was a pleasant stream. And now it's full of plastic—great rafts of it backed up behind drift logs caught along the bank. It doesn't have to be that way.

Bluegrass: Isn't that assuming responsibility on an individual level for that particular aberration, so to speak? I don't mean the creation of plastic, but the use of it . . . the disposal of it.

WB: If you could recycle it and you didn't recycle it, then you'd be irresponsible. But there's a lot of this stuff that's very hard to deal with responsibly. Automobiles, for instance. The automobile has done more damage probably than any single thing we use.

Bluegrass: In what respect?

WB: Air pollution, too many roads, too much pavement, this frenzy of "mobility," community destruction, child destruction—or I should have said teenage destruction. But the whole enterprise of the automobile—you can trace any number of extensive and serious damages to it. People begin to destroy their community when they begin to shop in other communities, for instance. There's lots of community and economic destruction that's assignable directly to the automobile. But what do you do? Owning an automobile is an interesting correction for anybody disposed to be self-righteous about these issues. A city person conceivably could get along pretty well without one, unless he or she wanted to go to another city. In the country we haven't got any public transportation. My grandparents had much better public transportation than I do. I don't have any. Not anymore. If I want to go to the airport, I've got to drive. If you have family members you're responsible for and they live more than walking distance way, you've got to have an automobile.

So our society's not only filled with problems that people can be smart and responsible about; it's also full of problems that individually we can't be smart and responsible about.

We have problems for which there are no obvious or easy answers. And it's important to know that.

Toward a Healthy Community:
An Interview with Wendell Berry
The Christian Century / 1997

Wendell Berry lives on a hillside farm in his native Henry County, Kentucky.
He has written more than 30 books of fiction, poetry, and essays, including
Another Turn of the Crank (essays) and *A World Lost* (novel). Berry has a passionate love for the land and a concern that people live in responsible relationship with the land and with one another. In his essays he links a scathing
criticism of the much-touted "global economy" with a call to renew and sustain local communities. Berry urges his readers to consider how their decisions and lives affect the community's land, its local economy, and its future.
We spoke with him about economics, the city, and his understanding of
community.

Christian Century: Several times in your writing you describe your hometown, Port Royal, Kentucky. What's happened there? How has it changed, and
what forces have been at work behind that change?
Wendell Berry: Throughout my lifetime, my community—like every other
community in the modern world—has become more and more peripheral
to its own consciousness. And this does not imply that there is a center that
has moved away. In the modern world there is no center; every place is
peripheral.

CC: Why has witnessing this change had such an impact on you?
WB: Because (to put the narrowest construction on the question) I want to
live in a good place, and I know that people can't live in good places unless
they know where they are and pay the closest, kindest attention to what they
do there.

My little community is no different from virtually any other little community in the modern world. It doesn't grant enough importance to itself. It concurs too much with the general assumption that every place is peripheral.

CC: You seem to have in mind the idea of a good or healthy community. What are the elements of such a community?
WB: First, the qualities of a healthy community don't include perfection; I don't think that there have been any perfect human communities. If you talk about the virtues of a given community, you must also discuss its problems and evils. A good community is one in which people understand that in order to have certain good things, they have to have them in common. That's all.

CC: What is involved in trying to maintain or recover such a community?
WB: Loving one another, taking care of one another, being thankful for the gifts of heaven and earth and our human forebears, taking good care of those gifts. In short, we must do good work; we must have a good economy.

CC: How do you define "economy"? Your understanding seems to be different from the understanding of economics as the study of moneymaking.
WB: Economy is our way of making a living. It connects the human household with the good things that sustain life. This involves the money economy and many other things that our present idea of "economics" excludes: good work, good care of the materials and other gifts of nature, faithfulness to one another in all relationships.

CC: What's wrong with "thinking globally"?
WB: You can't think globally. You can only think in detail. "Global thinking" is a distraction from thinking.

CC: Consumers are glad for and dependent upon food products that can't be raised in their own regions. What's wrong with depending on farmers 2,000 miles away for our food?
WB: As distance increases, knowledge declines. How many of us can know the real costs—economic, ecological, social, cultural—of food produced 2,000 miles from our homes?

CC: Some people choose the city because they want to be somewhat anonymous—at least as compared to life in a small town. Do you respect this choice, or do you find that the evils of the city's dependency outweigh its positive qualities?

WB: There are lots of good reasons to want to live in the city. I understand these; I've lived in cities and I'm obviously dependent on cities. No country person who has thought through the rural economic predicament can assume that we're independent; we're not.

But I don't respect the desire of anybody to live anonymously. Eventually people will have to acknowledge their dependancies. They'll make it anonymously to the point where they fall down in the street. Somebody with a name will need to pick them up.

Some modern people think of themselves as "autonomous." They've found a way to live while (or by) ignoring critical dependancies. This is an illusion, and I don't respect it. I hope people will give up the superstition that they can somehow get away from the problems that they're making.

Wherever they live, if they eat, people have agricultural responsibilities just as they have cultural responsibilities. Eating without knowledge is the same as eating without gratitude. What's the use in thanking God for food that has come at an unbearable expense to the world and other people? Every eater has a responsibility to find out where food comes from and what its real costs are, and then to do something to reduce the costs. All of us are now dependent on lots of products the origin of which we don't know and can't learn.

CC: How can our cities take steps toward becoming self-sustaining?

WB: It's hard to see how a megalopolis could ever have an intimate relationship with its tributary landscape. A megalopolis, by definition, couldn't have this relationship because it depends entirely on long-distance transport. I can't offer a blueprint for solving the whole problem, but in some places there are imaginable solutions.

For example, we have a considerable food-producing capacity in Kentucky and we don't have very large cities. We need to ask, "What that we eat here are we not producing here?" and then, "What that we eat could we produce here?" To the city people we country people need to say, "What do you eat that we can produce and that you would buy from us?" We must work in increments, doing little jobs, solving little problems. I see more and more people who are willing to do these small but important tasks. People everywhere can help just by recognizing the existence (inescapable except by death) of the land-based economy, and then by trying to understand the terms of their dependence on it.

CC: You've said that you're kept awake by a "difficult hope." Can you see specific examples on the American scene of a revived interest in creating community?

WB: All over the place. What we're seeing that's tremendously hopeful is an attempt to revive the principle of local economy—especially, right now, the principle of local food economy. Although the global economy devalues these local economies, it also opens niches in which they may be able to survive. The global economy does not serve locally grown food. But here in Kentucky, the Burley Tobacco Growers Cooperative Association has revived its old Commodity Growers Cooperative to market locally grown food to local people. Eventually this co-op hopes to market all rural products.

Small farmers would have a better chance to survive if they dealt with people they knew, and who knew them—rural or urban neighbors who would value them for their ability to grow products that are needful and good.

CC: Can you give us an example of how you and your wife, Tanya, make domestic economic decisions?

WB: So far as we can, for things we don't produce here at home, we like to deal with locally owned businesses. Even so, outside our home economy, we're as economically ignorant as most people.

CC: You often celebrate the health and solidarity of the Amish and their relationship to the land. What's your understanding of their religious foundation?

WB: The Amish are pacifists. That's an extremely important difference between them and the powers that be. They're not interested in making war. This means, among other things, that the focus of their life is the community and the church.

I'm interested in the ability of the Amish to put their community first, and to ask of any proposed innovation, "What will this do to our community?" They're willing to answer that question in the most practical ways, which means that there is no distinction between their economy and their religion;

in their daily work they practice their faith. This is unlike any other community or church that I know in the United States.

CC: Is it possible, given the centrality of the religious foundation, to apply a kind of Amishness to the rest of the society?
WB: Most of us, now, can't be Amish. But some of us who aren't Amish have begun to ask the Amish question about the effects of innovation on the community, and to resist the modern divorce between economy and religion—which is really just a version of the devastating old dualism of body and soul.

CC: What is your religious background?
WB: I was raised as a Southern Baptist. But I've always felt myself an outsider to the sects and denominations.

CC: You've written about your frustration with itinerancy in the rural churches, saying that pastors are moved too frequently. Is this still true?
WB: The denominations tend to use country churches to subsidize the education of preachers. Young "ministerial students" come to our little towns, many genuinely interested in being ministers, some even worth listening to. But just as they are about to get to know us, and get used to the fact that we're not going to become much better very soon, they get their degrees and off they go. It's a kind of teenage emotional rhythm that we're on here with the preachers. They come, and we love some of them very much. But they don't stay long enough to get past their illusions about us, or long enough for us to get past our infatuation with them. (Some, of course, "depart without being desired.") Most of these country towns have never been preached to by a preacher who knows them thoroughly and loves them anyway. I see some signs that this may be starting to change—at the initiative of individual ministers and congregations.

CC: Is there a role for the church in building the kind of community that you describe?
WB: This raises a problem that I can hardly define, let alone solve. Churches, sects, organized religions, denominations all come into being and cohere (insofar as they do) by agreeing on issues of doctrine and ritual, and by excluding all who don't agree. We know what a bloody business this is. Christians, ignoring their specific instructions to the contrary, have been

including and excluding, killing one another and also people of other faiths, virtually from the beginning. The "church"—in its organized forms—has always loved itself for excluding, and sometimes for killing, unbelievers and heretics.

Christianity (in its Western forms, at least) has also tended to exclude nature—the body's life and all that it depends on. Which is to say that it has not been interested enough in our economic life. It has been too easy to be "a good Christian" while destroying the world that (we are told) God loves.

Moreover, I think that most modern Christian churches have entirely lost their artistic tradition. You couldn't tell from nearly all the sermons I have heard that there is in English a great Christian literary tradition that includes sermons. And it is a wonder how much modern church architecture is either brutally ugly or rather tackily pretentious.

CC: Does the church, having pretty well excluded the great commonwealths of nature and human culture, yet have a role in building communities? I certainly hope so, but I'm as doubtful of the church as I am of myself. How are we to live up to what we've been given?

WB: I think that if Christians quit worrying about being "Christians" or church members and just undertook to do what Christ told them to do—love one another, love their enemies, take care of the helpless and the friendless and the unworthy and the no-account—then the "church" might sooner or later dissolve into something much better.

Edward Abbey warned conservationists that saving the world was "a good hobby." The same may be true for theologies and creeds. A church that believed in nothing and forgot all its own tradition and history would be perfectly worthless, of course. All the same, the human mind too readily imposes on God and becomes owlishly knowledgeable about his mysteries, when it needs to be humorous and forgiving. Which, of course, some Christians have sometimes been.

Our time increasingly requires of us the same free-hearted neighborliness, the same practical charity, that the Gospels require of us but the churches generally do not. The churches generally sit and watch and even approve while our society hurries brainlessly on with the industrialization of child-raising, education, medicine, all the pleasures and all the practical arts. And perhaps this is because religion itself is increasingly industrialized: concerned with quantity, "growth," fashionable thought and an inane sort of expert piety.

From where I'm looking, it seems necessary for Christians to recognize that the industrial economy is not just a part of a quasi-rational system of specializations, granting the needs of the body to the corporations and the needs of the spirit to the churches, but is in fact an opposing religion, assigning to technological progress and "the market" the same omnipotence, omniscience, unquestionability, even the same beneficence, that the Christian teachings assign to God.

CC: What sustains you?
WB: Well, youth did for a while! But I have been extremely fortunate in my friends and allies, and in my family: my parents, my wife, my brother, my children. Also (I'm almost afraid to say it) there are more people on the "side" I'm on than there used to be. All these small local efforts add up to something very encouraging.

I'm interested in how people ought to act in order to preserve the fundamental needs and the fundamental pleasures of life. Anybody interested in that question could be fascinated for two to three lifetimes without any trouble at all. The questions themselves sustain me.

CC: Do you see yourself in a prophetic role?
WB: No indeed! I have only taken part in a conversation that living people must carry on with the past, with books and with one another. I'm a writer, in some sense a spokesman, but I have said nothing, as an essayist at least, that didn't come out of that conversation.

CC: What is the connection between your fiction and poetry and the public themes of your essays?
WB: All my work comes from my loves and hopes. My essays come from a desire to understand what I love and hope for and to defend those things; they pretty much constitute a single long argument in defense. This has sometimes been laborious and dutiful work, and I have sometimes grown very tired of it. My work as a fiction writer and poet, in spite of the difficulties always involved, has been increasingly a source of pleasure to me—it is my way of giving thanks, maybe, for having things worthy of defense.

CC: Is your writing nostalgic?
WB: If you're making a criticism of the way things are, then you have to contend with readers who need to find a way to dismiss you. One easy (and silly)

way to dismiss my argument is to call it nostalgic. There are indeed things in the past that I look back upon with love. But I know that the past does not return. I have been a steadfast critic of the past and certainly of my own inheritance from the past. History demonstrates certain possibilities, both good and bad, that we had better not forget. But my argument will stand or fall by the validity of its concern for the preservation of necessary things. I've tried to learn from the waste or destruction or ruin of some things that we might have inherited from the past, and that we need now.

A Conversation with Wendell Berry

Lionel Basney and John Leax / 1998

From *Image: A Journal of the Arts and Religion* 26 (Spring 2000), 45–56.
Reprinted with permission from John Leax.

Anyone familiar with Wendell Berry's essay "The Specialization of Poetry" and his comments on the genre of the interview will appreciate the trepidation Lionel Basney and I felt driving up to the Berrys' Lanes Landing Farm in Port Royal, Kentucky, one hot July morning in 1998. Lionel had been there before. I had not. Wendell's wife, Tanya, waved to us from the porch and sent us off to the steep field where Wendell was mowing. To find Wendell at work instead of waiting for us put me at ease. It made the day somehow welcoming, our conversation a part of three lives.

We spent the day talking. We recorded nothing and took no notes. We moved from the dining room table to the living room to the woods and back. We told stories and asked each other questions. Often, after telling a story or making a comment, Wendell would laugh and say, "You couldn't put that in an interview." We could have, but we haven't.

At the end of the day, Lionel and I stopped at an all-night diner, ordered pie and coffee, and wrote questions on napkins. Lionel took them home and typed them up. I arranged them in a rough order and they formed the outline of the following interview that was conducted, one question at a time, by mail.

In August of 1999 our pleasant exchange of letters was interrupted. Lionel died in a swimming accident while vacationing with his family on the North Carolina shore. To keep Lionel's voice present I used questions he had written during our planning session at appropriate points in the interview.

John Leax: What does it mean to think of wholeness? The movement within the poem, "To Think of the Life of a Man," from *Openings*, requires something more than abstract speculation. The two halves of the poem imply a connection between thought and action. Having thought, the speaker is changed. He is "beyond the time" he might have been less than whole. He has accepted a responsibility. My response, when I first read this poem, was to feel the demands of that responsibility myself. Yet, as I've read and reread the poem over many years, I can't quite locate its power. What is the source of the recognition of moral responsibility? How does the speaker move from description to action? Does the power to move come from a moral context larger than the poem? From memories of people who have lived a certain way?

Wendell Berry: A poet ought to be able to speak with authority about his own poem. That is a reasonable idea, and the source of some embarrassment to this poet. I don't think my use of the word "whole" in that poem was fully conscious—as, of course, it isn't yet. Now it seems a matter of wonder to me that we humans, in our fragmentariness and imperfection, could have conceived the desire to become whole. Or that, troubled and violent as we are, we could have imagined peace. We have heard, anyway, on good authority, that we are made whole by faith and that our peace is in God's will—which means that we can't, by our own doing, be whole or at peace. And so when I said in my poem that I had thought of "the life of a man / grown whole in the world, / at peace and in place," I was defining myself as a human in terms stricter probably than I realized. But the terms, and the direction, were right. And the change the poem records, I still think, is the right change.

At the time of that poem I had begun to try—and with great excitement and pleasure in the effort—to make my own life whole in relation to a place. I was trying to understand the practical connections, in economy and work, that could join a person kindly enough to land and family and community. That was more than thirty years ago, and I'm *still* trying, which shows that the task of wholeness grows ever larger while we work at it. The task is endless, but so are the excitement and pleasure.

Lionel Basney: I think there's a familiar paradox here: we cannot create the vision of wholeness by anything we do, and yet it only comes clear to us when we commit ourselves to certain kinds of doing. "In law is rest / if you love the law. . . ." I think you would see this "doing" as pretty specific and concrete. So how did the practical project of reaching toward wholeness present itself to you thirty years ago? What were the salient circumstances of this "time that breaks in cutting pieces," and this place you hoped to "join . . . kindly"?

WB: Now I'm getting uneasy about these words "whole" and "wholeness." Maybe I led this conversation a little astray by referring to the faith that makes us whole, though I think we must speak of that. But the "whole" that faith joins us to is by definition not knowable, and there is not much to say about it.

Another, more humble kind of wholeness is health—which, to me, means feeling good and being in a good place, so you can go about your work cheerfully and without thinking about yourself all the time. This kind of wholeness *can* be talked about, but not easily. It tends to be intermittent—nobody feels good all day every day—and it is dependent on and intermingled with the greater wholeness. So you have to be careful.

This humbler wholeness, as I understand it, is the human birthright, what we are permitted to know about and are enjoined to work for. It is the lowly wisdom, the knowing in measure, the knowledge of "things at hand / Useful" that Raphael talks about in *Paradise Lost* VII and VIII; and it is what Dante means by the "*quia*" (the *what* as opposed to the *why*) in *Purgatorio* III, 37.

I suppose it is correct, then, to say that at the time I wrote "To Think of the Life of a Man," I was "reaching toward wholeness." But it would be wrong to suppose that I was walking around here saying to myself, "I am reaching toward wholeness." The fact is that I was merely full of practical visions and doing practical work that delighted me. The further fact is that some of my visions were impractical, and some of my work was frustrating and disappointing. So I may have been "reaching toward wholeness" with delight, but that very effort revealed the fragmentation and difficulty of the world I was working in.

The poem was written probably in the summer of 1967. Tanya and I had then been living for just two years in the first house we had ever owned, in which we hoped to live the rest of our lives. We had twelve or so acres of land, and were growing a lot of our own food. We had begun the effort to make ourselves a pleasing, productive place in the world—something I had admired always, and always wanted to do. And so I was appropriately delighted, and I think that is the appropriate state of mind for reaching toward wholeness.

It is reassuring to know that Dante's first emotion after emerging from Hell and seeing the stars is delight. I might have supposed, once, that he would have had to climb to the top of the mountain in order to feel delight, but that is wrong. Delight, for such a climb, is standard operating equipment. If you haven't in some sense been there, why would you want to go?

In 1967, this little local delight was surrounded, in my own awareness, by knowledge of strip mining, agricultural erosion, the decline of rural life, other damages of our ongoing domestic colonialism, and the torment of our war in Vietnam.

JL: I find myself responding to your phrase, "local delight." When I bought a house at the edge of a rural town, I expected to live there only a short time and then move "out." Before I moved, however, I thought I should explore some of the possibilities of the place. Twenty years later, I've concluded the possibilities are probably inexhaustible, and my exploration of the "local delight" continues.

This exploration seems to me to be twofold. Part of it, my writing, is a kind of public speaking. The greater part of it, however, is private and local action occurring as I live my life within a community, working at the daily tasks of making a productive household. These parts interact. The daily work gives rise to poems and essays that in turn commit me publicly to that work.

Would you comment on your sense of this interaction? I'm interested in the literary explorations in *Clearing*, where you write about work and commitment. I'm also interested in the practical community that stands behind essays on subjects like local forest management or NAFTA and GATT in *Another Turn of the Crank*. In other words, how do writing and social action prompt each other?

WB: Some possibilities of place *are* exhaustible. You can impoverish the soil, poison the water, and destroy native species. Human life in a place can thus be made exhaustible. How long it may take a place to recover from miseducation of the young, willful ignorance, and the legitimizing of sloth and greed is a question I don't think can be comfortably answered.

But what you can know and experience of a place and the amount of good work that can be done in it—those, I agree, are inexhaustible.

I don't know much about how writing and social action prompt each other. You may write a certain kind of essay (or speech) because you perceive a need for social change. That is direct enough. I suppose the prompting may work in the other direction too—you may perceive a need and then act because of something you have written—but that seems not so direct.

The important thing is to write as one who is involved, not as one wishing to be involved or as one feeling duty-bound to be involved. If you like your community, the issue of its survival becomes a part of your consciousness. Politics and poetry (if you are a poet) may thus become substantially the same concern. My own reluctance about public involvement does not come from any doubt of the connection between politics and poetry. I just don't like crowd scenes. The public part of my life is more dutiful than enthusiastic.

LB: I'm not clear on the distinction between "is involved" and "wishes to be." Does it mean—is the writer willing to stake more than writing on the fate of the community? To celebrate a community is to recommend it, and by that to put its ways out in public, on trial—and the trial will be decided, in part, by whether we stand by what we've written. Am I getting this wrong?

WB: I think you have it about right. But the community is not on trial, only in its life in confrontation with "the public." It is also on trial in its members' lives. And the issue I was talking about is that of a sort of formal unity in a person's life: the possibility that one's life, dwelling place, work, politics, faith, etc., all might be included in the same affection. I'm talking about my ambition—what has looked desirable to me—not my accomplishment, which of course falls short.

There certainly does have to be more at stake than writing. If your only contribution is writing or talking, then how can you mean what you say? Or how can you know you mean it?

LB: There's something else to be included in, or by, a writer's affection: the community speech. A healthy community doesn't talk about its health: its speech expresses health. No, that isn't quite right: it may talk about its own health sometimes. I think of Tol Proudfoot, a character from your fiction, saying: "You've got to *like* to live in this world. You can't just mortal it out from one day to the next for three score years and ten." The sign of health here, I think, is the verb—"mortal it out." Did you ever hear anyone say that? In what ways have you drawn on the speech of your place?

WB: Since I was born and lived my early life here, and have lived most of my later life here, and since all of my closest kin and many of my friends have lived here, I suppose that I speak the speech of the place myself. Or I speak the local speech and also another speech modified somewhat by reading and by the need to speak to people in other places. Among the great gifts I got from this place were intelligent older kinfolks and friends whose speech was not at all tainted by fashionable slang or professional jargon or the speech of the public media, and who therefore spoke with a wonderful, unostentatious freshness and expressiveness. I suppose I heard those people speaking the local names and telling the local stories before I was born. When I got old enough, I listened to them eagerly, and finally knowingly also. Nearly all of them are dead now, but still in my thoughts and language I am always under their influence.

So far as I remember, I never heard anyone but Tol Proudfoot say "mortal it out."

JL: The introduction of Tol Proudfoot and his speech to our conversation takes us to the fictive world of Port William and what you have called the "Port William membership." The first time I read the stories about Tol, I read them out loud to my wife. Read that way they were entirely successful.

But I felt uncertain about them when I read them silently. Your previous fiction led me to expect a more realistic world than I found in these stories. My sense now is that they are meant to be different. They have a tall tale quality, and I read them as stories that would be told within your fictional world. As you wrote them, were you deliberately creating another layer of Port William, an internal oral history, or were you simply having fun? Did writing them for *The Draft-Horse Journal* influence their content and style?
WB: I'm not entirely satisfied with a "realistic" art or a "realistic" world. Things are real to me that are not real to the "realists." There is certainly a layer to the reality of Port William that has to do with what you are calling "a tall tale quality"—that is, with stories that are remembered because they are extravagant and wonderful and that are improved and made more wonderful in the telling. As one of my mentors used to say, "There is no use in telling a pretty good story when you can tell a really good one." Nevertheless, it reassures me to know that behind many of the imagined events of those stories lie real events. And I am fully serious about some of the events, particularly the acts of compassion. I understand Tol Proudfoot as a legendary character and in some ways a comic character, but I have written nothing that I take more seriously than the title story.

Of course when I wrote those stories I was having fun. One of the purposes of writing stories is to enjoy yourself as much as possible. I take it as a solemn duty that I should at least attempt to be always writing for pleasure. Obviously there is difficulty in art, and sometimes the difficult is great—I don't mean to deny that. But if there were no pleasure, and great pleasure too, in the work and in the result, then I would do something else. Or I hope I would.

The *Draft-Horse Journal* has been a good home for my work—because Maurice Telleen, who until recently was the editor, has been for the last twenty-five years a steadfast friend and ally in the great cause of agrarianism. And I dearly love to be read by the readers of *The Draft-Horse Journal*. However, I try never to write for a specific audience.

LB: I think "Watch With Me" is a wonderful story too, and part of the pleasure it gives is like that given by a tall tale. But what makes you say, "I have written nothing I take more seriously"?

WB: I take "Watch With Me" seriously because I think it is a good story, because it shows the way a functioning neighborhood acts even when the act of neighborliness seems as ineffectual as the lost sheep's cry of desperation, and because I had a surpassing good time writing it. My instinct is to trust my own pleasure in my work, and to like best the things that give me the most pleasure.

LB: One of the story's threads is Nightlife's appeal to a story from the Bible (the ninety-and-nine)—and I believe I hear the Gethsemane story here as well ("Couldn't stay awake?"). Given Port William's history, the Bible's presence isn't at all improbable; but it isn't exactly "realistic" either. What is the proper way of describing your story's use of, or appeal to, the Biblical story? Would you be comfortable saying your story is doing some kind of religious work?

WB: It depends on what you mean by "realistic" and "religious work." My own sense of reality does not exclude, for example, the miraculous. And I don't see why it is not a part of reality that people in a Bible-based culture should be remembering Bible stories, or that they should be prompted in their actions by Biblical ideas. I think it is clear in the story that Tol Proudfoot is consciously acting the part of a loving neighbor, his brother's keeper, and even a good shepherd.

The assumption that religious work is done only by preachers, missionaries, and church musicians seems to me a symptom of decay in Christianity. I don't doubt that the people in my story are doing religious work when they try to watch over a desperate neighbor—or, for that matter, when they help each other in their farming. I see no reason not to think that I was doing religious work when I wrote the story, or that the story was doing religious work for me while I was writing it.

JL: Tol's keeping of his brother, Nightlife, is not an isolated action in your fiction. Ben Feltner watches over the young Jack Beecham. Jack, in turn, literally holds Mat until Mat's anger dissipates and he is restored to himself when Thad Coulter murders Ben. In a quieter moment Jack, much to the annoyance of the town women, sits beside Hannah as she nurses. Danny Branch's kidnapping of Burley from his hospital bed might be seen as the same kind of brotherly keeping.

I have no problem seeing those characters doing religious work. Nor do I have any question that the making of Port William is religious work, but I would suggest one thing; for it to be religious work, it must be done consciously—willed.

WB: About the necessity of religious work to be willed, I would have to say *maybe* so. Or sometimes. Doing good by conscious will is certainly necessary sometimes for some of us. But that is a grim way to live, and it increases the temptation to take credit for one's righteousness. Mightn't it be, if one surrenders one's will to the will of God, that one might do a good thing willlessly or merely willingly—because, given your commitment, the good thing is *all* you can do? Sometimes I'm a rather bewildered reader of the Bible, and this business of knowing always what is God's will is not very clear to me. But Jesus seems to me to have had some strong reservations about the efficacy of the human will—as when He made "a little child" the standard of goodness.

Anyhow, I don't think Tol Proudfoot went through a conscious debate about whether or not to watch over Nightlife. I think that, when the time came to go, Tol just got up and went, because he couldn't imagine what else he might do. He had no choice, and so will was not an issue.

JL: I didn't intend anything grim by my use of the word "will." What I had in mind is more a sense of acting on the basis of a prior commitment, the doing "a good thing will-lessly" that you describe. Had Tol needed to think about his action, he would not have been the kind of man the situation required.

Can you say when you came to the realization that Port William was going to be a larger creation than the setting for one or two books? More importantly, would you describe how you came to that realization and would you talk a little bit about the complexities of working backwards from *A Place on Earth* to invent a coherent history for your characters to have lived? I know, for example, you cut a chapter of *Nathan Coulter* to make Nathan a character more fitting to what he becomes.

WB: For the Port William novels and stories there never has been an overall plan. It would have been good if there had been one, I guess. But only sometimes, and only when I was writing the short stories has it been possible to foresee any continuation beyond what I was then writing. I haven't willed any of this work into being. I have only been willing to write what comes to me, *if* something should come.

This does involve some retrospective bother. I am aware (thanks to readers more attentive than I am) of genealogical and geographical inconsistencies amongst the several books. I am attempting now, starting with the new edition of *The Memory of Old Jack*, to go back and fix those things.

JL: Let me press a little bit here. You seem to be reluctant to indulge us when we ask you to be self-conscious about your work. I understand that. But my interest is that of a teacher trying to show students how to think about their writing.

WB: Well, let me see if I can do better. I'm finding it hard to talk about the involvement of will in my work because I don't understand it very well.

Once, I would have understood it better, but that was when I was young and determined to become a writer. For a while, then, I really was writing by will power, trying to learn how to write and to make a start. But I remember a moment—in 1965, or a little after—when I realized that I didn't *have* to be a writer; there were other kinds of work also that required artistry and offered satisfaction. From here, looking back, I can see what a defining moment that was. I had, in effect, decided not to be a "professional" writer, but instead, in the literal sense, an amateur: I would work for love. I would be attempting a life, not a career.

After that, I knew I didn't have to try to "think things up," or try to force myself to get "ideas for writing." Will power, as an initiating force, became less and less involved. I wrote what came to me. The will was in the workmanship. I wanted to make of what had come to me the best work of art I could. But that also involves fascination. For me, the issue of will in art is impossibly complicated by the fact of fascination. Have I done what I have done—in writing, but also in the fields and woods—because I willed to do it, or because I was irresistibly attracted to it and *wanted* to do it? I have done it, I think, for love.

That is true, anyhow, of the novels and stories and poems. The essays, I suppose, originate somewhat differently. Love and fascination certainly are involved, but also fear. I became an essayist in order to try to defend good and necessary things that are in danger. With the essays, the issue of will seems to me to become even more difficult and obscure.

Perhaps it takes a certain amount of will to hang on for a few decades in defense of losing (though, I believe, never lost) causes. On the other hand, maybe one enters these battles not because of will or choice, but rather because, loving the things one loves, one *has* no choice.

Implicit in virtually all of my essays is the impulse of agrarianism: the desire for an economy that would be careful of the land, just to human workers, neighborly, democratic, and kind to all the gifts, natural and divine, on which our life depends. To a considerable extent, my argument was my father's before it was mine; in it, I have been his ally, and I have as allies my brother, my wife, and my children.

So how does one figure in an advocacy that is a fascination, a privilege, and a necessary result of one's most essential affections? I don't know.

JL: Haven't you willed—using the word as you have defined it—all that you have written by your deliberate choice to live within your subject? And doesn't that choice make your work—again using your definition— religious work, the work of a good neighbor?

WB: My decision to return here to live in my native country is hard for me to understand as a "deliberate choice." What was there to deliberate about? I didn't know what was going to happen. In fact, people I admired told me I was making a big mistake, and I was afraid they might be right. And thirty-five years later, I can't prove that they were wrong. There is no "control plot"—no life as it might have been with which to compare life as it has been. There is just the fact that at a crucial point in my life I did what I *wanted* to do. Doing otherwise would have required far more will.

(Some things I do depend simply and clearly on will power: flying in airplanes, speaking in public, answering my mail—things like that.)

Coming here did one thing for my writing that I am sure of. It caused me—as you say, as I believe I once said myself—"to live within my subject." That means that my subject has never been reducible to mere "subject matter" or "raw material" for writing, which is the usage of professionalism and industrialism. Coming here made it possible for me to avoid that.

Is my work "religious work, the work of a good neighbor"? I don't think I'm the one to answer that question. I can only say that I hope so. My work, at least, seems to have made *me* religious (though, I confess, not very churchly).

LB: You've suggested the origins of your work vary from genre to genre. You have, in fact, echoed poem VII, 1994 in *A Timbered Choir*.

> I would not have been a poet
> except that I have been in love
> alive in this mortal world,
> or an essayist except that I
> have been bewildered and afraid,
> or a storyteller had I not heard
> stories passing to me through the air . . .

How have the different genres of your writing developed? How much does the thrust of your work in one genre owe to and depend on the work in the others?

WB: From the time I started wanting to be a writer, I wanted to write poetry and fiction. I remember feeling, for a while, that I would have to choose one or the other, but I got over that.

Of course, nobody can get through school (I hope) without writing essays. But I became an essayist after I returned to Kentucky in 1964, and began needing essays for one reason or another. I'm an *occasional* essayist. Most of mine have been written as speeches.

The second question I can answer only vaguely. At a certain time in my life I became aware that I sometimes solved a problem or gained an insight in one genre that would help me in another. I suppose this has continued. My work as a poet and an essayist, I think, has pretty certainly influenced my novel writing.

JL: In the early 1970s Lionel and I worked with a student who wrote an honors essay discussing the influence of genre on theme in your work. He argued that you explored themes first in your poetry, developed them in your fiction, and became an advocate in your essays. What you've just said suggests something more interesting than that analysis. Would I be on track if I said the precepts of your poems and the propositions of your essays are embodied—Flannery O'Connor would say incarnated—in the characters and community of your fiction? This would imply that the world imagined in your fiction then becomes a part of the physical world you live in. An example of this might be the way Jack Beechum, Mat Feltner, and Elton Penn turn up in the poems in *Clearing*.

WB: Now you are asking me to explain a mystery. I don't think I can honestly say that I "know" what is happening in my mind and imagination when I am writing. The mystery rests upon what I believe is an impenetrable fact: when you start thinking about how you write, you are no longer writing. The phenomenon to be explained has vanished, and you are reduced to examining "the evidence." I can tell—just as your student or you can tell, and only in the same way—that my poems, essays, and fiction all evidently are written by the same writer. But this is not a result that I consciously intended. It just happened, because I am one person, not three or four.

I am not sure at all of the process by which I have imagined the characters in my fiction, but I nonetheless feel sure that they are not embodiments of precepts.

I *do* agree that imagined things—works of art, mine and other people's—belong to the reality of the world I live in. A world devoid of imagination would be much smaller (in spite of "space probes"), and also less real.

JL: I'm finding it curious that though we began talking of wholeness in the world we have focused almost exclusively on literary topics. I'm finding it curious because I think each of us values literature, not merely for itself, but because we believe it makes things happen in the world. Lionel captured something of this when he wrote in one of his essays on your work, "Poetry teaches by affording a vision of, and by praising, a fruitful, moral, coherent way of life." What would you like your work to make happen in the world?

WB: I don't agree with Auden that "poetry makes nothing happen." But what it makes happen is a question that needs to be asked and answered with caution. The best art, I think, gives our highest impulses—reverence or love or compassion or gratitude—an imagery or a language or a story that is necessary to them, to their effective life in this world, and that otherwise they would not have.

Art, I think, can help to make life more full and abundant. It can help us to survive as "living souls," and not just as a "species." I hope my writing serves that possibility. But of course I am not the one to say whether or not it does.

JL: I have more questions. There are many topics we haven't addressed, but I think we have found an appropriate end to this discussion. Thank you for your willingness to spend yourself so generously over the last eighteen months.

Before ending, however, I'd like to say a couple of things about this process. I discovered your poetry in 1968. During my first year of teaching I read *The Long-Legged House* and *A Place on Earth*. Lionel discovered your work at about the same time, and as our friendship grew, we engaged in a long conversation with your books, a conversation that influenced how we lived our lives. This chance to question you came at a good moment in that talk. That I had to complete this interview without Lionel has been difficult. I am reluctant to say much in public about his friendship to me. It was enduring and it remains central to my character and thought. The part your work played in that friendship has been great and enriching.

WB: It is strange to think that this interview ends, months after his death, my long conversation with Lionel Basney. The three of us first met, I remember, at a reading in Pittsburgh about twenty years ago. We were together a few years after that when I came to Houghton College, where you both were teaching. And, as you said, we were together here in the summer of 1998. In amongst those encounters of the three of us, I would see Lionel from time to time when he and his family would stop by here on their visits to Ruth's parents in Wilmore, and from time to time we exchanged letters or talked on the phone. I am conscious of a big debt to him. First, of course, for friendship. And then for instruction, for he was a thorough, generous scholar. And then for his example, his great integrity, his care in everything.

Wendell Berry's Community

Anne Husted Burleigh / 1999

From *CRISIS* 18.1 (January 2000), 28–33. Reprinted by permission of *CRISIS* Magazine.

Wendell Berry, novelist, essayist, poet, and farmer, is a central contributor to the growing renaissance of Christian culture. Although he does not, in his lean careful writing, broach religion directly, he writes as one completely at home with the Christian tradition.

His readers are numerous and ever growing, drawn to his scriptural and Aristotelian-Thomistic view of the world, a world that he sees as a created order for which the Creator has appointed us stewards and trustees. Reverence is a hallmark of Berry's work—reverence for the gift of creation, for the sanctity of the Word, for the sacred uniqueness of his subjects.

Convinced of the "necessary and indispensable connection between language and truth, and therefore between language and deeds," Berry says in *Standing by Words*, "I begin with the Christian idea of the Incarnate Word, the Word entering the soul as flesh, and inevitably therefore as action. . . ." Our words, in sum, always refer to and assume the divine Word. Words are sacred; we dare not speak them falsely or lightly. False words, because they cannot possibly refer to God's Word, have no meaning. If words have no meaning, there is no way we can speak to each other in community.

Berry is too gifted and universal to be claimed by any one movement or literary tradition. He does, however, acknowledge the influence of the Southern Agrarians (see his essay in the January 1999 issue of *Oxford American*). Yet he has dared to do what, for the most part, they did not: to live the life he has written about. More than three decades ago, after writing and teaching at Stanford University and then at New York University, he took a position with the English faculty at the University of Kentucky and moved his family to Lanes Landing Farm at Port Royal, Kentucky, in his native Henry County. He and his wife, Tanya, have spent the succeeding years

restoring their beautiful hillside farm nestled along the banks of the
Kentucky River.

Wendell Berry's world is the landscape of hills and hollows, woods and
fields, and bottom land that covers much of central and northern Kentucky.
His fiction and poetry emanate from the locale in and around the little town
of Port William on the Kentucky River, which Berry loosely models after his
own Port Royal. The scene sometimes extends to Hargrave, the county seat
(that is, Carrollton, Kentucky), some ten miles away, where the Kentucky
River spills into the Ohio. Each of Berry's stories concerns some of the
characters from the same families, which Berry calls (significantly revealing
his definition of community) the Port William Membership. Most of the
membership are farmers, mainly of tobacco. Some are also shopkeepers and
country lawyers, like Berry's own father.

Once immersed in Berry's fiction, the reader, too, becomes part of the
membership. His characters are good people—Mat Feltner, Elton Penn,
Burley Coulter, Wheeler Catlett—devoid of trappings; neighborly; living in
faithful relation to each other; having common patterns of thinking and
doing; united in friendship, work, loyalty, memory of the past, hope for the
future, responsibility for each other, and love of a concrete place.

Berry's themes are marriage, community, land, and the fidelity that binds
us to all three. Trust, fidelity, standing by one's word, are the cement of all
human relations and therefore of marriage and community.

Marriage, in Berry's view, is the cornerstone of the community, the engine
that energizes human life. For most of us, marriage is the form of our lives, of
which, once again, fidelity is the cement. To break our word would be to
break the form. Without faithfully keeping our word, there can be no
marriage and therefore no community. Berry points out in his essay, "Poetry
and Marriage," that fidelity, standing by our word, "is a double fidelity: to
the community and to oneself." Only within the community can we achieve
our end to know and love others; within the community one is "at once free
and a member."

Berry, a traditionalist, is suspicious of faith in the unrooted individual
intelligence, preferring "faith in the community or in culture."

"Belief in culture," he says in his essay, "calls for the same disciplines as
belief in marriage." It demands patience, faith, and dedication to work. This
work "consists of the accumulation of local knowledge in place, generation
after generation, children learning the visions and failures, stories and songs,

names, ways, and skills of their elders, so that the cost of individual trial-
and-error learning can be lived with and repaid, and the community thus
enabled to preserve both itself and its natural place and neighborhood."

The logical handmaid of marriage is attachment to the land, to the
particular place where the couple forges a permanent union, a family, a
livelihood, and a partnership between generations. One's attachment to
place, especially in farming, is itself a marriage. As Berry writes in his poem
"The Current":

> Having once put his hand into the ground
> seeding there what he hopes will outlast him,
> a man has made a marriage with his place,
> and if he leaves it his flesh will ache to go back.

The point is always to seed what will outlast one's short span, and that
kind of effort can only be driven by love, the love that husband and wife
lavish sacrificially on a particular place, on behalf of those children who will
follow them. They expend themselves in love and work because those whom
they love have a value beyond time and beyond human understanding.

Anne Husted Burleigh, a *CRISIS* contributing editor, interviewed author
Wendell Berry at his Kentucky farm, April 25, 1999.

Burleigh: Your fiction takes place in one locale around the little town of Port
William on the Kentucky River. You write often of the Port William "membership." Is that your definition of community—a membership?
Berry: I suppose so. That's a term borrowed from St. Paul, whom I don't
always approve of, but if you remember Burley Coulter in the story, "The
Wild Birds," he takes that verse and carries it on to where I want it: "The
difference ain't in who is a member and who is not, but in who knows it and
who don't."

Burleigh: One of my favorite books of yours is *Standing by Words*. Is our
failure to stand by our words at the heart of the fragmentation of
community?
Berry: There certainly is a prevalent loss of trust operating in this society
now, and if you have enough people who don't think they can trust each
other, you've got some serious problems. There's a famous crisis of
confidence in government; a lot of people think it's useless to vote. If we can't

trust each other to do what we've said we'll do, cooperation is impossible. Cooperation means working together. If you can't work together, you can't have a community. Yes, I think that question of whether or not people stand by their word and take it seriously is a real issue. As I said in that book, I think the fundamental fact of a marriage is that you've given your word.

Burleigh: Marriage is one of the strong themes in your writing. What does marriage mean to a community, especially to a rural community? You always link marriage and land and community.
Berry: Marriage for me has great power as a metaphor or analog of other relationships. In an intact community, the marriage vows are given *before* the membership. The couple doesn't just exchange them with one another. The vows are given before witnesses, who are there partly because they are party to the contract. This young couple is pledging from now on to be to a certain extent predictable in their behavior. It's a terrible thing to say those vows. Something like that *ought* to be witnessed by people who will acknowledge that it happened and that these awe-full things were said. And in my own experience the sense of having loved ones' expectations directed toward me has been very influential, and it still is.

Burleigh: So the married couple always has that responsibility not only to each other, but to everybody.
Berry: Everybody in the community.

Burleigh: Everybody, whether living or dead?
Berry: The immediate parties to it are the couple themselves and their children. But it branches out. They're right at the center of the pattern, of the crisis of expectation.

Burleigh: When you write about marriage, you have a profound understanding of the complementary natures of men and women. How does this complementariness affect the health and integrity of the community?
Berry: It's one of the primary connections, one of the primary joints of the community, and if one marriage falls apart, that means that other people are going to have to take more responsibility. That is what a community is for. If you have family failures in an intact community, the community takes up the slack. If there are enough failures, then that becomes a community failure.

The community can't any longer take up the slack and repair the damage and look out for things.

Burleigh: Do you think a community can exist without religious belief?
Berry: Probably not. It's either some kind of an authentic religious impulse working to authorize right behavior, or reason alone. I have great admiration for reason, but I can see that it doesn't go but just so far, and I think, ultimately, you have to have religious faith for community life to work.

Burleigh: In one of your essays you say about marriage, "For a couple marriage is an entrance into a timeless community." Timeless implies that a community is eternal.
Berry: Oh, yes.

Burleigh: Have we abandoned the idea of marriage as a timeless community, of the family as part of a community with an eternal dimension?
Berry: My approach to religion has pretty much been from the bottom up. I never was very good at the top-down version, and my understanding of religion has grown from my understanding of the things of time, from family and community life.

Burleigh: The incarnational.
Berry: Yes, that's right. As a farmer, I understand what it means when Christ says He's a shepherd. I understand what it means when Scripture describes the first creation as a garden. That makes sense for me not because of revelation from on high but from revelation from below, so to speak, from my experience. And I can see the ways the things of time relate to the things of eternity analogically.

Burleigh: That's a Judeo-Christian view of things.
Berry: It's a traditional approach, especially for poets. Dante started with hell and worked his way up. He's another bottom-up man, it seems to me. But he started his testimony from deeper down than I did.

Burleigh: You would see our relation to the world as trustees, shepherds, stewards, and guardians.
Berry: Stewards. And enjoyers.

Burleigh: Enjoyers because the world is a gift, isn't it?

Berry: It's important to understand that we're given pleasures here. It's important to me to understand that there are heavenly things that are present here, in time, in flesh, wood, rock, water, and all the rest of it. These good things are sanctioned in a good bit of religious teaching as part of the revelation of eternity. The *pleasantness* of it seems to me to be extremely important. I don't like the dualism of heaven and earth, which always leads you to condemn the earth as something evil, as something to be suffered through in order to get to heaven. It seems to me that there is an interpenetration, a major communication, and that to know this world at its best is to know something heavenly. And the other way around, too. To know it at its worst is to know something hellish. That's how we know what to work for and what to hope for in this world. This seems to me to be sanctioned by Scripture.

Burleigh: The Incarnate Word?

Berry: Scripture says God loved the world, that the Incarnation *happened* because God loved the world. The implication of his Sabbath rest at the very beginning was that it was a day of appreciation and approval of what he had done. It seems wrong to condemn the world and wrong to refuse its decent pleasures. Why would you deny yourself a decent pleasure, which is the signal and sign of heaven in this world, in order to get to heaven? It doesn't make any sense—to me.

Burleigh: You have written beautiful poems called *Sabbaths*, about Sabbath rest and enjoyment of creation.

Berry: Those poems have been my way of thinking about the subject.

Burleigh: How is understanding of the Incarnate Word essential to our understanding of the relationship of language and truth?

Berry: I believe that we have to try to make our words faithful to reality. Language has to maintain its power of reference to actual things, and everything depends on that power of reference and that community of knowledge, or else the word doesn't get out.

Burleigh: In our age, people don't have common understanding of the same words.

Berry: That makes for considerable difficulties, especially if they don't talk carefully with one another. It is always good to talk with people who understand things differently from your way, but that requires careful talk. Any common effort obviously requires careful talk.

Burleigh: If we believe that words do refer to reality and our words have to be true, we still have to communicate with those who have accepted individualism and subjectivism. They operate on the premise that words really don't mean anything except what the individual wants them to mean. Can we bridge that gap?

Berry: No. All one can do is speak as truly and clearly as one can. I think one's abilities to correct anything are limited. It is important to know what the limits of your abilities are. A person can make a difference within a fairly small boundary. Not very many people can change very much.

Burleigh: They can't change the world, but they can change their little corner of the world.

Berry: Well, I know that you can improve a few acres. You can take good care of a few acres. Your ability to take care of other humans is more limited than your ability to take care of an acreage simply because humans, in the main, would rather take care of themselves.

Burleigh: Do you place yourself in any particular literary tradition, or do you consider yourself independent?

Berry: I have to feel, to a considerable extent, independent because I'm not authorized to speak for other people. I have to remember that. I have never been a part of a school or a movement and have never wanted to be. It seemed to be a good idea not to be. However, I have had exemplars and influences that I am perfectly glad to acknowledge, friendships that have formed me and made me what I am and such as I am. Not all of them have been literary by any means. I have a big debt to local talk, local conversation, and to family talk. I have depended a lot on writers who had a place as a subject—Thomas Hardy, Sarah Orne Jewett, William Carlos Williams, Faulkner, and others.

Burleigh: Do you consider yourself related to the Southern Agrarian movement? And, how do you define agrarianism?

Berry: Oh, yes. I owe them a good deal. I read *I'll Take My Stand* while I was still in college. Agrarianism obviously has something to do with agriculture, but it also has something to do with stewardship in the highest sense of the word. Agrarianism includes the high *art* of farming. It includes the practice of farming as an art. It always has something to do with family and community continuity. It has something to do with honoring not just divine gifts but also the human inheritance. It has something to do with the political sense, too, of economic and intellectual independence that is founded on land ownership. Going back very far, it has to do with the belief in the importance of small ownership, the small holding. Jefferson's agrarianism certainly has to do with that and so does Virgil's. Homer's *Odyssey* is informed by this old sense of obligation not just to the homeland but to the farmland. There are people who say there's an aristocratic agrarianism, and you can deny that only with difficulty. Jefferson's agrarianism included that, too, I think. But if you let the idea of a landed aristocracy go too far, then you eliminate the small landowners. If you are going to take democracy seriously, there has to be a balance in favor of the small landowners. There ought to be many owners, Jefferson said. The land ought to be owned in small parcels by many people, who use those parcels, who farm them and farm them well. It doesn't mean a lot of absentee owners.

Burleigh: If you are trying to explain this to city people, how do you tell them what benefit agriculture has on the moral lives of a country, of a culture?
Berry: A long time before you start talking about the moral benefits, you need to talk about the physical benefits. City people eat and they've got to worry, though most don't, about the dependability of the food supply. The fact is that most farmland requires close care to be used well. That is the agricultural justification for the small holding. It permits close care in a way that large holdings farmed by hired people or even owners on large machines can't be farmed well. The moral benefit of independent small farmers is that it broadens the connection of the whole society to the land, and it increases the number of self-employed people. This is the political value that Jefferson saw in the small farm. People who are economically independent can think and vote independently.

Burleigh: All of your fiction is set either before or right around World War II.
Berry: Some of it is later but the influence of World War II is paramount. That event is paramount in my fiction and my way of seeing the world because it made the greatest change in rural life that has ever happened probably in the history of the world.

Burleigh: Do you think the issue of rural life is the question of using technology in a humane and moral way?

Berry: That's right. The only example we have of that, of course, is the Amish example. The Amish differ from all other modern human beings in having had the good sense to ask of any innovation, "What would this do to our community?" That involves limiting the use and the effects of our technological abilities. There is no escaping that.

Burleigh: What we are technologically capable of doing doesn't necessarily mean that we morally have the right to use that technology.

Berry: What we are entirely capable of is destroying the world. It doesn't take too much sense or courage to say we mustn't do that. If we are not going to do that, that means we have got to establish limits somehow. I think it has come to the point at which we can't expect governments, corporations, bureaucracies, and agencies to change as fast as the people can, and I think a lot of people have changed. They are determining the change on a small scale that will finally add up to something significant. I believe in that possibility, and it is a source of hope to me.

Burleigh: You have regretted the specialization of modern life—of work, of university life, of poetry. How do you think that self-absorbed specialization has damaged our community life and our literature?

Berry: Your adjective is the right one. You have got to have specialization if you are to have vocation. People are differently talented and differently called to kinds of work. So specialization is going to happen. What you have to regret is the *isolation* of the specialists so that they're at liberty to judge their work by professional standards to the exclusion of any other kind. The ascendancy of professional standards in the universities and the professions is a very bad thing, I think, because it means that the specialists are all isolated in their specialty and are not thinking about the pattern that they have to fit their work into.

Burleigh: You once wrote, "To stay at home is paradoxically to change, to move. When poets and people of any other calling stay at home, the first thing they move away from is professionalism." What happens when work becomes professionalized?

Berry: It ceases to submit itself to the standards of community life or religion or health or any of those other standards that can cause us to ask the right questions about what we are doing. If you are an isolated specialist, you never ask what a proposed innovation will do to our community because you are not aware of having a community. Specialists are sometimes very selfless people, working long hours and even with altruistic motives, but if you work too long in too great isolation, you lose the sense of limits; you lose the sense of the effect of your work on other people.

Burleigh: Does our violent society have a relation to the loss of the sacred?
Berry: To me, it must have. The sense of the sacred is not very selective. I really take seriously that verse in the Book of Job that says that if God withholds "his spirit and his breath all flesh shall perish together and man shall return again unto dust." If you believe that, then our life here is critical all the time because we must use everything considerately, not just some things. If you think that every life is ensouled and sacred, then you have to behave differently toward all these people—fetuses, criminals, enemies—that we've decided it's all right to be violent toward, and also toward animals and inanimate things such as trees and stones. We would have to be much more careful. We would probably have to be poorer, but we would also greatly increase the opportunities of pleasure and joy. I think there would be payoffs if we were gentler. But I don't think you can be selective in your violence. If you are thoughtlessly violent against some designated group, you can't keep that from spilling over. There is such a thing as influence. Influence is real; it exists. If young people see older people solving their problems by violence, what can you expect except that they will try to do it, too? If they see human life generally depreciated, then they'll generally depreciate their own lives and the lives of other children. Promiscuity is self-depreciation and another form of violence and exploitation.

Burleigh: How do you address the restlessness and inability of many people to commit themselves to a place, a marriage, a community; they feel compelled to stay on the move?
Berry: Gary Snyder said the right thing: stop somewhere, just stop. Finally, this thing we are calling mobility keeps people from learning their lessons. They keep moving away from the problems they've caused. Their idea is that you can completely mess up somewhere and then go somewhere else, or you can completely succeed somewhere and go somewhere else. In either case you don't know what the effects are. Sometimes people cause worse effects by their success than they do by their failure. To go back to the metaphor of

marriage. What marriage does is say to you to stay and find out. It doesn't say what you are going to find out. When you think this is it, we are at a complete dead end here, the marriage says to you: wait, stay, and find out. Always you find out more. The thing is too great to be belittled by any decision that you can make about it. This is the same for your relation to the community or anything else. Wallace Stegner said that we Americans divide into two groups, boomers and stickers. The boomers are always thinking that something is better somewhere else, that whatever they have or whatever they are is no good.

Burleigh: Don't you think that young people are often disappointed when they end their college years and realize that they didn't tackle the big questions?

Berry: They may have read things of importance, but also they may have learned to read reductively as if, say, George Herbert were only writing about the superstitions of his day. If you think that we've outgrown George Herbert, you have missed the whole point. It is not just from the canonical Scriptures that the news of eternity comes. It can come from anywhere, anytime. People have been carefully instructed to not see that and to have ways to defend against it. If George Herbert isn't telling the truth, there is no use in reading him as an exercise in anthropology.

Burleigh: You pointed out in a recent article that poetry and literature can be read so that the text is important but not the truth of the content.

Berry: That's right. So that you can read *I'll Take My Stand* as merely or purely a literary work and not as a political work.

Burleigh: You've said that the subject of poetry is not words; it's the world, which poets and writers have in common with other people. That's part of the specialization, isn't it? Writers see their work as something aimed only for other writers and not really connected with the world.

Berry: It's too bad if you think that writers will be the people in charge of words and other people will be in charge of things. It has to be more complicated than that. Writers certainly ought to take pleasure in words and know about them. You've got to learn your art. There is a lot else to learn, too. The arts ought properly to be subordinated to the art of living. That brings it back into a kind of perspective. The only thing that can preserve the arts is the knowledge of how to live—ultimately how to live in a community. That's the vessel that keeps a culture alive. You can't keep it alive in books. It really has to be kept alive by example, by conversation, by daily talk and tasks.

Burleigh: All of your writing is connected to the world. I think that's why your readers love it.

Berry: Well, I like the world, so far. I think the world exacts a terrible toll on all of us who live in it. We lose our loved ones and witness a lot of destruction and damage. It's a hard place to live, but it also offers us all the opportunities we're ever going to get in this life. They are all right here. The pleasures, the opportunities, the chance to love each other. So far I am not a bit sorry that I've had the experience and the privilege.

Burleigh: What would you like most for people to say about your writing?

Berry: I don't allow myself that thought at all. That's not my business. My business is to write as well as I can. If people think it's good, then that's fine. But I don't think that thoughts of how you want people to think of you are allowed. I mean strangers. I am always trying to make a good impression on my wife, Tanya!

Burleigh: Well, you must have. How long have you been married?

Berry: 42 years.

Burleigh: You wrote in *Standing by Words*: "Nothing exists for its own sake but for a harmony greater than itself which includes it. A work of art which accepts this condition and exists upon its terms honors the creation and so becomes a part of it." Is that a summation of the way you view your work?

Berry: I still pretty much stick with that.

A Citizen and a Native: An Interview with Wendell Berry

Jim Minick / 2003

From *Appalachian Journal: A Regional Studies Review* 31.3–4 (Spring–Summer 2004), 300–13. Reprinted by permission of *Appalachian Journal.*

The Ohio River was up when I visited Wendell Berry and his wife, Tanya, on Sunday afternoon, November 16, 2003. So was the Kentucky River along which the Berrys live. Heavy rains in the mountains of Virginia, West Virginia, and Kentucky had brought on the flooding. At Carrollton, Kentucky, ten miles downstream from the Berrys' farm, the two rivers join at Point Park, and here the Ohio crested at 36 feet, 24 feet above normal. A mile upstream on the Kentucky River, the high water mark was at 22 feet.

"This isn't Appalachia," I thought, "yet how do you describe these hills?" They fall dramatically to the rich bottom lands and waterways, but they have only one side. Drive up the steep roads through narrow hollows, and you arrive on a rich, slightly rolling plateau of bluegrass.

The Berry farmstead rests on the side of one of these steep hills, where the bottom border is the muddy Kentucky River, and between the house and the river, a hillside pastures sheep and a single llama. The house, a two-story white clapboard built in the late 1800s, perches on a bench in the hillside, "guarded" by two palm-licking border collies.

Wendell Berry came out to greet me, and we moved inside, settling at the round kitchen table. Throughout the interview, Mrs. Berry, in a corner rocker, occasionally joined our conversation as she trimmed and collated sheet music for that night's choir practice. Later she cut vegetables and made soup, filling the small kitchen with warmth and the smell of good food.

Minick: I would like to start with some basic questions about your farm. How much land do you own, and how long have you owned this farm?
Berry: We have 125 acres, more or less. We don't know exactly. As you can see, it's pretty rough. The two crops we have here, besides the garden, are

grass and trees. I would say well over half of it is wooded. On the pastures, we have a small flock of Border Cheviots.

We bought the first twelve acres of it, the old landing property here, in the fall of 1964, about this time of year. We moved in the next summer.

Minick: I guess that's when you started writing *Long-Legged House*?
Berry: That was a little later. When we moved here, I was writing *A Place on Earth*. I built that camp house, where I do my work, in 1963.
Mrs. Berry: It was already there, just in a different place.
Berry: Then the right word would be I rebuilt it.

Minick: What was the history of the farm before you? What was it like before you bought it?
Berry: Well, we bought it in a good many tracts. We have six deeds. A good bit of it was pretty badly run down. The 40 acres downriver had been savagely bulldozed by developers. We spent a lot of money bulldozing it back together.

We've cleared some land and let the woods come back on some, but for the most part, we have kept clear what was clear. Some of it was overgrown with bushes. Around here you don't have to plant trees, they come.

Minick: I'm asking this to lead to this question: when you read from *Hannah Coulter*, your novel in progress, at Hindman [Settlement School Appalachian Writers Workshop in 2003], you talked about the way land shapes the characters. How has this place shaped you and how have you shaped it?
Berry: That's a difficult question because you can't give a hard and fast, provable answer. We've been here almost 40 years. We've raised our children and gotten older here. We've done our best to take good care of the place. We've made some mistakes, but for the most part we *have* taken good care of it. What we've done here is the intimate history of our life, and so it's hard to say more than that if we had not lived here we'd be different people and it would be a different place. But we don't have what experimenters call "control plots." We know that if nobody lived here it would go back to the woods. And that would be fine. I'm ready for that to happen, and it probably will, eventually.

Minick: In several places, you've written that one of your goals has been to make farming fit the farm, and I agree, but I've always wondered how exactly you do that?

Berry: That phrase is J. Russell Smith's, from his great book *Tree Crops*. To generalize his point, you could say that he understood that when the ground is steep you have to go with perennials. Wes Jackson [Director of the Land Institute, Salina, Kansas] is saying you've got to go with perennials anyhow. But as the slope steepens, the need for perennial cover increases. That means that you have got to have grass where you don't have trees, and it means that you mustn't overgraze the grass. So we are grass farmers primarily. There was a time, when I had more energy and fewer distractions, when we were growing all our grain and hay in the river and creek bottoms. That's difficult here because the river and creek bottoms overflow, and there was a stretch of four years when I lost everything I planted. Our son farms near here, and now we get the little grain and hay that we need from him.

Mrs. Berry: One of the reasons we have sheep instead of cattle on this land is because it reacts better with the sheep. We had cattle, and they're a little hard on it.

Berry: The grass cover is as good as a tree cover on a slope, but you've got to take care of it. We don't have cattle on these slopes because in the wintertime they plow it up just by walking on it. And they'll start a slip; they'll push the soil off the hillside.

I keep horses, but I keep them over in the creek bottom where the damage is minimized. I don't put the horses on the hills—if I can avoid it, let's say it that way. And usually I can avoid it. It's an absolute wrong to put them on hills in the winter, and I don't.

Minick: Do you grow tobacco?

Berry: I never have grown tobacco here. Until recently, when my neighbors were growing tobacco, I was always involved. Nearly every year of my life, except when I was away, I was involved in setting and cutting tobacco with my neighbors.

Mrs. Berry: We just don't raise tobacco on our farm. We still have our allotment. Our children are growing it now.

Minick: In your interview with Elizabeth Beattie, you said you always knew you wanted to be a farmer, even from a young age. Can you say why?

Berry: Nope, I can't say why. I was involved in farming from childhood, and my father lived and breathed it. Although he was a lawyer, he was a passionate farmer. It's hard to say why you love to do something. I love to write too, but I don't know why. I grew up farming. My grandfather, my father's father, was insistent on the importance of it. I grew up among people who simply could not conceive of farming as an inferior way of work, or an inferior art, or something for stupid people to do.

Minick: When I grew up, my uncle ran the family farm, but all of the other three brothers, including my father, were never really interested. I wonder why?
Berry: Well, our society teaches that you have failed if you can't think of anything better to do than farm.

Minick: So, why did your family counter that?
Berry: I don't know. They were just people who liked farming. My brother and I like it. Both of us are on farms. Both of my children are farmers. We're raising some fairly fierce agrarian grandkids.

Minick: Do your children also have off-farm jobs?
Berry: My daughter-in-law works for the post office. My son works as a furniture maker part-time in the old store down there [by the state road, within sight of Berry's house]. My daughter and son-in-law are full-time farmers. They have a winery on their farm near New Castle. And they are making very good wine, too.

Minick: How did you instill in your children and grandchildren this agrarian way which runs counter to our society?
Berry: You know, they just grew up in a farming family and among farming neighbors. Children know from what they see in you what you love and respect, and they grow up to love and respect it too. I suppose that's the way it works. They see that it can be done, and they see and hear judgements made, choices made, about quality. They see very readily, I assume, where you take your pleasure. We haven't run an indoctrination program exactly, have we, Tanya? We haven't set them down and told them what to do . . .

Mrs. Berry: No, we don't know what they're going to do. We usually find out later.

Berry: You have to leave your children free to choose. If they want to do it, then you want them to do it. Our son never wanted to do anything else but farm. Our daughter decided a little later.

Mrs. Berry: She didn't like it at all when she was a girl.

Berry: She married a farmer and then became a farmer. That's the way it's been. Our son has cattle, tobacco, and corn. He sometimes raises potatoes, and sweet potatoes.

Mrs. Berry: They both have been involved in the movement to try to make a local economy that will save the small farm.

Berry: Both our kids are pretty actively involved in this effort we have going on in the state [of Kentucky] to keep the legs under the small farmers. They are working on marketing locally and in Louisville. They are involved in the cause of the small farm. My father was, my brother and I have been, and now my children are.

Minick: What do you see happening to your farm in the future?

Berry: It's hard to believe that anyone is going to want to farm this place after I'm gone. It's too steep. It has no arable land on it that doesn't flood. I assume that the slopes will go back to the woods, maybe the bottomlands too. I don't know what the children will do.

Minick: How much development pressure is here?

Berry: We're not under pressure here.

Mrs. Berry: The county is. All the counties around here are. This county is changing really, really fast. All the roads are filling with new houses.

Berry: Nobody has approached us lately.

Mrs. Berry: And this floods so much down here, that there is some protection in that.

Berry: We don't own land that is developable for summer homes or city lot development. But urbanization is growing all around us. People are moving in and moving out. Population here is many times more transient than it used to be. When I was growing up here, people mostly were living on the places where they had always lived, and they and their children continued to live there for a long time. Now it is shifting. People buy houses and move in. Then the first thing you know, there is a "For Sale" sign up, and they're gone.

Mrs. Berry: The land prices have gone way up, too, so the farmers can't keep up.

Berry: The land prices have gone out of the reach of the farmers. People buy farms to "get away."

Minick: So what's your opinion on the conservation easement movement?
Berry: I'm for that. We intend to give a conservation easement on this place.
Mrs. Berry: That has saved a farm or two in the county, where the farmers have done easements and that's enabled them to go on farming.
Berry: Of course, the cost of petroleum may control sprawl in a few years more efficiently than the land trust movement.

We pause to watch their two dogs outside wander off. Berry conjectures that they're visiting a deer carcass up the hill.

Minick: Did you kill the deer?
Berry: I didn't. Somebody must have thrown it off the road. We are really over-populated with deer.

Minick: We are too. Do you hunt?
Berry: No, I used to when I was a kid, but not anymore. I couldn't hit anything now!

The dogs disappear and we continue.

Minick: I went to the Land Institute and heard you speak in 1996. I have always been fascinated with Wes Jackson's work, but I have wondered: what he does on the prairie, what's the equivalent here on hilly land or in Appalachia? What's the parallel system of agriculture?
Berry: Wes Jackson's work pretty well parallels the work of Sir Albert Howard. Wes says the native prairie should be the model for agriculture in the prairie states. But Howard said if you want to know how to farm, you need to look at the forest. So here we need to look at the forest. The message is everywhere the same. When you uncover the land, you expose it to erosion, and the steeper the ground, the more vulnerable to erosion it is. But virtually all land is vulnerable to erosion. One of the most eroded states is Iowa.

Minick: I'm curious about the plow and its future. How *much* will it be used, and *how* do you think it will be used?

Berry: Well, there's no doubt in my mind that people can plow pretty well. I know a hillside that an Amish farmer has plowed in strips for many years without noticeable erosion. He has used a two-way horse-drawn plow that's been reengineered a little so that it lays the furrow very forcibly up the hill. So instead of a shingled roof, you have the opposite—every furrow is a water catcher. I've been on that hillside in the fall when the dead furrows on the lower sides of those strips were still open. You can do that in some places, depending on the kind of soil you have, and the degree of the slope, but it has to be very lovingly and very thoughtfully done.

This means that in agriculture as in other work, you've got to address the problem of scale. And again the steeper the ground, the smaller must be the scale, if you are going to conserve the soil. If you're plowing steep ground, the scale has to be small. The scale can be a little larger on steep ground if you're grazing. But the same laws still apply—you don't want too many head of livestock passing the same gate or bottleneck, wearing a path on a steep slope. So you've got to control the scale. In the long run, I think J. Russell Smith and Wes Jackson are right. The steeper land needs to be under grass or trees or both.

We've also got to address the issue of local adaptation. Some things can be done without damage here in our river bottom, for example, that can't be done without damage on the hillsides or in Arizona. We've got to address the issues of fertility conservation and water conservation. And we've got to address the issue of genetic diversity. Plants and animals need to be adapted to the farm. There is a reason these sheep of ours do better on hills than other breeds.

Minick: How long have you used the Cheviot breed of sheep?
Berry: We bought the first ones in 1978.

Minick: Have you tried others?
Berry: A little, but we pretty much knew the kind of sheep we needed. The Cheviots come from the Cheviot Hills in Scotland. Hillsides are where these sheep belong. What we're looking for is a ewe that will have two lambs a year, mother and feed them well, on the hillsides and *on grass*. We don't feed any corn to our ewes. We feed a little corn to the lambs. The meat that leaves a farm like this ought to be mostly made of grass.

Minick: And the lamb market, how is it now?

Berry: I don't know. We disposed of our lambs privately. This year we have fewer lambs than customers.

Minick: So you direct market?

Berry: Yes.

Minick: In a different vein, I would like to explore the concept of nativeness a little more. How do you define the word "native"?

Berry: Native means born here. But it's possible now to be *born* here but not *made* here. You can live here and yet be made by imported nutrients and imported influences. If "native" is going to mean anything, you have to say you're born, nourished, and educated to a significant extent in and *by* your place, your local community.

Minick: I was re-reading "A Native Hill," and this one sentence struck me. You're talking about coming back, and you write, "Here, now that I'm both native and citizen, there's no immunity to what is wrong." The "citizen" part jumped out at me on this reading. What is the connection between "native" and "citizen"?

Berry: That essay "A Native Hill" is an early one, written a long time ago, partly in the exhilaration of rediscovering my own part of the world, of seeing it with the change of vision that came with the feeling that I was going to live here, that I was here for life. It was an exhilaration sobered by the understanding that we had made historical blunders here that would have to be corrected. To live here responsibly meant that you had to accept responsibility for those blunders and errors and find, if you could, suitable remedies and corrections. So the word "citizen" occurs in that sentence because of its implications of responsibility. A citizen consciously assumes responsibilities that belong to the place, responding to the problems of the place.

Minick: I've always been troubled by neighbors who have claimed nativeness, rightly so in one way, with their families living in this one place for five generations. And yet I look at how they care for the land, and it is worse, or not any better, than most of the non-natives. That has always troubled me. The word "citizen" has to come in there to make any sense.

Berry: It has to come in there. Wes Jackson has a book titled *Becoming Native to This Place*. As he understands it, it's a very complex process, becoming consciously native. You ask where you are and how you should behave within the local circumstances and limits.

Minick: I've spent a lot of time this past year thinking about, and hacking at, non-native, invasive plants on our farm. Are there any parallels here between plants and people in regards to this word "native"?

Berry: Yes. Exotic weeds and pests are a side effect of long-distance travel and commerce. They are out of context and out of control, like European exploiters on the frontiers of North America. We came here as a sort of weed species, and we're not over it yet; in some respects we're weedier now than ever. Our advantage over the nodding thistles and Japanese beetles is that we can learn where we are and consciously adapt, if we are willing to do it.

Minick: So, do you think you can become native to a new place even though you were not born there?

Berry: Well, we had better. It can't be easy, but the stakes are pretty high.

Minick: Let me ask you a little bit about your relationship with Appalachia. In the Hindman [Settlement School] speech you said, "This part of the world [implying Appalachia] has been a peculiar kind of inspiration for me," and I'd like to hear you explain that.

Berry: Did I clarify that? (Laughter)

Minick: No, that's why I'm here. What's your connection to Appalachia?

Berry: Well, I live on a river that begins as an Appalachian river. Of course, every time I look at that river, I know where it comes from. So that's a fairly intimate connection. Living downstream from somebody is a predicament, and you would ask certain things of the upstream people if you had the power to do it. You would be interested in what they do with their sewage, and the way they manage their mountain sides, and so on.

I live downstream from a very large number of Kentuckians, a lot of people in Central Kentucky, and a lot in the mountains.

This is a river I have loved all my life. And I know that it's a badly mistreated river, and so to live here is to be always in the presence of a certain sense of grief and loss.

Minick: Any other connections to Appalachia?

Berry: Gurney Norman and I have been friends for most of our lives, and he has been my teacher and guide in the headwaters. His writings and conversation have been invaluable to me. We have traveled through the mountains together a good many times, looking and talking. Our conversation has lasted for many years and many miles.

I met James Still in (I think) 1954, and his work and his example have had a continuous influence on me. He was a nearly perfect writer, a master, who set a very high standard for us younger ones.

And in 1965 Gurney introduced me to Anne and Harry Caudill. I had read Harry's book *Night Comes to the Cumberlands* in 1963, after I had decided to return to Kentucky from New York, and it had affected me profoundly. That book gave me the sense of citizenship that I needed. Tanya and I have a big debt to the Caudills and we have remained friends.

I could say more about my connections to Appalachia, but maybe that's enough.

In justice, I ought to add that my father's example influenced me in much the same way as Harry Caudill's. Like Harry, my father went away, got a law degree and came back to his home community. My father spent his life working for the Burley Tobacco Growers Cooperative Association, among other things. He was a country lawyer and a farmer. He helped start that Co-op.

Minick: Does it still exist?

Berry: Yes, it has served the tobacco farmers in this part of the country well for 60 years.

Minick: How big was it, in terms of number of farmers?

Berry: At present the count is 88,000 tobacco farmers in Kentucky with an average farm size of 150 acres. The Co-op represents the burley tobacco farmers in Kentucky, Missouri, Indiana, Ohio, and West Virginia.

That Co-op has been a remarkable thing, considering the independence of farmers. It has been put to referendum over and over again, and it has been voted in overwhelmingly every time. It has been a model program, and a good example of a proper governmental service to agriculture. It's a no-net cost program. It hasn't cost the public anything because it combines price supports with production controls. The program hasn't encouraged surplus production.

Minick: The reason I'm asking about the Co-op is because I'm part of a group trying to form one. We're going to have a sustainable forestry, vertical business. We're all going to be Forest Stewardship Council (FSC) certified.
Berry: That's the right thing to do.

Minick: Our leader, Harry Groot, has been doing this for several years, so he has a mill, a drying kiln, and a moulder. We have roughly 10,000 acres, but if it's to succeed, we need five to ten times that as a business. That just daunts me.
Berry: The local food markets are facing the same question. If you're conceiving your co-op as a marketer of raw products into the global economy, then the question of large quantities is applicable, and probably means that you're going to fail. If you are talking about marketing your timber locally to local mills, builders, furniture makers, woodworking shops, and other local enterprises, then you're not limited by small acreages and you can go ahead.

If you're trying to market Kentucky-grown food to Kroger, you've got to have big, uniform quantities, and you are going to be competing with people in, say, California who are working with bigger volumes than you are, inevitably, and probably you're going to get beat. If you're talking about marketing to local shops, stores, restaurants, governmental institutions, and so on, then it's a different proposition.

Minick: I hesitate to ask you this, but how would you define "local," if you were to put a mileage on it? That's a hard question, I know.
Berry: This is a conversation we ought to have, but I don't know if we can have it here or not. Anybody's authority to talk on this subject is questionable. But mileage, the radius of the operation, is going to depend on the cost of hauling. If you can keep the product price depressed enough, you can haul farther. If the cost of fuel goes up, that's going to reduce the radius, and the cost of fuel is probably going to go up. So you have to think about that.

Maybe 30 years ago, we went to a farming conference in Keene, New Hampshire, and I talked at length to a fellow up there who was running his own forestry and logging operation. He had, as I remember, 2500 acres of forest in the hills, and his technology consisted of a portable sawmill and an 8N Ford tractor. He could be, at his scale, a very thorough marketer. He could sell short logs to build a table. To build furniture, you don't need a 16-foot log. He could sell firewood. He told me he once filled an order for

30 hornbeam logs. Somebody wanted them for some reason, and he went and got them. This is the kind of thing, he said, that he could do on his scale, that a big timber company couldn't possibly do. I think that's the way you've got to think about your co-op. And you've got to carry it out locally to finished products. Saw timber, firewood, birdhouses, grapevine wreaths, mushrooms, herbs, Adirondack chairs, cherry desks, corner cupboards—the whole range.

Have you ever visited the Menominee forest?

Minick: No, but I've read a little about it.

Berry: That's really something to see, and people in Appalachia ought to know about it. Your co-op people should send a delegate up there. That's an astonishing example. What they have been doing essentially is what Jason Rutledge [the Virginia forester and horse logger] calls "worst-first, single-tree selection" forestry. So you've got a given boundary of trees and you're logging it at frequent intervals. And it's doing nothing except growing more timber and getting better.

Then you go and look at one of those "laminated strand" factories, and the timber they're using looks like somebody's post pile or a pile of firewood.

In the laminated strand process, they shred the logs, which means they can use anything, trees of all sizes. Such a mill can be supplied by clear-cutting. So it can be a forest-eating monster. It can use all trees without any discrimination at all.

What you're doing [with the forestry co-op] is the right thing. It's an exciting thing to hear about, but the answer to competing in the global economy (which means you've got to undersell everybody else to survive, which means you probably won't) is to develop the local economy to its fullest. Fill the local demand out of the local woods and sell finished products.

Minick: I guess this has been a struggle I've had. One of the leaders sees making flooring out of the low-grade wood as the way to make money but also improve the forest. Making flooring requires substantial investment in machinery, and so I guess it's all about scale.

Berry: It's all about scale. You don't want to get onto that ladder that the farmers get on where they get a bigger tractor and then they've got to have more land, then they need a bigger tractor and then more land, and they can't find a place to stop. They fail to reach a balance point. First thing you know, they're bankrupt. You don't want to do that. That means you've got to solve the scale problem, which means you've got to practice thrift and frugality and accept limits. You've got 10,000 acres. If you get the scale wrong, the next thing you know, you'll be buying outside your boundaries, taking anything, or you'll be over-cutting your woods.

You've got to watch the emphasis on volume because the demand for volume drives you out of scale, destroys the effort of local adaptation, and costs you too much money. If you were a big corporation, it would be to your advantage to talk about big volume, big scale, and big equipment. But you're competing against the big corporations from at the bottom end of the ladder. You have to limit scale, control costs, and emphasize quality.

Minick: You praise the Amish in much of your work, and I grew up in Pennsylvania among Amish where I've witnessed their virtues and their problems. In one interview with Jack Jezreel, you said, "The Amish point the way, but there are certain questions that I don't think they've answered, which is inevitable." I was wondering what those questions are?
Berry: Well, they're dependent on us, on the "English" economy, for supplies of all kinds and for such things as long-distance transportation. They're marketing their stuff into our economy. Their communities would be different if our communities were different.

Minick: I know you're busy with traveling and all. Roughly how much of your own food are you able to grow?
Berry: We grow virtually all our vegetables, though we buy out-of-season vegetables sometimes. We buy a lot of fruit, coffee, and tea, such things as that. We're not fanatics.

We occasionally buy breakfast bacon if we can find it locally produced. We used to raise our own hogs and cure the meat, and we used to keep a milk cow or two, but we don't anymore. This operation has to be kept fairly simple for a lot of reasons, but we're still eating mostly our own meat. We grow a pretty good-sized garden, for a couple of old folks.

Minick: So, what's your view of the current organic movement, and which is more important in buying food, local or organic?
Berry: "Organic" has now become an official term, a label, and it doesn't necessarily imply good farming. If I have to choose, I prefer locally-grown to

organic. But a growing number of people want food they can trust to be free of poisonous chemicals, antibiotics, hormones, engineered genes, and so on. That demand is encouraging the production of such foods locally.

Minick: I want to ask you about Harlan Hubbard because one time I remember your writing about how you wanted Harlan to help protest the construction of a nuclear power plant.
Berry: Well, I didn't ask him to, but I wondered why he didn't.
Mrs. Berry: The power plant was going to be built right across the river from Harlan and Anna's.

Minick: And you got frustrated by that until you finally realized *his life* is a protest.
Berry: Yes.

Minick: So I was wondering how that has translated into your life now?
Berry: We're doing our best to lead a life of protest. But we have a lot more modern conveniences than the Hubbards did, and our lives are different from theirs. I'm leading a much more public life than Harlan did. We have children and grandchildren, and so ours is a different situation. Still, we try not to have things that we don't need. We don't have a tractor, we don't have a TV, we don't have a fax machine or a computer or an answering machine.
Mrs. Berry: We're awfully behind on things like movies.
Berry: I mostly avoid screens. You can't keep children from seeing TV, but you can keep them from seeing it at home. And it's possible for children to discover they can be happy without it.

Minick: So, what's your opinion of the American Dream? Barry Lopez calls it a nightmare; do you agree? What might a new American Dream look like?
Berry: Obviously there always have been several American Dreams. Some people's American Dreams have become nightmares for other people. I think one's "dream" ought to be limited to what one's place can sustain indefinitely and by the requirements of stewardship and neighborliness.

Minick: Back to the Prairie Festival in 1996, I think it was Don Worster who gave a provocative speech about land ownership, if I remember right, basically saying that our current system is not working. A private land ownership is defunct and outdated and not working. I'd like to hear your opinion on that.

Berry: Because some people have been unwilling to give up the frontier spirit of really stubborn individualism, they've clung to the idea of absolute ownership. I don't remember exactly what Don was saying about it that day, but the idea of absolute ownership is fraudulent. It's fraudulent if you measure it by the religious traditions. The Bible says the earth is the Lord's, and the deed has *never* been transferred to any of us. It's fraudulent by the laws of ecology too.

On the other hand, all creatures are territorial. Even the most far-flying sea birds have their own nesting places that belong to them in a sense, that they come back to, and think of as home. You need some means in the law to safeguard the sense of belonging, of being at home, and to grant people certain privileges, certain rights of self-determination, within their homelands. But the culture also needs to instruct people that they are not the absolute owners of anything, not even of themselves. The Indians, or some of them at least, had the idea that you have to hold yourself responsible to the seventh generation of your descendants. Well, it was once easier to imagine the seventh generation of your descendants than it is now, but it's never been possible to *know* the seventh generation. What that requirement does is put you under the pressure and even the guidance of a mystery. You don't know what's going to happen, but you have to hold yourself responsible to the possibility that the human race will survive and will need the things you have.

Minick: So, to take that a step further, when that cultural means breaks down, which it has, how much should the government play a role in protecting the land?

Berry: The government ought to prevent people from destroying things outright. It's so obviously a question that the government needs to ask: what right does a mere person have to destroy forever a mountain or a watershed? And the government isn't asking that question. What right do we have to burn up all the oil and all the coal in, really, a very short time? Wes Jackson is saying that this is the "prodigal" era of our history. He means it's the era when we squander our birthright, the era in which we use up most of the fossil fuel and most of the soil.

There's such a thing as a principle of return. That you're a living creature implies that you have a right to take from the world what you need to maintain yourself, to live and go on. The compensating principle is the principle of return. You must take but you also must give back, so that the cycle completes itself over and over again. The Wheel of Life—of birth, growth, maturity, death, and decay—must turn, and it must turn in place.

Minick: I ask about the government's role because, are you familiar with the CREP program, the Conservation Reserve Program, which pays farmers to fence out streams? We just signed up for it, and yet my neighbors say cows have always pissed in the streams.
Berry: Well, they have. The buffaloes pissed in the streams before the cows. But the proper question is how often they do it and how many do it at the same time.

Minick: It goes back to being a citizen, the native and the citizen, doesn't it?
Berry: It does. There are lots of questions governing decisions like this. I'm quite sure that the government is not asking them all. A lot of it has to do with climate. How long, in this place, does it take for a trampled patch of ground to restore itself? How often does the disturbance occur? What are the numbers involved and so on? There are ranchers out West who are thinking well about these problems.

I can't fence my stream banks because of flooding, but I have dropped back from the edges. For the last two years when I've mowed my creek bottoms, I've dropped back 50 or 100 feet; it varies from place to place. I'm not sure what I'm doing. I'm not sure that by mowing them I wouldn't improve the quality of the sod. I am not seeing, because those bottoms are pastured, any significant growth of tree seedlings. I'll know what I'm doing in ten years, maybe, if I last that long. It interested me to do it. I knew the principle, so I thought I would try it.

The principle is the same wherever you're working—in pasture or field or forest. You need to use the place, but you need also to keep it healthy, keep it ecologically intact, while you use it. My friend Troy Firth says that a bad logger is thinking only of what he can get out of the forest, whereas a good logger is thinking of what will be left. So the principle is that you take out what the forest can produce and still remain a forest. The Menominee Reservation is obviously an intact forest ecosystem. There are ancient trees in it. North of there, where the forest was extractively logged, taking everything, you find a forest ecosystem that was destroyed 100 years ago, and it's still destroyed.

It just drives me nuts that in all the talk about eastern Kentucky, or the Appalachian mountains, nobody is willing to come out and say, "Look, it's the forest or nothing!" If you neglect the forest, then all you have left is these bastards who will move industry into the region to exploit the people as cheap labor.

Berry excused himself from the kitchen table to change in to his farm boots. I walked with him outside, and twice he told me, "I really want this to be good. I want to do right by this for my friends in eastern Kentucky."

The older dog already waited in the back of the truck, eyes focused on Berry, knowing that it could ride along to tend the other animals. But the younger dog, Maggie, wasn't here. "Wonder where she is?" Berry asked. He cupped his hands to his mouth and hollered, "MAGGIE," the second syllable ascending. The shout hit the hillside and came back to us. Soon the black and white pup scurried under the fence and hopped in the back of the pickup.

Berry headed out to feed his lambs.

Heaven in Henry County:
A *Sojourners* Interview with
Wendell Berry

Rose Marie Berger / 2004

From *Sojourners* 33.7 (July 2004). The following text is an expanded version from *Sojourners Online*. Reprinted with permission from *Sojourners*. 1-800-714-7474. www.sojo.net. All rights reserved.

Sojourners associate editor Rose Marie Berger and photographer Ryan Beiler spent a Sunday afternoon in February with Wendell Berry at his farm in Henry County, Kentucky. Berry is the author of more than forty books of fiction, poetry, and essays, including *The Unsettling of America*, *What Are People For?*, *Life Is a Miracle*, *Citizenship Papers*, and *The Art of the Commonplace*. He has farmed in a traditional manner for nearly forty years. Berry spoke with *Sojourners* about religious practice, Bluegrass country, defending against Wal-Mart, usury, and Jesus.

Berger: Tell me about this land, about this bioregion, about the history of your farm.

Berry: We're on the west side of the Kentucky River, in the Kentucky River Valley. Some people call this the Outer Bluegrass; there are other names for it. We have limestone soils. An old ocean or sea laid down these layers of limestone. There are lots of trees here. There are white, chinquapin, red, black, and shumard oaks. Those are the principle ones. And we have two or three kinds of ash, maples, several varieties of hickory, black walnut, sycamore, black locust, honey locust, cedar, basswood, red elm, slippery elm. We used to have chestnuts once. Tanya and I have 125 acres altogether, 75 here and about 50 on Cane Run.

This place where we're sitting today is the old property known as Lanes Landing. Twelve acres, more or less, the deed says. Tanya and I bought it in 1964 and moved in the next year. So we've been here thirty-nine years.

My mother was raised in Port Royal. And her father's land borders this. My father was born and grew up on a farm just the other side of Lacie. My brother lives there now.

This is tobacco country. We've lost two-thirds of the allotment in the last few years, courtesy of the global economy. Not the anti-smoking people. This is traditionally a mixed farming country. Tobacco was the staple crop, but we also grew corn and small grains. The small grains were grown as cover crops on the tobacco and corn ground.

The farms were around a hundred acres when I was a boy, on the average; they're about 150 on the average now. But the farming that was done here when I first knew it, in the 1940s and '50s, at its best, was very good farming. In addition to the crops I named, we raised cattle, sheep, and hogs, sometimes all three on the same farm. And every farm had a kitchen garden, a flock of chickens, meat hogs, and at least enough cows to supply the household with milk.

Berger: You really had a working, home economy. How does the local tobacco economics fit with the global economics? How has that shift from local to global been experienced here?

Berry: Tobacco acreages have declined here because the companies can fill their needs more cheaply elsewhere. The other products we grow are thrown into the world market to compete as best they can. With the help of subsidies, of course. In Kentucky we have always raised for export. One of this state's problems is that it hasn't added value to its agricultural products. I would say we are adding less now than ever. Louisville used to have two or three packing plants, for instance, and a stockyard. But no more. Most of the things that are produced in this state are shipped out, to have the value added elsewhere.

When you take away the subsistence economy, then your farm population is seriously exposed to the vagaries of the larger economy. As it used to be, the subsistence economy carried people through the hard times, and what you might call the housewife's economy of cream and eggs often held these farms and their families together. The wives would go to town with eggs and cream once a week, buy groceries with the proceeds, and sometimes come home with money. Or they'd sell a few old hens, that sort of thing. So that's the first lesson to learn about agriculture, as far as I'm concerned: it needs a sound subsistence basis. People need to feed themselves; next they need to feed their own communities. That's what we're working for now. We want to develop a local food economy that local producers will supply and that the local consumers will support. It's ridiculous that we should be importing food into this state while our farmers are suffering.

Berger: What are the models that are being used here in Kentucky to resist the economic pressure from the larger market?
Berry: Community-supported agriculture, farmer's markets, direct marketing of meat, that sort of thing. There's an effort under way to develop a retail market for local produce. But this is hard to bring about.

The local landscape used to contribute food to Louisville. There was a significant amount of truck farming going in those days. That's gone. The stockyard's gone, the packinghouses are gone. So there's Louisville economically and culturally isolated from its rich agricultural landscape. Which is ridiculous.

Berger: It's almost a process of reweaving the city life with its agricultural counterpart—its breadbasket.
Berry: That's right—building commercial linkages between the city and its local countryside. And there are good reasons to do that. You've got the prospect, to begin with, of better, fresher food. You've got the possibility that consumers could influence production.

You have the possibility that urban consumers, by fulfilling their responsibility to local producers, can make secure their local food supply in the face of various threats. The paramount one, now on everybody's mind, is terrorism, but there are also the threats of epidemic and disease. In other words, the influence of local consumers could work, not only to maintain farming in the local landscape, but also to diversify it. And American agriculture is badly in need of diversity. Another threat to the present food system, of course, is the likelihood that petroleum is not going to get any cheaper.

Berger: That happened in Venezuela a few years ago. They had an oil producer's strike and people lost their gasoline supply. As a result they couldn't truck food anywhere. Whole communities were starving because they couldn't get access to food in stores, and they didn't have any capacity to feed themselves.

Berry: What could be more terrible? There are lots of bad things that can happen to a food economy that's both extensive and centralized. There's no substitute for petroleum. And from what I read, the curve of discovery and production of petroleum is about to decline. To have a growth economy based on a declining fuel supply is bound to be stressful.

Berger: In *Life Is a Miracle*, you talk about cloning and genetic engineering. Genetically modified organisms are being promoted by agribusiness as "a way to feed the poor people of the world." What kind of ethical values should we be operating under when we think about cloning, GMO, and genetic engineering?

Berry: The first ethical requirement is a decent suspicion of the claims of people who have something to sell. I'm not reading anything that suggests that genetic engineering is increasing production. Some recent things I've read suggest that productivity of Roundup Ready soybeans is less than that of other varieties.

I think that the real reason for genetic engineering is to put absolute control of the food system into corporate hands. They don't want anybody— farmer or urban consumer or anybody else—to have anything whatsoever that they don't buy from a corporation at the corporation's price. In other words, economic totalitarianism is the goal. And I don't think the difference between political totalitarianism and economic totalitarianism is worth lingering over. If you're not economically free, if you don't have economic choices, you're not free.

Berger: Your collection of essays, *Citizenship Papers*, has been published recently and you wrote an amazing set of articles for *Orion* about the national security agenda. As I read through sections of the Patriot Act, I was reminded of an old poem of yours titled "Do Not Be Ashamed." It says, "Though you have done nothing shameful, / they will want you to be ashamed. / They will want you to kneel and weep / and say you should have been like them."

Berry: Well it's sort of normal to wish that things like that would not be applicable any longer and it's discouraging to see that they stay current. You wish that a book like *The Unsettling of America* would become obsolete, but it's more relevant now than it ever was. I don't think that national security can be achieved the way we're trying to achieve it. I don't think that being the strongest country in the world can necessarily make us the most secure country. And the fact remains that we're destroying our country ourselves.

It's easy to get the idea that we're stationing troops all over the world to protect our right to destroy our own country. I think that if you were seriously interested in security, you would make the country secure in its regions. You'd make it possible for the people to eat with far less public transportation. To do that you'd have to think in a different way. And we've got to face the likelihood that the people in charge are simply not capable of thinking that way. They've never thought in that way. Their doctrine is maximum force relentlessly applied. That's the doctrine of war. But it's also the doctrine of industrial agriculture. It's the way the industrial system works.

Look at the way we mine coal, for instance. Look at the way we're logging the forests. These are not sustainable procedures. They're not even conservative procedures. Wes Jackson has started calling this the "Prodigal Era." By that he means the era in which we're going to use up most of the topsoil and most of the fossil fuels.

Berger: It seems like it always comes back eventually to the individual's choice. Does one choose to live in an economy of grace, based on generosity, or in an economy of scarcity based on acquisition?
Berry: You have to realize that people are working very hard to remove that choice, to make it impossible to make such a choice. And they can do that simply by putting the land entirely under corporate control. It can happen. We're pretty well advanced into a corporate or capitalist totalitarianism. And it's a very strange thing to see happen, because we were lately so much afraid of communist totalitarianism. You can remove that choice we were talking about simply by making it impossible for small economic enterprises to survive.

You can use Wal-Mart as a weapon, for instance, to destroy the economic centers of small towns and small cities.

Berger: The method of disarming such a weapon is carving out a local economy, a local space, and defending it?
Berry: You've got to defend it; you've got to defend it economically. You've got to have some kind of fidelity between consumers and producers. The great corporations can use volume discounts to make it impossible for anybody else to be in business. And they are doing that.

Berger: And you have that partnership of slightly increased unemployment—no benefits, poor wages—so it's a push and a pull. People are pushed into the arms of Wal-Mart and Wal-Mart is pulling them with cheap products produced in labor conditions that are exploitative.

Berry: Healthcare and health insurance are so expensive that almost nobody can afford them. Most people can't.

Berger: How do you see that playing out in terms of the rural poverty here?

Berry: Rural poverty happens because people aren't being paid to take adequate care of their places. There's lots of work to do here. And you can't afford to pay anybody to do it! If you depress the price of the products of the place below a certain level, people can't afford to maintain it. And that's the rural dilemma we're in now. But you've got to see the connection between the poverty of the people and the impoverishment of the place. If you buy the products, and you don't give an adequate payment in money, then that means that the producer doesn't give adequate care.

The worst example of rural poverty we have right here is that of migrant farm workers. Well, they're "temporary workers," is the way to put that. They have no permanent jobs, so they have no equity in the places where they work. They're not shareholders, let alone entrepreneurs. They're not small farmers, they're not market gardeners, they're just temporary—uprooted, isolated, easily exploitable people.

Berger: One ends up lacking affection. The migrant workers perhaps don't have a particular affection for the place other than just the work and the money, and the place and the people and economy never develops an investment in them because they're on their way out.

Berry: That's right. Because they're temporary and replaceable. They're more readily replaceable than the slaves were. Also in Kentucky some corporations, Fruit of the Loom, for instance, have just left for places that are more exploitable than Kentucky. And then we have, west of here, the hog and chicken factories. That's another story of corporate abuse of places and people.

Berger: This organic mechanism of resistance is trying to establish a community/regional area and beginning to develop alternative models of connection between the producer and the consumer, and begin to create some trading zones that are micro-trading zones.

Berry: Yes. You can hope only to take it back a little at a time. There is no master plan. And I would be very suspicious of a master plan if I knew of one. It's got to happen a little at a time. You've got to confront the very difficult economic problem of making a local supply and a local demand come into existence simultaneously. I don't know that that's ever been done before in the way we will have to do it. And nobody knows how well it's going to succeed. But there are hopeful signs. It would be no trouble to take you and show you things that are working, but there are not enough of them yet.

Berger: I want to ask you also about Harlan and Anna Hubbard, about the influence they've had on your life. And also the tension between the nomadic, pilgrim experiment that they launched off into versus rootedness, staying in one place, making a deep commitment to a particular area.

Berry: Well, Harlan and Anna Hubbard were a married couple who began their life together by building a shanty boat and making a sort of epic drift down the rivers from Brent, Kentucky, above Cincinnati, to New Orleans and then on out into the bayous. In the early fifties, that journey having completed itself, they returned to Kentucky and bought a remote property, known as Payne Hollow, on the Ohio River in Trimble County. They built a house there and remained there, living mostly from their land and the river until they died.

They were musicians; they played duets every day of their life together. They played Mozart, Brahms, and Bach, those people. Harlan made prints, drawings, oils, and watercolors. And he was a writer. He published in his lifetime two wonderful books, one called *Shantyboat* that was an account of their trip down the rivers, and another called *Payne Hollow*, which is a distillation of their life at Payne Hollow. Their life was exemplary in a lot of ways. They did little harm. They lived abundantly, by their own efforts, and with a very small expenditure of money. In their frugal life they experienced much joy and made much beauty. They were teachers to a lot of people, and I'm one of them.

Berger: How did you come to meet them, originally?

Berry: By accident. A friend and I were on a canoe trip. We stopped there to see if we could get some drinkable water. We had replenished our water supply with the city water of Madison, Indiana, and we were finding it hard to swallow.

Berger: I've gone back and looked again at some of the ways that Harlan engaged his spirituality or religion, his reading of the Bible, and how at one point I think he said something about how he experiences the Bible not as revelation but as confirmation, and that he comes to these lessons in his life, and is sometimes surprised that the Bible also has come to those lessons. And I find that sort of engagement with Christianity very appealing in the sense that it feels very authentic, and lets the faith be a humanizing faith.

Berry: I think Harlan was a man with a very strong religious impulse, or religious nature. But I don't think the formal religions, the churches of this area, had much to offer him. It's hard to nail Harlan's religion down very firmly. I did the best I could in a chapter of my little book about Harlan and his work.

Thinking about Harlan as a religious man is quite different from thinking about, say, Thomas Merton as a religious man, because there's not a body of doctrine that Harlan subscribed to. He didn't endorse any creed. He was a man at large with his faculties and his gifts and his inspiration, his great relish of life and of his world, which he said was "heaven." You look to see what Harlan painted when he was "painting heaven" and you see landscapes of northern Kentucky and Payne Hollow.

Berger: What was your connection with Thomas Merton, the Trappist monk who lived here in Kentucky?

Berry: My connection with him was the photographer Ralph Eugene Meatyard, who has grown steadily in reputation since he died. Thomas Merton was interested in photography, and I guess that led him to Gene, who was no more conventionally religious than Harlan Hubbard. Gene was a wizard. He had an incredible gift of seeing and of picture-making. But let's don't say "incredible." It was perfectly credible when you saw what he could do. He had a very great gift. Merton could see that, and he made a friend of Gene. Gene and his wife Madelyn took Tanya and me down there twice.

Merton was a man who understood how to be a companion. He had a lot of humor, and I think he knew something about how to be happy or how to enjoy happiness when he had it. I liked him tremendously. He had a very lively countenance; a very bright, curious, amused eye.

When we went down there the first time, he just dropped it out casually, and I think with great secret amusement, that he was thinking about joining an Indian tribe. I think Merton was a profound Christian. Some people seem to think that when he went East he was abandoning his faith or his vocation.

I don't think he was at all. His talks to religious groups in Alaska (*Thomas Merton in Alaska*) on that last trip were wonderful.

Berger: He just seemed to be moving deeper and deeper, which in some ways made it easier to connect across a variety of spiritual expressions.
Berry: He had, I think, a very fortunate impulse to reach out to other religions. And we need to pay attention to that, because there are people now who would carry us right into a religious war. That's a big problem, I think.

Berger: The end of Christendom.
Berry: Well, Christendom is all right, but it doesn't have to exclude everybody else. It doesn't have to go to war against them. And it doesn't have to be so stupid as to condemn other faiths that it doesn't know anything about.

Berger: One of the lines in *Life Is a Miracle* says, "It's impossible to prefigure the salvation of the world in the same language by which the world has been dismembered and defaced." It's a brilliant line!
Berry: You've got to reach towards a better language, and you're not going to make it up from scratch; you've got to reach back into the tradition. Western tradition is not as impoverished as a lot of people would like to think, but you'd have to go back before the industrial revolution; you may have to go back farther than that. Of course, the Bible has a perfectly adequate language, but it's suffered a lot of thoughtless wear.

Berger: Some of the work being done, more by poets rather than theologians, in reclaiming the roots of biblical language—digging in for what almost intuitively or artistically makes sense rather than the science of translation—seems to bring life back.
Berry: If you're a writer and you are at all inclined to speak as a Christian in some way, you realize very quickly that the conventional language is pretty much useless. It takes a long time to get past that, or it has taken me a long time. People in conventional Christianity have spoken lightly and sometimes frivolously of God for a long time. It's a word that needs to be used sparingly, in my opinion.

Any religion has to have a practice. When you let it go so far from practice that it just becomes a matter of talk something bad happens. If you don't have an economic practice, you don't have a practice. Christians conventionally think they've done enough when they've gone to the store and shopped. But that isn't an economic life. It isn't an economic practice. If you take seriously those passages in the scripture that say that we live by God's spirit and his breath, that we live, move, and have our being in God, the implications for the present economy are just devastating. Those passages call for an entirely generous and careful economic life.

Berger: There are a number of explorations and economic models in the scriptures, in terms of the Sabbath economics, jubilee economics, but there's not enough experimenting among Christians or people of faith with alternative models of economics.

Berry: There's a fairly explicit attempt back there in the early books of the Old Testament to see that property doesn't accumulate into too few hands. There's a real attempt at economic democracy. The idea of the Jubilee year is a deliberate affront to what we now call capitalism. There's a lot that's been said, not just in the Bible, but in the biblical tradition in literature, on the subject of usury. Dante was pretty explicit about it. It would put you in hell because it implied, among other things, a contempt for nature. It's an attempt to go around the natural world and human work and make money grow out of itself. It's an attempt to make value grow in the abstract, without work, without a real product. As lots of people have said, this goes against the real economy of the world. Ezra Pound has a great canto on usury, two of them as a matter of fact. "With usura hath no man a house of good stone." Nobody can have good things when you let money become its own value.

Berger: As the epigraph to *Citizenship Papers* you quote 2 Peter 2:3, "And through covetousness shall they with feigned words make merchandise of you." I don't know that I have ever heard that phrase in this context. Suddenly it becomes revolutionary.

Berry: Yes. The gospels, and sometimes the epistles, are pretty revolutionary. They propose a revolution of about 180 degrees.

One of the popular versions of the Bible has in the back an index of great stories and great chapters, and not one of them from the gospels.

But Christ was quite explicit, for instance, about his pacifism. You can't be more explicit than "Love your enemies." He did run those people out of the temple, but he didn't kill them.

People are always talking about the first church. The real first church was that gaggle of people who followed Jesus around. We don't know anything about them. But he apparently didn't ask them what creed they subscribed to, or what their sexual preference was, or any of that. He fed them. He healed them. He forgave them. He is clear about sin, but he was also for forgiveness.

Berger: Well there's so much in that way of engaging people—and the sin and forgiveness model's a good one—that is all about promoting life and opening up possibilities for life. It's never about shutting life down, closing people off, stopping them in their tracks. It's about opening up possibilities for people.

Berry: That's right. That's right. A completely decent and authentic way of putting it, I think.

Berger: Of all your writing, *Life Is a Miracle* is the one that I think is the most brilliant because it calls into question the entire myth of progress.

Berry: You know, it helps an old man to hear that!

Berger: There are not enough people who are asking questions about the post-Enlightenment era, and the myth of progress and where it's taking us. Even our contemporary Christian mindset is just built on this myth that the world just keeps getting better and that the past was worse than the present.

Berry: It gets taken for granted, that's why it's so easy to attack. People are handing out this stuff without thinking about it.

Berger: How is that myth of progress operating on us as people, and what are the reasons for calling it into question, or subverting it?

Berry: Well, that's two questions, isn't it? How does it operate on us? It substitutes this infinite advance toward better and better life in the material sense for the old pilgrimage, which you make by effort and grace, to become a better person. And I guess that's the reason you need to subvert it if you can. It takes people's minds off the important things. It becomes, at it's worst, a kind of determinism: all we have to do is just passively go along and things will get better and better, and we'll be happier and happier. That's why we need honest accounting.

I think all the time about the medical industry's emphasis on longevity. It's a substitution of quantity for any idea of completeness or wholeness or any sense of real fulfillment or real worth, so that you prolong life past the time where it's worth living, and then you brag about it. Without any acknowledgment of the possibility that somebody's life might become a burden, or that some things are worse than death.

Berger: Death becomes simply an inconvenience to be shuddered away.
Berry: As if it might not at some point be a great relief. As if it might not be a blessed deliverance.

All the questions about progress reduce to the question of what your measures are. And what is the measure of progress? It is possible to measure the progress of the last two or three hundred years in soil erosion. We can measure it in the rate of species extinction. We can measure it in pollution, in the toxicity of the world. Those things, like power and speed, are perfectly measurable.

But we need also to raise the questions that are not quantitative. How happy are people? What do we make of all this complaining? How healthy are people? How are love and beauty faring? What do we make of all this doctoring and medication that's going on all the time at such a great expense? That's not to deny that this so-called progress has given us things that are worth having. A hot bath every night is a good thing. I affirm that it is good, and wish to record my gratitude. There are other good things, but real harms also have been done.

Beth Newberry: How does your identity as a writer connect to a region, a place, and a land?
Berry: Well, I was born here, not in this house, but in this county. I grew up in these little towns, and in the countryside, on the farms. All my early memories are here. All the voices that surrounded me from the time I became able to hear were from here. Tanya and I came back here in 1964 and have lived here for 39 years, raised our children here. How could you draw a line separating this place and my identity? If you've known these places from your early youth, that means that you have a chance to know them in a way that other people never will.

I think often of the importance of a language spoken by people who are really local, who really know where they are and have lived there a long time; that language has a particularity about it that no language of bureaucracy or government or the university can ever have. It has a designating power that's utterly precise. Knowing the landscape in common and knowing it intimately, minutely, that has to be the basis of a language. That's where it starts, and you can raise it up from there, in successive levels of abstraction. But if you lose that power to particularize and designate precisely, in some sense you don't have a language anymore. So having a common tongue can mean that at one level you have the dictionary in common, you have the English vocabulary. But to have a common tongue in the sense that you can speak in detail, knowledgeably and responsibly, about a well-known place, a well-known ecosystem and a well-known human community, is quite another thing.

Berger: Is there a tension between self-sufficient communities and balkanism? Is there a danger of isolation in developing sustainable communities? If a community withdraws into itself so much, or becomes removed from a larger system of relationship, is there a danger of setting up enemy tensions between communities? Prejudice?

Berry: I'll honor the question if you will acknowledge that this can happen in cities as well as in the country. People are always saying that these terrible things happen in little towns and rural communities, but of course they happen in cities just as readily, and for the same reasons. I suppose the direct way to deal with this is to point out that no community is or ever can be entirely self-sufficient. It's dependent on other communities, not only for supplies, but also for conversation and goodwill.

We're a pretty bad species in a lot of ways and in other ways a pretty good one. We can become a warrior civilization and live by piracy; on the other hand, we're capable of lovingkindness, of genuine affection, of generosity, of friendship, of peaceability, of forgiveness and gratitude. It's a question of where you want to put your influence, how you want to apply the little means that you have. It's too easy to say that country people are provincial and prejudiced, as if the worst things that humans are capable of hadn't also risen up in cosmopolitan, highly sophisticated, urban civilizations. That's just a passing of blame. If you can blame it all on people out in the provinces then you don't have to worry about what's going on in your urban neighborhood or in your urban soul.

One of the oldest human artifacts is the trade route. People were trading in obsidian and other rare things long before history. So we know there's going to be trade, we know that you can't isolate a culture and keep it going without cultural interchange. You can't live without influence, you can't live without change, you can't live without trade.

The serious question is whether you're going to become a warrior community and live by piracy, by taking what you need from other people. I think the only antidote to that is imagination. You have to develop your imagination to the point that permits sympathy to happen. You have to be able to imagine lives that are not yours or the lives of your loved ones or the lives of your neighbors. You have to have at least enough imagination to understand that if you want the benefits of compassion, you must be compassionate. If you want forgiveness you must be forgiving. It's a difficult business, being human.

The Short Answer: An Exchange with Wendell Berry
Preservation / 2005

From *Preservation* 57.2 (March/April 2005), 49. Reprinted with permission from *Preservation*, the magazine of the National Trust for Historic Preservation.

Q: You often write and speak of "community." What is it?
A: A community—a real community—would be a place and all of its native or benevolently naturalized inhabitants. The human part of it would be responsibly conscious of the having-in-common of which the community is composed.

Q: Are community and "place" the same? Must community have a geographic location?
A: Yes. Otherwise the word becomes merely a figure of speech. "Networks" or professions, for example, are often called communities, but they are only metaphorically so.

Q: Do we have to be rooted in a place in order to preserve it?
A: No, but we need to have settled into it conscientiously as our permanent home. We have to give up the idea of going to "a better place" or of "going west" to escape our troubles or messes.

Q: Much effort has been invested by many in preserving rural America. Where are we?
A: We're still losing. We have made it almost impossible, economically, to preserve good farmland, good farming, or even good farmers—although we don't know, we haven't asked, how we will survive for long without them.

Q: Is the historic preservation movement helping to save what you call the "economic landscapes" of farms and other cultural aspects of the land?

A: It is not helping enough. No movement is helping enough. This is because the present economy is inherently destructive of land and other necessities. The way to save farmland is by farming it well. To do this, it is necessary to save farmers who know how to farm well.

Q: But in today's economic situation, can these still be small farmers?
A: Yes. If the necessary markets and other economic supports are in place. There are prosperous Amish farms of 100 acres or less. A few acres of vegetables can provide a decent income, given a decent market.

Q: What role do communities in cities have in helping rural communities?
A: Urban communities eat. Rural communities produce food. The present economy throws these communities into competition with one another—as if "cheap food" at any human or ecological cost is a triumph of capitalism. But there is no correlation between the cheapness of food and either quality or sustainability. If we're interested in quality and sustainability, then we have to think of local food economies based on cooperation between consumers and producers.

Q: Does volunteerism still work in rural areas, or anywhere?
A: Volunteerism, as I understand it, is a way of compensating for economic or social failure. If you have an economy that impoverishes land and people, as now, then decency will try to compensate by various kinds of volunteerism. But the only effective answer to economic destructiveness is a better economy—an economy that takes proper care of things, as an economy is supposed to do.

The idea of the current crop of "conservatives"—that government can cater to greed and leave charity to volunteers—is vicious, and it can't work. The "liberal" idea—that the failures of a greedy and wasteful economy can be effectively patched by government services and regulations—is also hopeless. There is no way to get a good result from an economy that institutionalizes greed as an honorable motive and excuses waste and destruction as "acceptable costs."

Q: What should government's role be, in rural areas and cities, in building community?
A: To do for the people what the people can't do for themselves. The people, either as individuals or as local communities, for instance, can't protect

themselves against trusts and monopolies. They can't stop the likes of Wal-Mart from destroying locally owned small businesses. Such destruction damages the economic life and health of the country as a whole; it weakens the country, and the government should not allow it. As another example, the government can ensure a decent income to farmers at little cost by means of price supports *with production controls*—as in fact it did under the New Deal. The government, in short, has the power to see that the economy fulfills its proper function: to take good care of things; to put things, including land and people, to the best possible use.

Q: Ours is a culture preoccupied with growth, both economic and physical. Is it possible to not grow, yet not die?
A: Creatures who grow beyond the carrying capacity of their habitats will die. So the right question is: will we restrain ourselves, or will we die?

How Can a Family "Live at the Center of Its Own Attention"? An Interview with Wendell Berry

Holly M. Brockman / 2005

From *New Southerner* 2.1 (January/February 2006). Reprinted by permission of Holly M. Brockman.

Holly M. Brockman: I've heard you use the term "useful" in some of your talks, and it certainly permeates all your essays and other writing. What does usefulness mean? Who is somebody who is useful and why?

Wendell Berry: There's a kind of language that obscures its subject. Such language makes it harder to see and to think. By the word usefulness I mean language or work that enables seeing, makes clarity. Wes Jackson's work and language have been wonderfully useful to me in that way. Harry Caudill too, by his books and his conversation, helped me to see and think and make the radical criticism. Gary Snyder and I agree on a lot of things, but his point of view is different from mine and it has been immensely useful to me. Some differences make for binocular vision.

HB: And what does it mean in the context of human daily living and beyond? Let's say into the corporate world?

WB: Usefulness stands in opposition to the frivolous. John Synge wrote about the Aran Islands where the people were poor and yet all the useful things in their life were beautiful. The issue of usefulness has a kind of cleansing force. If you ask, "Is it useful?" probably you're going to have fewer things you don't need. You are useful to your family if you're bringing home the things they need. Beyond that, maybe you are useful to other people by your work. The corporate world is much inclined to obscure this usefulness by making and selling a lot of things that people don't need. For instance, a lively and important question is how much light we use at night and what we use it for and need it for. I'm old enough to remember when the whole

181

countryside was dark at night except for the lights inside the houses, and now the countryside at night is just strewn with these so-called security lights. How much of this do we need? How much of it is useful? We have a market-place that is full of useless or unnecessary commodities. I don't want to be too much of a crank, but there are many things that people own to no real benefit, such as computer games and sometimes even computers.

HB: How does your notion of usefulness differ from the old Protestant work ethic?
WB: The Protestant work ethic has never been very discriminating about kinds or qualities of work or even the usefulness of work. To raise the issue of usefulness is to call for some means or standard of discrimination. The Protestant work ethic doesn't worry about the possibility of doing harmful work or useless work.

HB: In order to be better stewards of our own lives and therefore those resources around us—land, soil, each other—how do we work toward a more sustainable, community-oriented life?
WB: I think you have to begin with an honest assessment of the value or the possibility of personal independence. What is the limit of individualism or personal autonomy? Once you confess to yourself that you need other peo-ple, then you're in a position to look around your neighborhood and see how neighborly it is, starting with how neighborly you are yourself. The question of stewardship naturally follows. How careful is your neighborhood of the natural gifts such as the topsoil on which it depends.

HB: Large chunks of what used to be taken care of by family members—caring for children, the elderly, and education—has been outsourced to cor-porations in the form of daycare, preschool, and corporate sponsorship of education initiatives. You've written extensively about this and that these are signs of familial breakdown. Why is it a breakdown and what impact does it have on a family?
WB: The issue here is the extent to which a family is like a community in its need to live at the center of its own attention. A family necessarily begins to come apart if it gives its children entirely to the care of the school or the police, and its old people entirely to the care of the health industry. Nobody can deny the value of good care even away from home to people who have

become helplessly ill or crippled, or, in our present circumstances, the value of good daytime care for the children of single parents who have to work. Nevertheless, it is the purpose of the family to stay together. And like a community, a family doesn't stay together just out of sentiment. It is certainly more apt to stay together if the various members need one another or are in some practical way dependent on one another. It's probably worth the risk to say that families need to have useful work for their children and old people, little jobs that the other members are glad to have done.

HB: What are some things we can do—small things, perhaps—until we actually make a commitment on a broader scale, to initiate husbandry (whose trajectory will be felt globally) to ourselves, our families, and our communities?

WB: I think this starts with an attempt at criticism of one's own economy, which may be the same thing as good accounting. What are the things that one buys? How necessary or useful are they? What is their quality? Are they well grown or well made? What is their real cost to their producers and to the ecosystems in which they were produced? Almost inevitably when one asks these questions, one discovers that they are extremely difficult and sometimes impossible to answer. That frequently is because the things we buy have been produced so far away as to make impossible any stewardly interest on the part of the consumer. And this recognition leads to an even better question: how can these mysterious products brought here from so far away be replaced by products that have been produced near home? And that question, of course, leads to all manner of thoughts and questions about the possibility of a better, more self-sufficient local economy. What can we neighbors do for one another and for our place? What can our place do for us without damage to us or to it?

HB: Is it possible to reshape our thinking in baby steps or must we make sweeping changes?

WB: Oh, let's be against sweeping changes and in favor of doing things in small steps. Let's not discourage ourselves by trying for too much or subject ourselves to the tyranny of somebody else's big idea.

HB: If everything is left to the individual and the community, how can each avoid being so overburdened that no one has much time for activism and intellectual pursuit?

WB: In other words, how can you have a livable life and do everything? Everything ought not to be left to individuals and communities. Government exists to do for people what they can't do for themselves. Farmers individually or in their communities, for instance, can't enact effective programs for price supports with production control so a government can do that, and at one time our federal government did do that. Maybe I'd better say at this point that I am an unabashed admirer of the tobacco program of the New Deal.

HB: Many progressives live transitive lives (you included, having spent time in New York, California, and abroad) having fled small towns for the more intellectually stimulating environment or a college town. How do we close that gap and encourage progressives and intellectuals to find safety and comfort outside an academic setting?
WB: The geographer Carl Sauer said, "If I should move to the center of the mass I should feel that the germinal potential was out there on the periphery." I think there should always be some kind of conversation between the center and the periphery. So you need people in the periphery who can talk back to the people in the center.

HB: What encouraged you to settle back in your hometown of Port Royal, Kentucky, after finding rewarding intellectual and academic success?
WB: It was clear I'd be thinking about this place (Port Royal) the rest of my life, and so you could argue that I might as well have come back so as to know it. But that's only a supposition. The reason I came back was because I wanted to. Tanya and I wanted to. We hadn't been homesick but when we started down the New Jersey turnpike with the New York skyline behind us, it was exhilarating.

HB: How do we encourage progressives to settle down, and where should they stay? Would you see possibility in them forming communities among themselves or would you see them successful in joining already established rural communities where they might not feel initially welcomed?
WB: Well, people do form intentional communities. I have visited a few that seemed pleasant enough. But I've never lived in one, and so I don't really know about them. I'm not willing to say, as general advice, that urban people

should move to the country. I've never advised anybody to give up a well-paying city job and try to farm for a living.

HB: Rural, community-based living has the thinking, stereotyped perhaps, that there is an innate distrust of outsiders. Do you see truth in this thinking? What can be done to re-shape this thinking?
WB: There's truth in it, but it's also true that distrust is a major disease of our time, wherever you live. I don't have any idea what can be done about that. The only way to stop somebody from distrusting you is to be trustworthy and to prove it over a longish period of time.

HB: Do you believe community-based living has historically bred conservative rather than progressive ideas?
WB: That depends entirely on the community you're in. Communities of coal miners have supported the union movement. Small farmers have in this part of the country supported the tobacco program. On the other hand, I suppose that if you live in a community that is thriving, providing good work for its members and unthreatened by internal violence, you would probably try to conserve it. I suppose that Amish communities have tried to be conservative that way. If you live in an enclave of wealth and privilege, probably you tend to be conservative in a more familiar way. And, in my opinion, that is the wrong kind of conservatism.

HB: Many people grow up in small towns and find great comfort in their natural and familial surroundings, but their thinking and ambitions aren't rewarded there either by lack of jobs or lack of embracement of ideas—certainly, a misuse of the community's resources. How can youngsters and young adults be encouraged to stay home and still be fulfilled?
WB: This question depends on what you mean by intellectual stimulation and whether or not you can get it from the available resources. It's perfectly possible to live happily in a rural community with people who aren't intellectual at all (as we use the term). It is possible to subscribe to newspapers and magazines that are intellectually challenging, to read books, to correspond with like-minded people in other places, to visit and be visited by people you admire for their intellectual and artistic attainments. It's possible to be married to a spouse whose thoughts interest you. It's possible to have intellectually stimulating conversations with your children. But I've had in my own life

a lot of friends who were not literary or intellectual at all who were nevertheless intelligent, mentally alive and alert, full of wonderful stories, and whose
company and conversation have been indispensable to me. I've spent many
days in tobacco barns where I did not yearn for the conversation of the
college faculty.

HB: Farmers markets and co-ops where people buy a share of a farmer's
harvest and pick it up weekly or bi-weekly have gained in popularity. So
have weekly, predictable roadside stands. Why is this so important to a
community?
WB: Well, the obvious reason is that a good local economy feeds the local
community. But markets of the right kind and scale also fulfill an important
social function. They are places where neighbors, producers, and consumers
meet and talk. People come to the farmer's market to shop and might stand
around and talk half a day. Country stores have fulfilled the same functions.
People feel free to sit and talk up at the Hawkins Farm Center in Port Royal.
It's a great generosity on the part of the Hawkins family, and a great blessing
to the community.

HB: Why is providing food to a local community so important in
sustaining it?
WB: Because the most secure, freshest, and the best-tasting food supply is
local food produced by local farmers who like their work, like their products
and like having them appreciated by people they know. A local food system,
moreover, is subject to the influence of its consumers and the dangers and
vulnerabilities of a large, high-centralized, highly chemicalized, industrialized
food system held together by long distance transportation. A locally adapted
local food economy is the most secure against forms of political violence,
epidemics, and other threats.

Rendering Us Again in Affection:
An Interview with Wendell Berry

Katherine Dalton / 2006

From *Chronicles: A Magazine of American Culture* 30.7 (July 2006). Reprinted by permission of Katherine Dalton.

Wendell Berry is the author of over forty books and has been writing about conservation, community, and the necessity of good farming for over four decades. His novels include *The Memory of Old Jack*, *Jayber Crow*, and *Hannah Coulter*; among his collections of poems are *A Timbered Choir* and *Given*; and some of his more recent books of nonfiction are *Life Is a Miracle* (a response to Edward O. Wilson's *Consilience*), *Citizenship Papers*, and a small book of extracts from the Gospels, *Blessed Are the Peacemakers: Christ's Teachings about Love, Compassion & Forgiveness*. He is a native of Port Royal, Kentucky, where he has lived most of his life. From it he has drawn the imagined world of his fiction, Port William. He and his wife, Tanya, raise sheep on a farm overlooking the Kentucky River, and both of their children live and farm with their own families nearby. He spoke to contributing editor Katherine Dalton at his home in April.

KD: Why do you write fiction in addition to essays and poetry?
WB: To take that question seriously we're going to have to wander around awhile, maybe. But to start with I'm a storyteller. I like to tell stories. This country's full of stories, and it has a storytelling style that's economical and loves a punch line. Both my grandmothers told me stories, and my grandfather—my mother's father—told me a lot of stories. I grew up listening to stories. I think it's fairly common in cultures that are still oral—and this one was, when I was growing up—people will go out and do something they think is pretty remarkable and they'll be telling the story to each other before they get home. One might tell it and then another might tell it and thus they improve upon it. My granddaddy said there was no use telling a pretty good story when you could tell a *really* good one.

And that suggests maybe why you depart from the essay into fiction. I've been thinking about this for a long time, because the reason for writing what we call fiction seems to be the desire to tell a *whole* story. And to stick strictly to the truth, what we call nonfictional truth—to tell the story that really happened—is invariably to have an incomplete story. Nobody ever knows all the facts. Time passes, gaps come into memories, and so on. The impulse is an artistic one, the impulse toward wholeness. You may be dealing with your experience, with things that you remember, but they may come scrambled, they may even come from different times in your experience, and you can put them into a story and give them a coherence that they don't have in factual reality.

I've spent a good deal of time this winter writing another little novel called *A Visit to Port William*, and it has two points of view: the point of view of Andy Catlett at the age of nine, and the point of view of Andy Catlett as a man of my age. It deals with the difference between the mind that thought a four-mile-an-hour team of mules was going quite fast enough and the mind that leans against the bulkhead of an airplane and pushes at 500 miles an hour.

The experience that I had as a child is inevitably skewed by being forced into the geography and the *dramatis personae* of Port William and the Port William fictions. And yet memory and imagination can be put together in a kind of coherence, and the two points of view give dimension that it wouldn't otherwise have. Again, it's that impulse toward wholeness—not that art can ever satisfy that impulse, not that it will ever be completely whole, but fiction gives scope to the purpose of wholeness that nonfiction doesn't allow. You have to qualify nonfiction all the time by saying things like, "Well, as best I remember," or, "I don't remember what happened in the next few minutes, but . . ." To make an imagined thing is to place it in a landscape where wholeness seems in reach.

The other thing you're trying for is meaning, of course, which is not separate from storytelling in the quest for wholeness. But ultimately too for pleasure. You wouldn't do it if there weren't a deep pleasure in it, within reach, along with the other things that are within reach that may not be so pleasant.

KD: If one of the laws of thermodynamics holds that the universe tends toward disorder, there is another law of humanness that we would desire to create at least a small corner of order out of that disorder. Is that what you are trying to do?

WB: I think the great writers have always understood the difference between nature and human nature. Nature just clatters along as it will, absorbing its losses, ignoring its losses in a sense, and human nature comes along with checks—charity, hospitality, generosity, love, loyalty, those things. Of course my fiction has tried hard to escape the boundaries of what passes for realism, to pose a question that the realists usually don't deal with: what if a group of people in a little community were conscious of being members one of another? That has required imagination, not factual memory.

KD: Is beauty necessary to art? I ask because beauty is not a given anymore, and in fact the goal of many works of art seems to be something entirely different—to be ugliness, or perhaps the strong reaction evoked by ugliness.
WB: I think beauty is necessary. The effort to make something that's beautiful is just infinitely worthwhile, but this doesn't mean that you don't have to take big bites of ugliness. You've got to acknowledge that it exists. And yet the overall attempt is to go beyond that to the point at which the ugliness is somehow redeemed.

I'm trying again to write about *King Lear*, and *King Lear* probably has some of the ugliest scenes of all of Shakespeare. The scene in which Lear in his oblivious self-absorption subjects his daughters to a love contest—played right, it would be horribly ugly. The scene of the blinding of Gloucester is almost unbearable. The play has to hold those scenes and deal with them somehow, include them in a larger vision that is redemptive and even beautiful.

I think the great quest of *King Lear* is to imagine clearly the point at which some redemptive force can enter into the context of the play. And I think it does. When Edmund, Gloucester's bad son, dispatches a soldier to kill Cordelia, he says, "men / Are as the time is." It's a flatly deterministic view of human nature: if you live in a bad time, you're going to be a bad person. To me that's a sort of evil absolute that Shakespeare seems to pitch the whole play against. All the good and faithful servants in that play—Kent, Edgar, Cordelia, even the Fool, and finally Albany—they all exist to controvert that principle that men are as the time is. And to my sense those characters are very beautiful in their courage and goodness and faithfulness.

The other sort of absolute evil in that play is Gloucester's line, "As flies to wanton boys, are we to th' gods; / They kill us for their sport." Edgar's great effort is to save his father from the despair of that line. The perfect self-pity

of that line is just horrible. I think Shakespeare had the courage, one, to face
things like that and, two, to try to imagine what in the human soul was
redemptive, was counter to that negative force. And to me that courage gives
lines and acts of great beauty to *King Lear*.

It's not a sentimental view of beauty. It doesn't say that you can put beauty
in one pan of the scale and ugliness in the other, and heap up the beauty
until it outweighs the ugliness. There is an engagement, a life-or-death
engagement, and beauty wins by hanging on, not by heaping up.

KD: Why then is there so much emphasis on ugly books and ugly paintings?
Is that related to our artistic emphasis on being original?
WB: It may be that if you have an ugliness within you then the quest to be
original will bring ugliness out of you. But I think that's the least complicated
view of it. The other view has to do with a sort of lower order of the courage
I was talking about, the courage to face so-called reality, to face the worst for
fear that you'll be surprised by it. But I don't altogether understand this. I
don't understand why some people prefer to believe that "men are as the
time is."

Related to this is the idea that whatever we have is inevitable, that there's
really nothing you can do about the ugliness or the awfulness of human
experience. An advocate such as I have been has heard that word "inevitable"
over and over and over again. Why isn't it smartest and most sophisticated to
say that ugliness is inevitable, make replicas of it, call it art, and sleep better?
Be rid of it, in that sense. But the advocates that I am for and have found as
allies are not people who reconcile themselves to the inevitability of anything
bad. They commit themselves to acts of foolish loyalty, like Kent. Well, what if
we're losing it all? What if there is nothing to gain? What if this old man I'm
loyal to is going to lose everything? I'm still going to be right here; I'm still
going to go on.

KD: Is the common ground among all these people faith? Religious faith? Is
it possible to go on without a religious faith?
WB: It may not be faith according to some kind of a sectarian doctrine. But
the faith is that experience is somehow redeemable. That to be on the right
side in this fight between good and evil, between compassion and heartless-
ness, between beauty and ugliness, is without limit rewarding. It's the "without limit" part, not necessarily a doctrine, that makes it religious. People are

more likely to do it, I think, if they have religious faith, but that's maybe beside the point. Even C.S. Lewis, you know, made a place for the adamant rationalist in *That Hideous Strength*. There is a rationalist in there who doesn't believe in any of the wonders that are going on, and Lewis honors that: the strict, the absolutely strict or devoted rationalist or empiricist is a thing of wonder. The thing that gets awful is when the empiricists don't understand that their faith in rational intelligence can become superstitious.

I've been reading a book by Harold Morowitz, *The Emergence of Everything*, and in there he talks about what he calls an "epistemic circle." In the epistemic circle you begin with mind, and you go through the constructs of reality, and you end up again with mind. And he says he's more comfortable with this than he is with either the idealists or the realists—the idealists who say the mind is the only important reality or the only reality, and the realists who say the objective, factual world is the only reality. What he's saying is that there is some kind of interchange going on between what's in here and what's out there, and that you are never going to get to a final, objective, provable truth: "We will never have God's knowledge of the thing in itself."

KD: Maybe there's some comfort in that.
WB: I think there is. Cézanne was not painting exactly what he saw, and he was not painting what he dreamed up; he was painting an imagined world that was parallel to the world he was looking at. Between those two worlds, the imagined and the real, there are points of contact, so that one is somehow measured by the other. I've written about Barry Lopez's paragraphs in *Arctic Dreams* in which he talks about the cultural landscape as a superimposition on the real landscape. The cultural landscape, the known landscape, the landscape of memory, is never going to correspond exactly to the actual landscape. But if it doesn't correspond more or less exactly, the penalties can be harsh, especially in the Arctic.

So what Morowitz is calling the epistemic circle is simply a predicament that human life is in. And there *is* relief in it. What is claustrophobic is the idea that there is a human system that's entirely adequate. To me that's intolerable. I can't stand it in religious people; I can't stand it in non- or antireligious people. It's frightening because the next logical step from that is a totalitarian government that has all the answers.

In fact, the adjustments between the cultural landscape and the actual landscape can't ever be made finally, and can't ever be made in one place for another place. It means something lively and necessary is going on in adequate local cultures.

KD: I'm sure you've studied other traditions and other faiths—
WB: A little.

KD: —why are you a Christian and not something else?
WB: I'm a Christian in a sense I'm uneasy to talk about. From a sectarian point of view I'm a marginal Christian. But then I'm a marginal person, I'm a marginal writer. But I do know the Bible; I've had the sound of the King James version in my ears and mind all my life. I was never satisfied by the Protestantism that I inherited, I think because of the dualism of soul and body, heaven and Earth, Creator and creation—a dualism so fierce at times that it counted hatred of this life and this world as a virtue. From very early that kind of piety was distasteful to me. Nevertheless, I am devoted to that old translation of the Bible, and I'm devoted to the literary tradition that we call Christian. I have studied that, and I'm still studying it. It doesn't mean that I don't know enough about Islam or enough about Buddhism to have learned things from writers in those traditions, valuable things, and I don't think the truth is going to turn up anywhere without a divine origin. I think if it's true, then it's of the party of truth and it's allied to the truth of our tradition.

KD: Why did you pull together Christ's teachings on love and forgiveness in *Blessed Are the Peacemakers*?
WB: I'm moved every time I get into the Gospels by the generosity of Christ's talk to His disciples and the people who followed Him around. That seems to me to be the real first church: just a bunch of people coming along to hear. And Christ didn't exclude anybody; there was no test, there was no creed to sign, people came because they thought this man was speaking the truth and He spoke it to them in an extraordinarily generous way.

I think the story of the Resurrection in the Gospel of John is astonishing. It's so beautiful, so dramatic, done with so little dialogue—just a few words— and I am always overwhelmed by it.

But I'm not answering your question. My motive, I think, was the feeling that something fundamentally ungenerous, unforgiving, and implicitly violent is—as usual, I'm afraid—creeping around organized Christianity, and I wanted to look again at what Christ actually said in, for example, the Sermon on the Mount.

I don't think that you can know the Gospels and know history and not see that something is badly amiss. Something is just wildly *off* in the history of Christianity. I think it is the constant resort of Christians to violence, to what they call "just wars."

A thing that Shakespeare also is concerned with is the opposition between force and affection or gentleness or good and faithful service. Early in *As You Like It* Celia says to Rosalind, "what [my father] has taken from thy father perforce, I will render thee again in affection." That theme keeps cropping up, and Shakespeare pushes it to the wall in *King Lear*.

It's this necessity of merely standing by that so impresses me. I think the good ministers must feel it often and often here in these small communities. There they are: something absolutely awful has happened to one of their people, and they are standing by. Often there's nothing they can do, nothing, and yet there they stand on the impulse to make up in generosity, in constancy, in affection and compassion, what has been taken away by force. I've been there, you've been there; you're standing by somebody you love. You can't help, but you're going to stand. And this is an extraordinary thing. It can't be affirmed except by faith. It's affirmed, that is, in contradiction of everything that the world is telling us is worth something.

And I think that's exactly the spirit of the Gospels, and that's exactly the spirit of that little book [*Blessed Are the Peacemakers*]. If you're going to commit yourself to this, then go ahead and do it, and don't try to get logical about the consequences. You'll have to deal with the consequences as they come, and you're not going to know beforehand what they are. That seems to me to be the real Christian commitment, and it certainly coincides with commitment of other kinds. We see examples of this all the time, and our tradition will tell us what to make of them, if we pay attention to our tradition. Why do mothers love their disappointing children? They do it absolutely; there's something inexpressibly good about that. And yet if you try to keep books on the necessity of it, you'll find yourself profoundly frustrated. It's just not going to work out in some kind of accounting.

It's like trying to get your mind around the Amish, who really do act Christian. If you love your neighbor as yourself, you're going to wind up with an economic return, which is very funny, because you can't love your neighbor on the condition of an economic return.

KD: Some people who've read the New Testament have had difficulty reconciling parts of St. Paul with Jesus. Have you had this problem, and how do you resolve it?

WB: Jayber Crow calls him that exasperating, indispensable man St. Paul. St. Paul is the second wave; he's the administrator, he's the organizer, the founder, in a way, and so he puts us into funny binds. There's nothing to do about that except to start wherever you are in history and make the best of it you can. I think you have to recognize that there are some conflicts in the New Testament. Jesus went right straight into the face of authority, it seems to me; he lived hour by hour as an insult to instituted authority. So for that matter did St. Paul, but St. Paul wrote that remarkable passage in Romans requiring us to subject ourselves to "the powers that be"—which plays hell with the Founding Fathers, Thoreau, Gandhi, M. L. King, et al. These are not Gordian knots to be cut by somebody's sword; these are difficulties to be suffered and lived with.

KD: A book I read recently reminded me that after World War II, Great Britain continued to have rationing and food shortages for years, to the point where many people were not getting enough to eat. Part of the problem was that Britain had become a net importer of food. Since the attacks here in 2001, we've talked a little about the safety of the food supply, but has there been any serious discussion about the necessity—for national security—of being able to grow enough food to feed ourselves both now and in the future?

WB: Not that I know of. I think there really is something like a national insanity, and this fiction we have that we are living in a service and knowledge economy is insane—just horribly misleading and dangerous. Because of course we live in, and from, the land economy. We have no choice; there's no escape from the land economy. From eating. From needing clothing. From needing shelter and warmth. The fossil fuels come from the land economy and they can't come from anywhere else. There are hard-headed realists now who think you're a sentimentalist for talking this way—a bucolic idiot. But of course you're not, as I have to keep reminding myself.

There are several of us who have been insistent for a long time that if you want to eat you've got to have land to produce the food from, and you have to have people who know how to make the land produce, and people moreover who know how to take care of the land in production—if you want to keep eating. And we've been involved in a kind of exercise in futility. It's been clear for a long time that the powers that be were not going to hear this argument—that they were not going to be reachable by the mere sanity of saying that we live from the land economy. Still, one is called upon to keep saying it. But maybe it's instructive to be thrown back repeatedly on the need to make an act of faith, and one shouldn't complain.

KD: You continue to teach high school students occasionally, and you have grandchildren whose education you're deeply interested in. How should we educate our children in a world that is so often pushing them where we don't want them to go? Are there certain subjects we need to teach? Is there too much school and not enough time at home?
WB: Well, that's a decent starting place. There is too much school and not enough time at home. Not enough time with parents. There's not enough working with parents. But we've invented a world now in which it's often dangerous to work with parents, or parents aren't available, or parents can't have their children on the job. Nevertheless, to have committed other people's lives to this world, as you have your children's, is an extremely serious thing, and it establishes a priority that people don't think about until they have children.

I think that the issue of education really does need to be re-ransacked. You know the Amish don't educate their children formally past the eighth grade. But this doesn't keep the Amish from learning as much as they are capable of learning, and some of them are capable of learning quite a lot. For instance, there are Amish factories that are run by eighth-grade-educated Amishmen who have taught themselves enough mathematics and physics to calculate gear ratios and to design complex manufacturing procedures. They are capable of mastering as much mechanical engineering as they need. They don't have to bring in a mechanical engineer to solve their problems for them. That to me is a kind of a marker. That brings into question our now rather facile assumption that everybody needs to be at least a bachelor of arts.

KD: You make this argument explicitly in *Hannah Coulter*, that college ruins the son of Hannah's who was most suited to and most loved farming.
WB: It's a story that happens over and over. I also had in mind the kids who become biologists because they love the outdoors, and they end up computer modeling, or in molecular biology. I've been increasingly convinced that the

careerist/professionalist paradigm is dead. You just can't assume, as I think a lot of college professors still assume, that if you merely pursue your specialty your work will be used for good. I just don't think that is assumable any longer.

I don't think the education industry has been asking the essential question: What must we teach? What do we owe the young? It's *not* just a good living, and it's *not* just employability. It's *not* just job training. What do we owe them that can possibly prepare them for the experience of living in an unpredictable world? The education industry doesn't accept the inherent tragedy of that. We don't know enough to teach the young. We don't even know enough to decide what they need to know. But we've got to make a gamble. We're going to be surprised, they're going to be surprised; we know that.

That idea we had back in the '60s and '70s that everything had to be "relevant" was a joke on this subject. Nobody knew what was going to be relevant. Nobody ever knows what is going to be relevant. The question is, how do you prepare young people for a world in which *anything* might turn out to be relevant? We've come probably to the necessary conclusion, tragic and foolish as it may be, that we have to require them to learn certain things. But we haven't backed up to the point at which we can suffer those decisions as they need to be suffered. Certain things are going to be required. But then certain things are going to happen in anyone's experience that weren't foreseen by their teachers.

I'm working a morning a week now with [his two youngest grandchildren] Emily and Marshall. And when I say "working with them" I mean I work and they work. There are little cross-references occasionally. They say, "How do you spell so-and-so?" or I say, "Did you see that great blue heron that just flew up the river?" And those are teaching situations. But I'm not the taskmaster; I don't make the assignment.

I can't say that I'm teaching a great deal, but the situation is relaxed to some extent, and it's structured at least to the extent that they feel obliged, since I'm at work, to be at work. What will come of it I'm not sure. Eventually I'll assign them a book to read, and we'll talk about it. I did that with [granddaughters] Katie and Virginia. We'd talk about *King Lear* and at the end of our conversation they'd get up and give me a kiss and say, "Goodbye, Granddaddy," and be off.

I had that kind of education in farming to a considerable extent. I learned a lot of extra stuff, wonderful stories, wonderful talk, wonderful English. I was being taught but as a rule nobody was trying to teach me. Sometimes very demanding lessons were taught. Sometimes somebody was trying to teach me, and did.

KD: Would you give an example?

WB: An example is in a poem that I wrote. There used to be Hop Club dances around here. They would be held in a high school gym, or in the old dance hall over at the Oddfellow's Park in Eminence. They'd start at 10 o'clock at night, they'd end at 2 o'clock or 3 o'clock in the morning; quite a lot of liquor would be consumed, lots of very interesting dancing would be performed and, you know, there were added attractions. Maybe there'd be a breakfast afterward at somebody's house. One time I went through the whole gamut of one of those nights and presented myself to work in tobacco cutting the next day. My employer (who was in fact my teacher) never paid any mind to me at all. I got in in time to sleep maybe an hour; he waked me up as if it were any other morning. He went out ahead of me as usual and expected me to follow, and I made my way through that terrible day. It got up in the evening, with still a long way to go, and I became aware that he'd stopped to watch me fumbling along. After a while he said, "That social life don't get down the row, does it, boy?"

KD: Who was this?

WB: It was Owen Flood [a neighbor and friend, now deceased], who was having a marvelous time. It was one of the best days of his life, I imagine. But you know it was profoundly instructive, the way he did it. It was an educational work of genius, really.

KD: They say you learn by doing, or in this case, by not doing.

WB: By being unable to do, almost, and yet having to do. And I think that what the education industry has not thought of is the kind of education that simply takes advantage of opportunities in the shared life. For that, there has to be a shared life; parents and children and neighbors have to be sharing their life, and then beautiful times occur in the midst of work. Suddenly everybody's having a good time, suddenly everybody's having something good to say, suddenly something awfully funny has happened, maybe to you, and you're the hero of the story everybody's telling. We need to pay attention to those things, for they can be profoundly instructive as well as profoundly pleasurable.

I think maybe sports teams experience that. Coaches probably are laying for teaching opportunities: "Now, do you see what you did just then?" Or if you're a freshman English teacher and you at all know what you're doing, you know you can't *make* good work happen; you're just standing by to say, "Now do you see what you did? That's the way it ought to have been done. If you've done it once you can do it again." Essentially you're reduced to two sentences: one is *That ain't it*, and the other is, *That's it*. And parents are fixed that way, too: "Did you see how you did that? That was right. Remember how it felt to do it right." My daddy used to say, "Now you see that?"—and he'd point to a good bunch of cattle on a good pasture. "Don't forget it. Remember that and you'll always know what's good."

KD: Looking through the history of the Burley Co-operative I read a few speeches of your father's and thought I could see the germ of your style in him. I think you argue like your father did—like a lawyer.
WB: One of my brother John's old law partners, Ed James, said that John is a lawyer with the mind of a poet and I'm a poet with the mind of a lawyer. [Laughter]

My father had very strong syntax, and he could put a cracker on the end of a sentence that sometimes was just devastating. He was a man who was pretty thoroughly disciplined, and he was hooked on language.

KD: Your daughter, Mary, says he'd look around the room at a meeting and take the hardest chair. Is that true?
WB: It could be. John says he was always poking and prodding and urging any group he was in, but he was never in a place of obvious prominence. If they were taking a picture, he didn't want to be in front.

KD: You've been writing professionally for close to fifty years. A lot has changed in that time. In areas of particular interest to you, outside of your family, has anything changed for the better?
WB: Oh yes. Things have changed for the better, but the better is not in any way near to a win. There is a kind of alliance in this country of people who want to take care of things—children, dark nights, the land, good

architecture, forests, ecosystems, rivers, and so on. I don't know the degree of competence there is in this movement. I don't feel much assurance that we know how to take care of much of anything over the long haul. But the sense that things need to be taken care of is growing, and it's a good thing.

We're really stuck now with this word "sustainable." We haven't sustained anything for very long. We've been here in Kentucky for 230-some-odd years now since the first settlers, and we've lived at a very considerable cost to our place. There's much less soil here than there was when we came; the great forests are gone; a lot of coal has gone; God knows how much farm produce has gone, and a lot of soil with it; the land and water quality are worse. So we can't say we've sustained much. But we've got to use the word; we've got to talk about sustainability. That's a good thing; that's an improvement.

We've got these care-taking organizations, as I'll call them, and if you're familiar with the politics of these organizations you know there's a lot of discouraging things going on in them—territoriality, competition for grants. A lot of people who are on the same side are competing with each other. There's an infamous competition between the farmers and ranchers and the conservationists. They've got the same enemies, there's every reason to cooperate, and yet they have this cherished animosity. But the organizations also are doing good work. Necessary things are getting accomplished. People are learning. The conversation is expanding.

There was a father and mother and daughter and son-in-law here yesterday who have a family business up in Indiana. Their thinking is clear; their work is good; they're succeeding. They were getting I believe nine cents a pound for their hogs, and the father went to the supermarket to buy a ham and realized he couldn't afford it. It was an epiphany. He realized that he had to control more of his economy. He was merely working as a sort of slave for the corporations because he didn't control processing or marketing. So they've started processing and marketing locally their own and their neighbors' livestock, and they're doing well.

KD: Is this family running a small slaughterhouse?
WB: They were farming, and they realized they had to add value to what they produced; they realized they had to sell directly to customers. Then they reached a point at which they saw they could buy the small processing plant that they were using. And what is most impressive to me is that they're hiring local people: their neighbors are working for them, their son-in-law is working for them, their son; they're processing meat and furnishing jobs. This is

real "job creation"—because it's local; it's happening among neighbors. Their clientele has grown to the point where they can't supply the demand from their own land, so they're processing meat for their neighbors also. They're not trying to buy their neighbors out; they're saying, Come and join us; this will help you and you can help us.

What's really interesting, and what we have to latch onto and understand, is that this is an example of a cooperative economy. We've been taught to think that the only economic virtue is competitiveness. This is a faith: I'll get into it for all I'm worth, seeking the maximum advantage for myself; and then you'll get into it for all you're worth, seeking the maximum advantage for yourself; and then this will result in good—which is a preposterous notion. The other way, and we have to learn this from scratch, is the way of cooperation or neighborliness: people asking what they can do for one another that will be mutually helpful.

There are good things going on. When hope sets out in its desperate search for reasons, it can find them now. It can find people who know what they're doing. When the impact of expensive energy finally lands on us, we have to hope that we'll have the teachers and the examples that we need.

Wes Jackson [of the Land Institute in Salina, Kansas] and I have been conducting a conversation about cheap energy for a long time. Take almost anything you can think of, and subtract cheap petroleum from it, and try to imagine what you've got left. The education industry, for example, is solidly founded on cheap petroleum. Almost everything you can name, if you subtract cheap petroleum from it, either it disappears or it changes radically. So we're going to need teachers.

My guests and I had a pretty interesting conversation yesterday about whether we need to be evangelistic about the available solutions. I said no, because when you're being evangelistic you're oversimplifying. Evangelists are wanting people to join the church, not to live a Christian life. So what you have to do is go ahead and do what you know how to do, and do it as well as you can, and then be there to answer questions when people realize they need your answers. Otherwise, you're oversimplifying, and that just won't do. That's wrong.

I've understood that my job as an advocate has been to speak of the issues in something like their real complexity. People have assumed that eating is a very simple business, and I've been forty years trying to explain that it's really a complex business. It starts way, way back before the dinner table—even before farming there are questions that have to be dealt with.

In the Service of Hope—A Conversation with Wendell Berry

Marlene Muller and Dennis Vogt / 2006

Printed here for the first time by permission of Marlene Muller and Dennis Vogt.

Q: In your novel *Jayber Crow*, Jayber tells us, "Now I have had most of the life I am going to have, and I can see where it has been . . . and I have this feeling, which never leaves me anymore, that I have been led." Do you share that feeling with Jayber? Is this an experience you only have when you are older? Is there some assurance along the way when, like Jayber, you are "cut completely adrift" or "wandering in the dark woods of error?"

Wendell Berry: Your reference to Jayber's feeling that he has been "led" forces me to realize that he can say that more easily than I can. Jayber, after all, has only himself and his story to account for, whereas I am taking part in an interview about my work, which means that I now have a responsibility that is different from Jayber's. The issue you've raised is that of vocation or calling. This is an issue I take seriously, and my authority here is Ananda Coomaraswamy, who took it seriously. Coomaraswamy said, "The artist is not a special kind of man, but every man is a special kind of artist." I take this to mean that every one of us is called, by God or by our inborn gifts or talents, to work that is our own. And Coomaraswamy said further that in traditional cultures "the principle of justice" was "that each member of the community should perform the task for which he is fitted by nature." This may be a little difficult to take hold of in an age of "job creation," in which most people are thought to be without vocation and are expected to be employees and to work for bosses. Even so, I think that Coomaraswamy was right. Jayber, as he looks back on his life, feels that he was called to be a member and a servant of Port William. Looking back on my own life, I have a similar feeling—that I was called to do the work I've done. Like Jayber, I was a long time figuring out what my calling was and making a response that seemed to me to be creditable. It was an awkward business. There was of course some error and misconception. I really can't imagine how it could have been otherwise, and of course one learns from one's errors and misconceptions, and perhaps this learning gathers toward an outcome that is in some way substantially different from error and misconception. I don't want to make too strong a claim or pretend to too much understanding, but my experience has caused me to believe that help does come. It comes by way of inspiration, and it comes from friends and books met with at the right time.

Q: Speaking of friends, you spoke at Denise Levertov's memorial service in Seattle in early 1998. How did you come to know her, and how has your life and writing, particularly your poetry, been informed or influenced by her?
WB: My friendship with Denise Levertov began, as I said at the memorial service, with a letter she wrote to me in the summer of 1959. She wrote in response to a poem I had published in *Poetry* magazine. The letter was characteristically generous and encouraging. I began to read her soon after that, and then we met when I went to New York to teach in the fall of 1962. We met at a reading that she gave with David Ignatow at the Mannes College of Music. Tanya and I were living then, with our two young children, in an apartment in New Rochelle, and I was teaching at University College of New York University in the Bronx. Denise and Mitchell Goodman, her husband, were living on the top floor of an old four-story commercial building at 277 Greenwich Street. Early the next spring, that is the spring of 1963, the loft on the third floor of that building became vacant. We were not especially happy in New Rochelle, and so we moved ourselves into that loft on Greenwich Street. That was a move from an uninteresting place to an interesting one, and from a place where we knew no neighbors to a place where we had Denise and Mitch for neighbors. And they were good neighbors.

I have to reply to the second part of your question with some hesitancy, because I think it would be extremely difficult for a writer to demonstrate how and how much his work has been influenced by the work of another writer. But I have no hesitation at all in saying that Denise's work was important to me then, and it has remained important to me. I have no doubt that I learned a lot from her attitude toward her work and her way of thinking about it. She was utterly dedicated to her work, and she was unremittingly interested in her own work and in that of other poets. She could be passionately partisan about poets and poetry, but I don't think she felt competitive with other poets. I know for sure, and from my own experience, that she could be wonderfully instructive and encouraging to a younger writer. I have always felt largely and deeply indebted to her. And I have continued to be encouraged by her example and her work.

Q: In *The Letters of Denise Levertov and William Carlos Williams*, there is an exchange between the two of them in which Denise appears to push against her friend and mentor in order to claim more deeply her own voice. She writes, "That poem you were distressed by . . . has to be the way it is because it sounds the way I think and feel about it, just as close as I can make it . . . And I believe fervently that the poet's first obligation is to his own voice—to find it and use it . . ." And in your poetry cycle, "In Extremis: Poems About My Father," you write of temporarily knowing your father as enemy as you argue over the Vietnam War.

As a man of letters, have there been times when you've had to intentionally resist respected teachers in order to follow the path you sensed was set before you, and if so, did the breaking away bring you closer to where you needed to be within yourself, as well as with the other person, as it seemed to do between you and your father, and between Levertov and Williams?

WB: The letter that Denise wrote to Dr. Williams is remarkable and entirely admirable. I can easily imagine Dr. Williams grinning when he read it. All teachers and parents, and a lot of friends too, have undoubtedly met this sort of resistance and suffered the inclination to resent it or oppose it. But the good ones probably have learned to be grateful for it. Scared by it of course, for there is a large possibility of error on both sides, but grateful for it too. One likes to see the young people claiming their lives, especially if they do so with the sort of responsibility that Denise demonstrated in her letter to Dr. Williams. For a young person who intends to realize his or her vocation, this sort of break is simply necessary. It is unavoidable. But of course that does not mean that the break is absolute. These "breaks" simply require the relationship to grow up.

Q: In Ralph Meatyard's book of photographs of Thomas Merton, there are pictures of you in 1967 with Merton, Denise Levertov, and your wife Tanya at Merton's Kentucky Hermitage. How did that gathering come to be? What do you recall about your conversation and impressions of that day?

WB: I really don't know how that trip came about. Gene Meatyard and Thomas Merton became friends, I suppose, because of their mutual interest in photography. Gene Meatyard was an extraordinary photographer, and so maybe I should say that they may have become friends because of Thomas Merton's interest in Gene Meatyard and his work. I suppose that by 1967 Merton's opposition to the war in Vietnam was widely known, as I suppose Denise's opposition also was. Maybe because of that, or because of an interest expressed by Denise, Gene invited her to come along on a visit to the monastery. Having invited Denise he then invited Tanya and me and our daughter Mary. We ate with Merton at the Talbot Inn in Bardstown, and then went to his hermitage where we visited through the afternoon. It's hard to remember details of a conversation that took place nearly 40 years ago, but I know that Denise and Merton were mutually cordial, mutually respectful, and that they talked together for a long time about the war and about the things that people were doing in protest.

Q: You have actively protested the war in Iraq through your poems and through your books of essays (such as *Citizenship Papers* and *The Way of Ignorance*). Does your opposition to this war echo in word and deed your opposition to the Vietnam War? Do you think opposition to the war would be more effective if Americans "took to the streets" as so many did to protest the Vietnam War, and as they did early in the Iraq War?

WB: I have not taken part in any public demonstrations or meetings against the present war in Iraq. That does not mean that I will never do so. But, to tell the truth, I don't like mass meetings and demonstrations— "taking to the streets," as you put it. I don't think such affairs are inherently anti-democratic, but neither are they democratic. They put large numbers of people at the disposal of the loudest or most prominent voices. And they lead to dangerous oversimplifications—that is, to slogans, to what can be said quickly and loudly. In a crowd of demonstrators, it is easy to forget that the people on your side may sometimes be wrong, and that the people on the other side may sometimes be right. The democratic way is reasoned argument in honest language and in good faith. My own bias is for the way of argument. But as the means of public argument are reduced, public demonstrations are increasingly validated. Even so, "taking to the streets" is a bad sign. It, like the need for it, is a symptom of the decay of democracy.

Q: Regarding Coomaraswamy's observations that "each member of the community should perform the task for which he is fitted by nature." Some
would argue nature has pushed women only into childrearing, housekeeping,
and caregiving roles and that modern society has liberated them from these
constraints of nature. How should vocation, the task for which one is fitted
by nature, relate to roles of men and women in marriages and households?
Do children have their own vocations or is this only an adult issue?

WB: We have to acknowledge that we're talking about this issue of vocation
in an age made unique in all of human history by the abundance of supposedly cheap fossil fuel. This has enabled us to make assumptions about vocation, work, and leisure that would not have been possible for most people
until about the middle of the twentieth century. At present some people
would argue as you suggest in your question. A more ordinary and I think a
more realistic argument would be that nature has pushed us *all* into
childrearing, housekeeping, and caregiving. Because of intellectual fashion, it
has become too easy in our time to assume that childrearing, housekeeping,
and caregiving, along with all the varieties of manual work, are somehow
undignified and unworthy. And we have attempted to lighten and improve
them by means of gadgets and institutions. But I would argue that these are
the most basic and the most noble vocations. How can we live, or how can we
live for very long, as a people if we don't take care of the children, keep
house, and give care to all things needing care? I think the hierarchy that
places work done away from home above work done at home is utterly
phony. Also phony, and dangerous, is the idea that "the arts" and other
vocations "of the mind" are too exalted to be interfered with by the daily and
necessary work of the world.

I don't believe in slavery. I don't believe in a life so burdened with work
that one cannot write or read or sing or dance or listen to music or paint or
look at paintings or take pleasure with one's family and neighbors. On the
other hand, I don't believe in being too smart or important or talented to
take part in the daily maintenance of the world. I don't see working away
from home as a liberation or an exaltation for men or women either. I need
to add that by "home" I mean a household with a household economy, a
place where all members of the family always have work to do in their own
support.

I wouldn't expect a child to be conscious of having a vocation and I
wouldn't recommend urging a child toward some vocation picked by the

parents, which is a way to ruin childhood. But I don't think it ruins childhood at all for a child to be given tasks to perform that are useful to the family and that contribute to the economic maintenance of the family. Such work, I think, can give a child a sense of worth that is not available any other way.

Q: Your work makes many readers (us) yearn to live, to have a "membership," in a pastoral place like Port William among the sort of folks able to sustain the countryside and the village. Do you think it is possible to experience life in a similar order of satisfactions and affections in neighborhoods, suburbs, and cities? If so, what do you think such a life would look like? Where would a person begin in order to attain it?

WB: I certainly do think it is possible to live as a member in a city or a suburb or wherever you are. For help here I will quote some sentences of Burley Coulter's, in which he is perhaps improving on St. Paul: "The way we are, we are members of each other. All of us. Everything. The difference ain't in who is a member and who is not, but in who knows it and who don't." So I guess I would say that a better question is whether or not you can know yourself as a member in a city or a suburb or wherever you are. When enough people in a place know themselves as members, then I believe the place will change for the better. That's a statement of faith, necessarily, because most of us now don't live in such a place. There are exceptions: monastic communities, so-called intentional communities, and a few traditional agrarian communities such as those of the Amish. But most of us live in places and in neighborhoods dominated by the influence of individualism, by the endlessly justified selfishness of the consumer economy, and by the principle of competition. But we don't, as individual people, have to submit to the shaping of those influences. We can imagine a difference and a better thing. And we can change ourselves. I suppose what begins this is an insight something like Burley Coulter's.

Q: "Wild" Burley did not lead the kind of life that would have been approved by the members of the local church. The Port William membership, one he recognized, named, nurtured, celebrated, and gave his life to, seems far closer to the Body of Christ St. Paul describes than what passes these days for membership in local churches. Do you see it this way as well? What does "Bishop" Burley know that many pastors seem not to know?

WB: No doubt people need bishops of one sort or another, and no doubt Burley Coulter was not one and should not have been one. He is not an institutional person, and he has no "official position" on anything. I have known a good many such people, and I am strongly prejudiced in their favor. If, as I said earlier, Burley improved on St. Paul, he did so only by telling a more comprehensive truth. All of us humans and all the creatures are, in fact, members of one another, whether we know it or not. St. Paul's beautiful metaphor is right; it only needs to be more inclusive. I suppose Burley understands that this all-inclusive membership implies and requires an unofficial and unconditional neighborliness and compassion. I don't see why pastors, who stay in the same place long enough, could not exercise the same sort of neighborliness and compassion.

Q: Hannah noted, "This membership had an economic purpose and it had an economic result, but the purpose and the result were a lot more than economic . . . work was freely given for work freely given. There was no bookkeeping, no accounting, no settling up. What you owed was considered paid when you had done what needed doing." Does a genuine membership always have to have some economic purpose, some armature of regularly exchanged work done by people who live near one another?
WB: The answer, I believe, is yes. To have a viable community, or as you say a "genuine membership," its members must need one another's help and must be practically useful to one another.

Q: What does Hannah mean when she says, "The membership includes the dead"?
WB: When people who know one another have lived in the same landscape for a long time, they are surrounded by reminders of the dead in one another's faces and in the landscape itself. In such a community the dead are bound to linger on as influences, as the subjects of memories, conversations, and stories. I assume that's what Hannah means.

Q: Your response brings to mind these lines from your poem "Elegy": "The best teachers teach more / than they know. By their deaths / they teach most. They lead us beyond / what we know, and what they knew." I am curious, do you think there is a limit to the number of members "who know they are members," who can maintain the quality of membership present in the Port Williams stories?

WB: I don't think the Port William story can be accounted for according to the terms or assumptions of realism. In writing about Port William over the last 50 years, I have more and more consciously asked myself to suppose that a group of people in a little community do consciously understand themselves as a membership. This sort of supposing is as much addressed to imagination as it is to observation. I don't think realism, by its terms, can suppose any such thing.

I doubt that there is in reality an imposed limit of the number of members who know they are members, but in Port William, as everywhere else, there are some who are not members and some who do not want to be members.

Q: Hannah, a grieving widow, says, "There are always a few who will recite their complaints, but the proper answer to 'How are you?' is 'Fine.' . . . Should you fall on your neighbor's shoulder and weep in the midst of work . . . No, you are fine." It is fair to say, the regnant premise in our culture is that openness and "honest sharing" followed by talk therapy are the means for dealing with trouble and suffering. Is Hannah's way outmoded?

WB: Hannah says that this has to do with shame and fear: "shame for the terrible selfishness and loneliness of grief, and fear of the difference between your grief and anybody else's." If I understand her, she means that it is wrong to overvalue your own grief in the presence of somebody else's, and that it is also wrong to permit your grief to be depreciated by somebody else's false sympathy or indifference. And so she is right, I think, when she speaks of this also as having to do with courtesy and honesty.

No, I don't think Hannah's way is outmoded, if by "outmoded" you mean that it has been replaced by something better. It is apparently not in the nature of some people to want to speak of their deepest feelings. And there is a reasonable doubt that those who would like to speak of their deepest feelings ever have a language adequate for doing so. There is, as Hannah says, "a terrible selfishness and loneliness" in grief.

Your question seems to me perfectly good and proper. All the same, I would not like it to distract from the occurrence in my Port William novels and stories of a good many occasions when two people face each other and speak in complete mutuality and sympathy. I am remembering, for example,

Nathan's proposal to Hannah: "I know you're afraid. And so am I. But can you see a life here?" Those brief sentences have a context. And in their context they say everything that needs to be said.

Q: I was rereading *The Hidden Wound* the other day. In your afterword you say of the campus meetings, "Speakers and hearers seemed to be in perfect agreement that whites were absolutely guilty of racism, and that blacks were absolutely innocent of it. They were thus absolutely divided by their agreement." You go on to say, "If love was present at those public meetings, it was the self-love of self-righteous anger and the self-love of self-righteous guilt." It seems to me this has a passing resemblance to the politically correct discourse current in modern universities wherein European culture is deemed oppressive and all others are deemed liberating. Is this a fair observation in your opinion? What is your take on the current state of American universities?

WB: I have never, so to speak, lived in a university, and I haven't taught in one since 1993, and so I think I'm the wrong person to ask about the current state of American universities. I am well aware, however, of the *consequences* of what is going on in American universities, and in some of my essays I have had plenty to say about those. I am certainly aware of the current fashion among some intellectuals of disparaging European culture or Western civilization as somehow a total failure, or as something of no worth whatsoever. This, I think, is fashion, not criticism. Criticism is the exercise of judgement, of discrimination, of careful observation and comparison. It does not condemn the best with the worst or the worthy with the worthless. At the very least, these condemners ought to acknowledge the existence of a long tradition of dissent from the prevailing violence and greed. They should remember people like William Blake, John Ruskin, Henry Thoreau, and Martin Luther King, and try to be honorable members of that company.

Q: In your poem, "How to Be a Poet" from *Given*, you write: "Breathe with unconditional breath / the unconditioned air," and "Accept what comes from silence. / Make the best you can of it." Also from *Given*, in "Sabbaths 2000" you write: "I stand and wait for light / To open the dark night. / I stand and wait for prayer / To come and find me here."

Some people might recognize this kind of breathing and standing as "contemplative being." I have read an expansion on the Coomaraswamy quote that says, "The contemplative is not a special kind of person, every person is a special kind of contemplative." Is paying attention to life through silence, listening, and waiting the place where prayer and writing poetry begin for you? Do you experience similarities between prayerfulness and writing poetry? How do you understand and experience "contemplative awareness" (if you would use that term) in your life of faith and in your writing?

WB: I am not willing to go much beyond the language of those poems. That is, I don't feel that I can talk with much authority about prayer and contemplation. My life does not at all resemble life in a monastery or a zendo, where a daily order of prayer or meditation is followed. My life seems to be given shape, when it has a shape, by the daily demands of living on our farm. And those demands, if I meet them in time, usually permit me also some time, varying with the seasons, to read and write. As I go about my daily work of farming, reading, writing, and the other pleasures, bothers, and duties that my life involves, things come to me that, because they give light and are moving to me, need to be written. And then, as soon as I can find the time, I take up the task of writing.

Q: Steinbeck wrote in his preface to *The Winter of Our Discontent* that "Readers seeking to identify the fictional people and places here described would do better to inspect their own communities and search their own hearts, for this book is about a large part of America today." Certainly your essays send folks back to their own being in the world, but do you feel the need to protect the Port William membership and their "context" that you referred to earlier, from well-meaning readers who might diminish their liveliness by talking and writing and analyzing so much about them? Aren't well written stories intended, maybe in large part, to return us to our own lives, to wake us up to what's right in front of us?

WB: There is what can only be called a literary industry in existence in the colleges and universities today, and I think that any writer should be wary of this. From what I've seen of it, and I try not to see too much of it, this literary industry can carry one very far from what I think of as reading, appropriate criticism, and writing. My own belief is that the purpose of writing is to do justice to its subject, not to please readers or to improve them or to set them thinking about their own problems. Those things must come as they will, as side effects. A writer's duty, as far as I am concerned, is only to do justice to the subject.

Q: Speaking in the fall of 2004 to a group of students at the University of Washington, you said, "My deal with the muse is if she leaves me alone, I leave her alone." You also commented, "Things come to me. If they didn't, I would not try to go to them." Why wouldn't you try to go to them? Do you experience a good kind of detachment from your writing, and if so, how did you come by it? Do you feel the freedom not to write?

WB: I suppose the answer to this question is that I don't consider myself a professional writer. I don't associate what is now known as "professionalism" with anything I do. I am an amateur: I do my work for love of it. Especially as a writer, I don't go looking for work, and I don't feel that I have a duty to be writing all the time. I am a small writer as I am a small farmer. If the work did not give me pleasure, I would not do it. There are other good and pleasing things to be done. A long time ago, after a good many years of being virtually obsessed with the idea of being a writer and trying to succeed as a writer, it came to me that I could lead a perfectly happy life without writing anything at all. That was a tremendous relief. It made the world larger, and it made me a better writer than I had been before.

Q: You are frequently referred to as a "prophetic voice." Just for fun, I did a web search on "Wendell Berry" and "Prophet." My search engine returned 23,201 hits. Are you comfortable in being thought of in this way?

WB: William Blake thought the words "poet" and "prophet" designated pretty much the same person. And of course we all ought to be prophets in the sense that we should see the truth and tell it. Nevertheless, being called a prophet makes me uneasy because I think it puts me into a category that implies that I am in some fundamental way different from other people, and therefore am not to be paid much attention to. "Poet" seems to me to designate the same sort of category. It's as though you have some highly unusual disease that most people would rather not catch.

Q: You have written extensively on the threats to people and places posed by unconstrained large and distant powers, among which are "free" markets, industrial economies, blind acceptance of technology, political fecklessness,

and regulatory malfeasance. In your recent essay "Compromise, Hell!" (*The Way of Ignorance*) you declared the destruction of our country is not necessary. "It is not inevitable, except that by our submissiveness we make it so." Do you see any evidence that individual Americans are becoming less submissive to these powers? Do you have hope that the powerful can be turned from general contempt for small places to respecting and caring for them?
WB: The single goal of the industrial economy, from the beginning of the Industrial Revolution, has been the highest possible margin of profit. That is to say that its single motive has been greed. This economy justifies itself as a sequence of innovations that it calls "progress." But it is progress for the sake of the biggest possible profit. Industrialism is the most effective system ever devised for the concentration of wealth and power. Its most characteristic "progress" has been the increasing ability to concentrate wealth and power into fewer and fewer hands. People are talking now about the imperialism of the United States, but the real imperialist power is that of the corporations that are in charge of the global economy. Those corporations have no national allegiance and no patriotism. They simply employ or purchase governments to serve an ambition for wealth and power that is global. The United States government, at present, is a hired servant of this corporate imperialism.

So far as I can see, the only effective answer to an imperialist global economy is the development of local economies. This may appear to be a slim hope, but it is also a real hope. To begin with, the global economy is dependent on cheap petroleum, and the signs are everywhere that the era of cheap petroleum is over. From now on, it is going to be more and more expensive to conduct a long-distance economy. Another weakness of the global economy is its extreme vulnerability to international disturbances. Another weakness is that, on its own terms, it is self-destructive. It does not observe what Sir Albert Howard called "the law of return." It takes from people and nature and does not give back. It is founded upon the waste and destruction of its own sources, which is to say that it is failing even while it thinks it is succeeding. The paramount question is not whether or not it can be sustained, for it cannot be, but how much and how many will be destroyed by its failures.

In opposition, efforts to develop and defend local economies are now under way all over the world. These efforts are being made because people everywhere are in fact becoming less submissive to the global economy and its political servants. And so, yes, I do have hope, and my purpose in everything I do is to serve that hope.

Q: What goodness and satisfaction has writing brought you over the past 50 years? What do you hope writing will bring you in the years ahead?

WB: Writing is difficult. Sometimes it is a struggle. My workdays as a writer do not invariably please me. But in general I have taken a lot of pleasure from doing my work. I like to write. The ideas and inspirations that have come to me have been deeply satisfying gifts, and it has given me pleasure to try to realize them in words as fully as I can. I agree with Robert Frost who said in one of his letters that he hoped to communicate to the readers of his work "what a *hell* of a good time I had writing it."

At present I have a number of things that I would like to write, and so I still have an agenda of work. If I am still writing on the last day of my life, that will be fine with me. However, if the well should go dry, I hope I will have sense enough to quit going to it with a bucket.

Index